中国—东盟法律评论

韩杼滨

中國—东盟法律评論

2011年 第1卷·第1期

China-ASEAN Law Review

Volume I Sep. 2011 Number 1

■ 张晓君 主编
Zhang Xiaojun Chief Editor

■ 中国—东盟法律研究中心 主办
Sponsor by China-ASEAN Legal Research Center

厦门大学出版社 XIAMEN UNIVERSITY PRESS | 国家一级出版社 全国百佳图书出版单位

目 录

中国、东盟国家国内法各论

中国—东盟自由贸易区的司法及实务合作

学术综述

附录

Contents

DOMESTIC LAWS OF CHINA AND ASEAN COUNTRIES

JUDICIAL AND PRACTICAL COOPERATION IN CAFTA

ACADEMIC SUMMARY

APPENDIX

发刊词

刘　飏

中国法学会常务副会长
中国—东盟法律研究中心理事长

2011年是中国和东盟建立对话关系20周年。回首往昔，中国和东盟国家齐心协力，克服艰难险阻，成功走出了一条具有亚洲特色的区域合作之路，实现了前所未有的发展与繁荣。2011年也是《落实中国—东盟面向和平与繁荣的战略伙伴关系联合宣言的第二个五年行动计划》的开局之年。展望未来，中国和东盟国家的多样性必将转化为加强交流合作的活力和动力，在相互学习和相互借鉴中增进彼此的理解和信任，实现各领域合作的深化和拓展。在这样一个承前启后的特殊时期，我欣喜地看到，由中国—东盟法律研究中心编辑的、汇集了来自东盟和中国法律法学界专家研究成果的《中国—东盟法律评论》正式出版。

伴随中国—东盟自贸区货物贸易、服务贸易、投资等领域一体化进程的深入，自由贸易区内各种复杂新颖的法律问题层出不穷。在此背景下，加强中国和东盟法学、法律界的交流与合作，对于保障自由贸易区顺畅运作、深化区域合作的内涵，加强和充实中国—东盟战略伙伴关系，具有迫切的现实意义。

《中国—东盟法律评论》的出版应当常态化，要为本地区的法制建设提供一个常态化的交流平台。来自不同国家和不同领域的专家学者可以实时关注本地区出现的可能影响自贸区顺畅运转的各种问题，积极为中国—东盟自贸区涉及的法制建设献言建策，探究一整套适应国际规则和惯例，符合自由贸易区实际需要，能够被自由贸易区成员普遍接受的自贸区经贸和投资保障机制、司法协助体系、民商事争议解决机制以及法律协调机制，以防止和减少商贸风险和投资纠纷，逐步完善成员方各自的经贸法律规范，为推动中国—东盟自由贸易区法制建设进程做出有益贡献。

《中国—东盟法律评论》的出版，更为中国与东盟间政界、法学、法律界和商业界架设起一座文化沟通的桥梁。《中国—东盟法律评论》的作者来自于东盟国家和中国的政界,法学、法律界和商业界,广泛代表各自所在国家、组织和职业团体的观点和意见,不同思想和观念之间的碰撞与协调,必将增进中国与东盟之间法律的相互理解,为促进本地区政治、经济和文化等各方面的和谐发展尽绵薄之力。

"中国—东盟法律合作与发展高层论坛"自创立以来,一直秉承"合作、发展、共赢"的精神,积极致力于中国—东盟间的法律交流与合作,并于2010年结出累累硕果:"中国—东盟法律研究中心"在中国法学重镇——西南政法大学成立。在中国法学会的大力支持下,《中国—东盟法律评论》的创刊出版,为"中国—东盟法律研究中心"的实体化建设写下了浓墨重彩的篇章。

我期待着,研究中心能够以《中国—东盟法律评论》出版为契机,围绕自贸区经贸、投资、争端解决机制、各国法律协调和区域法制建设中具有全局性、战略性、前瞻性和实践性的重大法律理论和实践课题,进行深入的研究、探讨和交流,为促进本地区的法律法学合作和交流作出不懈的努力,为本地区的和平、稳定与繁荣作出积极贡献。

2011年9月

An Inaugural Statement in Honor of the First Issue of China-ASEAN Law Review

Liu Yang
Executive Vice-president of China Law Society
Chairman of China-ASEAN Legal Research Center

The year 2011 marks the 20th anniversary of the China-ASEAN dialogue relations. Looking back at the past decades, China and ASEAN countries have come a long way together from removal of misgivings and obstacles to successful opening of a regional cooperation with Asian identity, and achieved mutual growth and prosperity unseen in history. The year 2011 as well witnesses the beginning of The Second Five-year Plan of Action to Implement the Joint Declaration on ASEAN-China Strategic Partnership for Peace and Prosperity. Looking ahead to the future, there is no doubt that the common pursuit of peace and prosperity and the gaps in reality and individual diversities existed between China and ASEAN countries will turn into the incentive and motivation for enhancing exchange and cooperation, and China and ASEAN countries will push forward mutual understanding and trust in the process of learning from each other and further deepen and expand the cooperation in all areas. In such an extraordinary year inheriting the past and ushering in the future, I am absolute delightful to witness the official first issue of China-ASEAN Law Review, which is edited by the China-ASEAN Legal Research Center and will collect the findings of professionals of law from China and ASEAN countries.

Along with the speeding up of the integration process of the trade in goods, service and investment in China-ASEAN Free Trade Area (CAFTA), unprecedented legal problems are therefore on the increase accordingly. Under such circumstance, to strengthen the exchanges and cooperation in the field of law in the region will attach practical significance to the smooth functioning of CAFTA, enrichment of regional cooperation and promotion of China-ASEAN strategic partnership.

China-ASEAN Law Review will provide a persistent communication platform for the construction of local legal system, on which professionals and scholars from different nations in various domains will be able to follow up problems that may affect the normal operation of CAFTA in time and actively put forward proposals and ideas in legal system construction, concerning the making of a whole set of legal systems in China-ASEAN FTA, including FTA trade and investment guarantee mechanism, judicial assistance and civil and commercial dispute settlement mechanisms as well as legal coordination mechanism, which are in line with the international rules and practices, to the practical requirement of FTA and generally acceptable to FTA members, to prevent and reduce business risks and investment disputes ultimately, to gradually improve individual business rules of law of each member as well as to facilitate the progress of China-ASEAN FTA legal system construction. Furthermore, the publication of China-ASEAN Law Review will open up a new channel available for exchange of ideas among government officials, legal professionals and entrepreneurs from China and ASEAN countries. Since the authors of China-ASEAN Law Review come from ASEAN countries and Chinese government, law sectors and business world, their viewpoints will broadly represent that of their respective countries, organizations and professional societies, accordingly, the collision and merger of diverse ideas and concepts will for sure enhance mutual understanding, promote mutual trust and support so as to exert a vital and positive influence in facilitating the harmonious development of local politics, economy and culture. The China-ASEAN Forum on Legal Cooperation and Development, since its initiation, has been adhering to the idea of "Cooperation, Development and Win-win" and engaging in the legal communication and cooperation between China and ASEAN, out of which great success has been achieved. In the year 2010, China-ASEAN Legal Research Center was founded in Southwest University of Political Science and Law-a dominant quarter for legal studies around China. The publication of China-ASEAN Law Review will open a brand new chapter for the construction of the Legal Research Center in operation.

I sincerely hope that the China-ASEAN Law Review will grasp every opportunity and find out its own characteristic in a profound perspective, in the mean time, lead in the academic frontier, advocate theory innovation, follow closely to the judicial process and seek new channels for cooperation based on CAFTA major topics of general, strategic and foresighted importance in principle as well as in practice, to make it into the most influential domestic and international authoritative publication and to provide legal and intellectual support for the development of regional integration in an all-around and sound way.

Finally, I honestly wish that the China-ASEAN Law Review will gain success on every step!

September 2011

编者按

欢迎读者拈读《中国—东盟法律评论》(《评论》)。作为第四届"中国—东盟法律合作与发展高层论坛"的重要成果,"中国—东盟法律研究中心"推出的学术出版物,诚如中国法学会常务副会长——刘飏女士在发刊词中所言,本刊旨在"为本地区的法制建设提供了一个常态化的交流平台"的同时,"为中国—东盟政府界、法学法律界和商业界架设起一座有效沟通的桥梁"。

《评论》第一卷主要收录了来自中国、菲律宾、缅甸、文莱、印度尼西亚、越南等六国作者在第四届"中国—东盟法律合作与发展高层论坛"上的演讲稿或参会论文共17篇,一定程度上反映了中国及东盟国家法律人对本地区法律问题的最新研究成果,探索、合作的精神也在思想碰撞的火花中发展显现。

在"中国—东盟自由贸易区"基础问题栏目中:菲律宾司法部总检察长办公室的Maria Cristina P. Rilloraza女士分析了中国—东盟自由贸易区(CAFTA)的地缘政治及经济因素,指出CAFTA的建立将推动中国与东盟国家在经济、政治、国家安全及法律等领域的全方位合作。印度尼西亚法院系统的Ifa Sudewin女士、Elyta Ras Ginting女士及Joni先生分析了印尼国内的公平竞争法律问题,并建议建立CAFTA下的相应法律框架以解决垄断与不公平竞争贸易行为。西南政法大学的张晓君先生、徐忆斌先生剖析了CAFTA规则的不足,并提出了相应的完善建议。复旦大学法学院的何力先生指出CAFTA的成功有可能推动接近欧盟模式的东亚共同体的建立。西南政法大学的王玫黎女士认为源于亚洲的和平共处五项原则,作为国际法的基本原则,也可作为处理中国—东盟关系的法律准则。广西师范大学法学院的杨丽艳女士指出CAFTA目前的"浅层一体化"模式存在诸多缺陷,中国与东盟国家应进一步推进其深层一体化发展。

在"中国—东盟自由贸易区法律问题专论"栏目中:文莱仲裁协会的Colin Yee Cheng ONG先生探讨了CAFTA争端解决机制进一步完善的空间。广西大学法学院的魏艳茹女士指出应进一步完善《中国—东盟投资协议》的审慎措施、根本安全例外等条款。

在"中国、东盟国家国内法各论"栏目中：越南—中国—东盟法律信息咨询中心的 Nguyen Xuan Anh 先生考察了越南国内法与 CAFTA 间的契合性，指出各国双赢局面的实现，将促进其对 CAFTA 的进一步自觉、自愿遵守。缅甸总检察长办公室的 Win Myint 先生介绍了缅甸商法改革的历史及现状。西南政法大学的赵万一先生介绍了中国公司法的发展现状，并就中国公司法进一步完善提出了建议。越南河内法律大学的 Lee Lai 先生、Ruanru Zheng 先生也梳理了越南投资法律制度的演变及完善进程。

在"中国—东盟自由贸易区"的司法及实务合作栏目中：西北政法大学的王瀚先生强调了各国司法协助对 CAFTA 争端解决机制的重要性，分析了各国为区域争端的仲裁裁决提供司法协助时应遵循的有关原则。西南政法大学的张春良先生指出 CAFTA 的统一私法纠纷排解机制存在欠缺，并探讨了将外国法查明制度 CAFTA 化的问题解决途径。云南大学法学院的陈云东先生、米良先生，分析了法律服务在中国—东盟自由贸易区运行过程中的体系、特点及重要性。万益律师事务所的凌斌先生，北京大成(昆明)律师事务所的马巍先生也在其各自文章中探讨了 CAFTA 建立提供的法律服务机遇，律师服务能力提升与区域合作构建等问题。

《评论》蒙中国法学会会长韩杼滨先生为本刊题写了刊名，厦门大学出版社给予大力支持，中心咨询单位和咨询委员等给予了热情关心和帮助。编辑部在此表示诚挚的谢意。

《中国—东盟法律评论》编辑部

2011 年 9 月

Editors' Note

Welcome to the first issue of the China-ASEAN Law Review (CALR). According to Ms. Liu Yang, Executive Vice-president of China Law Society, our CALR, which is an important outcome of the Fourth China-ASEAN Forum on Legal Cooperation and Development and the academic publication designed for China and ASEAN law professionals by China-ASEAN Legal Research Center, aims to "provide a persistent communication platform for the construction of local legal system", and "open up a new channel available for exchange of ideas among government officials, legal professionals and entrepreneurs from China and ASEAN countries".

The first issue of CALR mainly includes seventeen articles collected from speeches or forum papers by authors from Brunei Darussalam, China, Indonesia, Myanmar, Philippines and Vietnam in the 4th China-ASEAN Top Forum on Legal Cooperation and Development. Those papers to some extent reflect latest research achievements of China and ASEAN countries' lawyers to local and regional legal issues, spirit of exploration and cooperation obviously develops from the collision sparks of thoughts.

In the CAFTA Fundamental Issues column, Ms. Maria Cristina P. Rilloraza, from the Office of the Chief State Prosecutor of Department of Justice of Philippines, analyzes the geopolitical and economic factors in CAFTA, and provides that establishment of CAFTA would prompt a comprehensive cooperation between China and ASEAN countries among all fields of economy, politics, national security and so on. Ms. Ifa Sudewin, Ms. Elyta Ras Ginting and Mr. Joni, from the court system of Indonesia, review the unfair competition issues in Indonesia, and suggest solving the monopoly and unfair competition issues by establishing relevant legal framework in CAFTA. Mr. Zhang Xiaojun and Mr. Xu Yibin, from the Southwest University of Political Science and Law, remind us of the shortages of the CAFTA rules, and provide some suggestions for improving. Mr. He Li, from the Fudan University School of Law, asserts that the success of CAFTA will facilitate the establishment of an East Asian Community similar to the European Union. Ms. Wang Meili, from the Southwest University of Political Science and Law, concludes that the Five Principles of Peaceful Coexistence, as the basic principles of the international law, origin from Asia could be the legal guidelines for China-ASEAN relations also. Ms. Yang Liyan, from the Law School of Guangxi Normal University, analyzes shortages of current "shallow integration" CAFTA, and points out that both China and ASEAN countries should further their "deep integration".

In the CAFTA Legal Issues column, Mr. Colin Yee Cheng ONG, from the Arbitration Association of Brunei Darussalam, explores the possibility of improving the dispute settlement mechanism of CAFTA. Ms. Wei Yanru, from the Guangxi University, suggests improving the prudential clause and essential security clause of the China-ASEAN Investment Agreement.

In the Domestic Laws of China and ASEAN Countries column, Mr. Nguyen Xuan Anh, from the Vietnam-China-ASEAN Legal Information and Consultancy, compares Vietnam domestic law and CAFTA rules, and concludes that the realization of win-win situation among China and ASEAN countries could foster a more voluntary attitude for cooperation to CAFTA. Mr. Win Myint, from the Attorney General's Office of Myanmar, outlines the history and current situation of reforms of Myanmar business laws. Mr. Zhao Wanyi, from the Southwest University of Political Science and Law, describes the current development situation of China Company Law and makes some suggestions. Mr. Lee Lai and Mr. Ruanru Zheng, from Hanoi University of Law, outline the evolution and improvement of Vietnam's Investment Legal System.

In the CAFTA Judicial and Practical Cooperation column, Mr. Wang Han, from the Northwest University of Politics and Law, emphasizes the importance of legal assistance to the dispute settlement mechanism of CAF-

TA, and analyzes the complied rules for governments to offer legal assistance to arbitration of regional disputes. Mr. Zhang Chunliang, from the Southwest University of Political Science and Law, points out the defects of unified private law dispute resolution mechanism under CAFTA, and explores the caftalization of proof of foreign laws as a problem solving way. Mr. Chen Yun-dong and Mr. Mi Liang, from the Law School of Yunnan University, outline the importance, role and status of the legal service under the CAFTA. Mr. Ling Bin, from the Guangxi Wanyi Law Firm, and Mr. Ma Wei, from the Beijing Dacheng Law Firm, offers their views on issues such as the legal service opportunities offered by the establishment of CAFTA, how to improve lawyer service, and the construction of regional cooperation in their respective papers.

In particular, the editorial board would like to express sincere gratitude to Mr. Han Zhubin, president of China Law Society, for his generous inscription for CALR, and generous support from Xiamen University Press, and the Advisory Organizations as well as Advisory Members of the Center, for offering us a great deal of constructive advice during the publication of our CALR.

Editorial Board of China-ASEAN Law Review
September 2011

中国—东盟自由贸易区的基础问题

CAFTA FUNDMENTAL ISSUES

The Geo-political and Economic Imperatives of the China-ASEAN Free Trade Area

Maria Cristina P. Rilloraza

Maria Cristina P. Rilloraza, prosecutor of office of the chief state prosecutor of Department of Justice

Content

Ⅰ. Introduction

The establishment of China-ASEAN Free Trade Area (CAFTA) on January 1, 2010 marked an important milestone in the development of China-ASEAN relations. It is the world's third largest regional free trade area, after European Union (EU) and North America Free Trade Area (NAFTA). CAFTA has a significant trade and development implications for Southeast Asia. However, as this agreement contains not only economic matters but also explicit political content, it stirs academic interest and contending views among activists and scholars in developing countries.

The rise of China has prompted frequent discussion and concern in the United States. Much of this discussion has focused on the future economic and security threat China may pose to the United States. In contrast, for the ASEAN member states, China's growing status as a global power is not a future challenge but a daily reality.

The idea of forming CAFTA as a free trade bloc dated back to the Asian financial crisis in the 1990s. At the third China-ASEAN Summit in Manila in 1999 then, Chinese Premier Zhu Rongji reiterated China's readiness to enhance its ties with ASEAN free trade district. His proposal got positive response from leaders of ASEAN nations.

The events that shaped the CAFTA include the accelerated globalization, the recent Asian financial crisis, China's entry into the World Trade Organization, the terrorist attacks in the South East Asian region, the 9/11 terror attacks on the United States and the reorientation in the U. S. security policy.

CAFTA is important to ASEAN. As a rapidly growing economy, China offers enormous potential for the largely small and export-oriented ASEAN member countries.

Ⅱ. The Association of South East Asian Nations (ASEAN)

A. History

The Association of Southeast Asian Nations (ASEAN) has its roots in previous regional groupings such as: SEATO (Southeast Asian Treaty Organization, 1945) the ASA (Association of Southeast Asian Nations, 1961), MAPHILINDO (Malaysia, Philippines and Indonesia, 1963) and ASPAC (Asian and Pacific Council, 1966).

On August 8, 1967, with the signing of the ASEA Declaration (also known as Bangkok Declaration), ASEAN was established.

B. Membership

The five founding members of ASEAN are: Indonesia, Malaysia, the Philippines, Singapore and Thailand.

On January 7, 1984, Brunei became the sixth member of ASEAN.

At present, ASEAN has ten member countries, namely, Singapore, Brunei Darrusalam, Malaysia, Lao PDR, Vietnam, Cambodia, Myanmar, Philippines, Indonesia, and Thailand.

As embodied in the Bangkok Declaration, the ASEAN "is open for participation to all States in the Southeast Asian Region" subscribing to the Association's aims, principles and purposes.

Aside from abundant natural resources, the region is a developing market with a strong potential demand for consumer goods, capital goods, and technical skills.

It has one of the fastest economic growth rates and membership countries have projected annual growth expansion rates from five to seven percent.

The heads of government of member countries are the highest authority of ASEAN. Whenever necessary, summit meetings are held to discuss problems and to give renewed direction to ASEAN.

C. Aims and Purposes

ASEAN desires to establish a firm foundation for common action to promote regional cooperation in Southeast Asia in the spirit of equality and partnership and thereby contribute towards peace, progress and prosperity in the region.

To achieve its goals, the ASEAN shall seek to:

a. accelerate the economic growth, social progress and cultural development in the region through joint endeavors;

b. promote regional peace and stability;

c. promote active collaboration and mutual assistance on matters of common interest;

d. provide assistance to each other through training and research;

e. collaborate for the uplift of the standard of living of the region's people;

f. promote Southeast Asian studies;

g. maintain close cooperation with international and regional organizations with similar aims and purposes.

D. ASEAN Cooperation

ASEAN member countries have forged several cooperation agreements on different aspects, particularly on economy, science and technology, social development, drugs and narcotics control, culture and information, politics, and with countries which are dialogue partners.

Economic cooperation is a key aspect of ASEAN cooperation. It encompasses both intra-ASEAN cooperation as well as extra-ASEAN cooperation with Third Countries (non-ASEAN member countries) and international organizations. ASEAN economic cooperation extends to the following fields:

a. Finance and banking

b. Food, agriculture and forestry

c. Industry, minerals and energy

In the field of political cooperation, pursuant to the ASEAN Declaration (1967) and the Declaration of ASEAN Concord (1976), ASEAN member countries coordinate their positions and take common stands whenever possible on several international political issues.

E. The ASEAN Charter

The ASEAN Charter, which was signed on November 20, 2007 in Singapore, entered into force on December 15, 2008. The Charter provides the legal and institutional framework for ASEAN to be a more rules-based, effective and people-oriented organization. The ASEAN Foreign Ministers and the Secretary-General of ASEAN met on December 15, 2008 at the ASEAN Secretariat to welcome the ASEAN Charter's entry into force. The Charter can serve as the basis for speeding up and strengthening regional integration. By virtue of its provisions, ASEAN community would be resting on the pillars politico-security cooperation, economic cooperation and socio-cultural cooperation. It also provides for ASEAN's elevation into a rules-based and people-oriented organization with a legal personality. H. E. Dr. Surin Pitsuwan, the Secretary-General of ASEAN, pledged to protect and uphold the ASEAN Charter in letter and in spirit for the benefits of all the peoples of ASEAN.

Ⅲ. The China-ASEAN Free Trade Agreement (CAFTA)

A. History

The idea of a free trade area between China and ASEAN was first proposed by Chinese Premier Zhu Rongji at the November 2000 China-ASEAN Summit. In October 2001, the China-ASEAN Expert Group on Economic Cooperation issued an official report recommending a "WTO-consistent ASEAN-China FTA" within ten years. A month later, at the November 2001 China-ASEAN Summit, the relevant leaders endorsed the ideas of the

Expert Group and the negotiation process officially commenced. Then, at the Eighth China-ASEAN Summit in November 2002, the ASEAN leaders and Chinese Premier Zhu Ronjgi signed the "Framework Agreement on Comprehensive Economic Co-operation" (CAFTA Framework Agreement). This agreement has served as a roadmap for the development of the free trade area. As laid out in the CAFTA Framework Agreement, a free trade area covering trade in goods between China and the original six ASEAN members is to be completed by 2010. The remaining four ASEAN members are expected to fully join by 2015. The CAFTA Framework Agreement is a ground breaking document, for after individual ASEAN members had previously created free trade agreements, ASEAN as an organization had never before made such a pact with an outside entity. Moreover, the CAFTA Framework Agreement was China's first free trade agreement with a foreign entity. Since the CAFTA Framework Agreement, both China and ASEAN have entered into negotiations with other countries regarding free trade agreements.

The objectives of the CAFTA Framework Agreement as stated in Article 1 thereof are the followings:

a. strengthen and enhance economic, trade and investment co-operation between the parties;

b. progressively liberalize and promote trade in goods and services as well as create a transparent, liberal and facilitative investment regime;

c. explore new areas and develop appropriate measures for closer economic cooperation between the parties;

d. facilitate the more effective economic integration of the newer ASEAN member states and bridge the development gap among the parties.

In order to establish China-ASEAN FTA within ten years from the taking effect of the CAFTA Framework Agreement, and to strengthen and enhance economic cooperation, the parties, in accordance with Article 2 thereof, shall adopt the following measures for comprehensive economic cooperation, to wit:

a. progressive elimination of tariffs and non-tariff barriers in substantially all trade in goods;

b. progressive liberalization of trade in services with substantial sectoral coverage;

c. establishment of an open and competitive investment regime that facilitates and promotes investment within the China-ASEAN FTA;

d. provision of special and differential treatment and flexibility to the newer ASEAN member states (Cambodia, Lao PDR, Myanmar and Vietnam);

e. provision of flexibility to the parties in the ASEAN-China FTA negotiations to address their sensitive areas in the goods, services, and investment sectors with such flexibility to be negotiated and mutually agreed based on the principles of reciprocity and mutual benefits;

f. establishment of effective trade and investment facilitation measures, including, but not limited to, simplification of customs procedures and development of mutual recognition arrangements;

g. expansion of economic cooperation in areas as may be mutually agreed between the parties and formulation of action plans and programmes in order to implement the agreed sectors/areas of cooperation;

h. establishment of appropriate mechanisms for the purposes of effective implementation of the framework agreement.

An "early harvest programme", to accelerate the establishment of the CAFTA, specified that tariffs on certain products would be eliminated over three years beginning January 1, 2004. A longer time-frame (no later than January 2010) was accorded to Cambodia, Lao PDR, Myanmar and Vietnam

An Agreement on Trade in Goods and an Agreement on the Dispute Settlement Mechanism of the Framework Agreement on Comprehensive Economic Cooperation between ASEAN and China entered into force on January 1, 2005. Authorities indicate that since the tariff reduction began, there has been a boom in imports and exports between China and ASEAN, and a narrowing trade imbalance.

It needs to be mentioned that there is also an Agreement on Trade in Services of the China-ASEAN Free Trade Area that was signed in January 2007 and entered into force on July 1, 2007.

B. The birth of CAFTA and its motivations

On January 1, 2010, China-ASEAN Free Trade Area (CAFTA) came into effect. Although some remain skeptical about the implementation of CAFTA and its impact on trade and industries in ASEAN countries, many ASEAN countries have been adjusting their economic structures and activities to remain competitive, and also to complement the Chinese economy.

Under CAFTA, China and ASEAN will inevitably increase intra-regional trade and investment as trade barriers are lowered and costs reduced. With access to a larger and more integrated market, businesses in the region become more competitive due to economies of scale. A more integrated market also tends to attract more inward investments from developed countries, creating employment and increasing economic welfare of member states.

China and ASEAN nations enjoy geographic advantage in their economic cooperation, and their economies are highly complementary to each other. Before taking effect, it is projected that CAFTA will benefit both sides and help lift world economy out of any financial crisis. It will also help enhance cultural exchanges and integration in the region and the mutual understanding between China and ASEAN nations.

Cooperation between China and ASEAN nations covers economic, political, cultural, environmental, security and many other spheres, and the CAFTA offers further impetus to their comprehensive cooperation.

Apparently, at the end of 2009, China has overtaken the US to become ASEAN's third largest trading partner. With the CAFTA in force, China may soon overtake Japan and the European Union to be ASEAN's largest trading partner. To enhance the positive effect of such relations, ASEAN countries may have to continue their efforts in adjusting their economic structures so as to reduce direct competition and create more room for complementarities with the Chinese economy.

Worth noting that at present, data show, as the world's third largest FTA, CAFTA has a combined GDP of US$6.6 trillion, a market of 1.9 billion people and a total trade of US$ 4.3 trillion. As any other FTA, the CAFTA would likely bolster ASEAN-China trade, which has already risen at a dramatic pace. The removal of trade impediments has lowered costs of transactions, further increasing China-ASEAN trade volume and enhancing economic efficiency. Moreover, since the implementation of CAFTA on January 1, 2010, more than 90% or over 7,000 products have been traded between China and the six members of ASEAN, i. e. , Brunei, the Philippines, Indonesia, Malaysia, Thailand and Singapore, tariff-free.

Ⅳ. Conclusion

In sum, although increasing trade and investment ties have caused China and ASEAN to become more economically interdependent, these relationships are still trailing the region's economic relationships with the United States and Japan, but the gap is narrowing.

The China-ASEAN relations are characterized as economic cooperation at first hand. Such relationship has been developing from economic cooperation to other areas of cooperation. The agreements between China and ASEAN, has gradually evolved and been formulated, thus extending their relations initially from economic aspect to political, security and legal fields and on many other areas of cooperation between the two sides.

CAFTA is expected not only to improve the economic but also the political and social relations between ASEAN and China, building on existing geographic proximity, as well as historical and cultural ties. The free trade area as a regional bloc, will bring about regional peace and prosperity in China and Southeast Asia as well as contribute to a balance of power in East Asia and provide for a louder and more effective voice in the international fora.

Truly, the forging of the China-ASEAN Free Trade Area came as a milestone in the annals of China-ASEAN relations, in that if continued to be carefully and transparently implemented, will improve not only the economic but also the geo-political conditions in the China-ASEAN region and thus may well serve as a model for regional cooperation not only in Asia, but in other parts of the world as well.

References:

—Handbook on "The ASEAN Basic Information", The Third ASEAN Summit, December 14—15, 1987, Manila, Philippines.

—ASEAN Documents Series, 2002.

—Foreign Relations Journal, Volume X, No. 4, December 1995.

—Implementing the Roadmaps on ASEAN Community 2015, ASEAN Annual Report 2008—2009.

—China-ASEAN Free Trade Area in 2010, A Regional Perspective, by Sarah Y. Tong & Catherine Chong Siew Keng.

—The ASEAN-China Free Trade Area (ACFTA): A Legal Response to China's Economic Rise? by Alyssa Greenwald.

中国—东盟自由贸易区在地缘政治及经济上的必要性

Maria Cristina P. Rilloraza
菲律宾司法部总检察长办公室代表

内容摘要

2010年中国—东盟自由贸易区的成立对于中国—东盟关系的发展具有非常重要的里程碑意义。本文首先对东盟的历史、成员构成、目标与宗旨、东盟内部合作、东盟宪章进行分析,进一步对中国—东盟自由贸易协定的历史、中国—东盟自由贸易区的产生以及发展进行阐述,进而指出,中国—东盟自由贸易区的成立强化了中国与东盟之间在经济上的相互依赖程度,并将推动双方从经济合作扩展到政治、国家安全以及法律等领域的全方位合作。

关键词:中国—东盟自由贸易区;经济合作;地区发展;地缘政治

目　次

The Legal Issue Related to China-ASEAN FTA: From Indonesian Judge Perspective

Ifa Sudewi & Elyta Ras Ginting & Joni

Ifa Sudewin, vice-chief of District Court of General Jakarfa of Indonesia

Elyta Ras Ginting, vice-chief of District Court of Surabaya

Joni, Judge of Bogor District Court

Content

Introduction

After the establishment of the China-ASEAN FTA in January 2010, almost 90 percents of trade products (approximately 1516 tariffs posted in the industrial manufacture) now enjoy zero tariffs from 5 percents. It is predicted that China's rapid economic growth will affected Indonesia economic growth significantly and thus China itself would enjoy great profit from Indonesia. The argumentation is based on Indonesia's territory with 1904569 kilometers and populate of 230130000 be assumed as a potential geographical market for China's products and services. Prior to FTA commencement, many China's product such as agricultural products and manufacturer were selling massively throughout Indonesian territory and China's products compete fairly with domestic product within the quality and price rate.

However, compared to the recent China's rapid economic growth, many experts doubt that there would be unbalance within free and fair trading relationship between the two countries in the future. Until now, Indonesia has not yet fully developed its market system to compete with other Asean member countries, particularly with China after enter the FTA in 2010. Therefore, Indonesia's domestic market would not be ready to compete in free trade like its counterpart countries such as Singapore, Malaysia, Thailand and Philippines. In addition, the FTA, which promote free trade, would likely to influence the small-scale medium to business which produce the alike product imported from China in the relevant market. Even agricultural products such as early harvest product like fruits, cannot compete in free trade market without the government policy to protect the domestic product. For example, when China's oranges sold massively in Indonesia, the local oranges' price fell down to the lowest and caused loss to the oranges' farmers.

Recently, to deal with the establishment of China-ASEAN FTA framework, Indonesian government has established the technical commitee to guard the implementation of the framework. One of the supervisory areas is the entry of goods to Indonesia to prevent smuggling. The government is also dealing with anti dumping and to watch whether the goods exported to Indonesia have been accomplished with the state of origin notes. However, the framework has nothing to do with the trade competition between Indonesia and China. Until now the government has not taken any action to enable the local products to compete fairly and equally with China's product which selling broadly within Indonesia. Whereas, the FTA establishment between China and Indonesia obviously display a number of important legal issue, particulary in the fair competition trade law. This paper is about Indonesian judge's perspective about legal issue related to China-ASEAN FTA commencement and proposed to describe the regulation concerning fair competition practice in Indonesia and how the business actors deal with the regulation.

Ⅰ. Governing Law

In the past, Indonesia had no specific regulation regarding with competition trade practice. All trade practice in Indonesia must be comply with general law such as Indonesian Criminal Law and Civil Code and all trade practice shall be based on economic democracy with due attention to balance between the business actor's interest and the public interest. After Indonesia hit by economic crises in 1998, the Government and the House of Reperesentatives proposed the draft law concerning competition trade practice in order to satisfied the Letter of Intent proposed by the International Monetary Fund (IMF) which urged Indonesia to reform its market system and to promote competition in trade practice. On March 5, 1999, the Law Number 5 of 1999 concerning against Monopolistic Practices and Unfair Business Competition was signed into law and after some additional grace periods the Law Number 5 of 1999 fully enacted on March 5, 2000. The Law No. 5 of 1999 is proposed to:

a) Safeguard the interest of the public and to improve nation economic efficiency.

b) Ensure the certainty of equal business opportunities among the large, medium or small-scale business actors.

c) Create effectiveness and efficiency in conducting business activity.

d)Regulates the agreement and business activities and also provides how the business actor should behave to market behaviour, market price, market share, market structure and to dominant position in the relevant market in order to achieve fair business practice accordingly.

Basically, the Law No. 5 of 1999 concerns with three points: 1). prohibited agreement in trade practices, 2). prohibited activities in trade practices and 3). abuses of dominant position in trade practice that may result in monopolistic practices and unfair business competition. Therefore, the prohibition concerned by the Law No. 5 of 1999 are monopolistic practices and unfair business competition. Accordingly, such prohibited practices are proved from the agreement or from the business activities relate to the trade practice. On the other hand, the dominant position does not violate the Law of No. 5 of 1999 but depend on how the business actor deal with its dominant position. The Law No. 5 of 1999 prohibits the business actor abuse its dominant position by conducting concentration of power and therefore dominant position has relevance with merger and acquitition. The law provides that the business actor in dominant position have to undergo investigation before merger and the legality of merger activity is subject to the Company Law which deal with general provisions of merger and acquitition.

The context of monopolistic practice and prohibited activities is defined in general term and provided in Article 1—2 and 1—6 of the Law No. 5 of 1999 :

· Monopolistic Practices:

Monopolistic practices shall be the centralization of economic power by one or more business actors resulting in the control of the production and/or marketing of certain goods and/or services thus resulting in unfair business competition and potentially harmful to the interest of the public.

Unfair business competition:

Unfair business competition shall be competition and business actor in conducting activities for the production and/or marketing of goods and/or services in an unfair or unlawful anti competition manner.

Ⅱ. Prohibited Agreements

The law prohibits some agreements tending to establish some condition which results to occurence of monopolistic practice or unfair competition. There are 16 (sixteen) agreements that may violate the Law No. 5 of 1999 including:

1. Oligopolies:

An agreement to exercise control over production or marketing of goods cooperatively which may gives monopolistic practices or unfair competition. The bussiness actors should be alleged or deemed to control over production and/or marketing of goods if two or three business actors take control more than 75% of market share of one specific kinds of goods.

2. Price Discrimination:

Business actors are prohibited to enter an agreement supposed to require purchaser to pay different price with another purchaser for the same goods.

3. Price Fixing:

An agreement with competing business actor to stipulate prices which must be paid by purchaser for goods in the same relevant market. This provision does not apply to agreement made in the joint venture sector.

4. Predatory Pricing:

An agreement with competing business to set prices below the market price which result to unfair business competition.

5. Control Over Re-sale Pricing and Supply:

An agreement contains conditions that the good's recipient may not re-sell or re-supply goods which are received previously under price than the agreed price if that condition may result in unfair business competition.

6. Market Segmentation and Carving:

An agreement among the business actors to divide marketing territory or allocating market relating to goods if that division may result in monopolistic practice or unfair competition.

7. Boycott:

Prohibits business actor to enter an agreement with its competitor which may hinder other business actor/competitor from engaging in the same business conducted domestically or internationally. The agreement which contains agreement to reject sale of any goods of any other business actor also considered to boycott activity if the agreement may cause loss to another competitor or cause to limit another business actor to sell or to buy goods in the relevant market.

8. Cartel:

An agreement between a group of business actors to regulate production and marketing of goods in order to influence the prices in the markets. The agreement is prohibited if the said agreement may result in occurance of monopolistic practices or unfair competition.

9. Trust:

An agreement to cooperate in formation of larger federation of business among the business actors by protecting and securing the existence of each business member in order to control production or marketing of goods. This agreement is prohibited if the said agreement may result in occurance of monopolistic practices or unfair competition.

10. Oligopsony:

An Agreement among business actors group to control purchases or receipts of supplies jointly in order to control the price of goods in relevant market is prohibited if the said agreement cause them jointly to control 75% of market share of one specific kinds of goods.

11. Vertical Integration:

Prohibits the business actor enter an agreement with other business actor in order to control a number of a series products of specific goods where each production series constitutes product of manufacturing or continuing processing directly or indirectly if the said agreement may result in occurance of monopolistic practices or unfair competition.

12. Tying Agreement:

Prohibits the agreement among the business actors which contains some conditions that:

1) The goods receiver will only supply or will not re-supply goods to particular business actors or to particular place

2) The goods receiver must be prepared to buy other goods from supplier

business actor

3)Condition to give particular price or discount provided the goods receiver must be prepared to buy other goods from the goods supplier and will not buy the same or the similar goods from other competitor

However, certain agreements and business activities are exempted from by Law No. 5 of 1999 including:

a)Agreements related to intellectual property rights

b)Agreement regarding technical standards for goods/services products provided such agreement does not restrain or impede other business actor to compete

c)Agreement intended to implement applicable laws and regulations

d)International agreement ratified by the Government

e)Small scale business's activities

f)Activities of business cooperative aimed at serving its members

g)Agency agreement that do not include resale price maintenance

h)Agreement for the purpose of research and development

i)Export agreement

Ⅲ. Prohibited Trade Activities

According to the Law No. 5 of 1999, some trading activities of the business actors are prohibited if such activities likely to prevent other competitor to enter or to compete in the market share. In order to determine whether the business activities are prohibited by the Law No. 5 of 1999 are measured by *rule of reason* or *per se illegal* approach. *The rule of reason* approach is applied to:

a)Market division

b)Cartel

c)Trust bid rigging

Whereas, *the per se illegal* approach is applied to business activities including:

a)Price discrimination

b)Exclusive dealing concerning resupply

c)Trying agreement

d) Reciprocal Dealing

e) Exclusive dealing

f) Abuse of dominant position

g) Cross share ownership

According to the Law No. 5 of 1999, the business activities where a firm or group of firms take control over 75% of market collectively are presumed conducting oligopoly and olygopsony. Monopoly or monopsony practice occurs when a business actor control over 50% of market and impede production which prevent other competitor to enter the market to compete in the same market. Other trading activities such as dual position, share ownership, merger, acquisition and consolidation may be prohibited if such activities results to restrain or prevent other competitor to compete in the market share, to limit market and technology development and to restain other competitor to compete in the relevant market.

Share ownership activities are prohibited and considered to unfair competition if:

a) One group of business actors controling more than50% market share of one particular kinds of goods

b) Two or more business groups controlling more than 75% marketshare in one particular kinds of goods

Dominant position might violate the Law No. 5 of 1999 if a business actor control over 50% (for a group of firm control over 75%) of market and the business actor abuses of its dominant position by conducting any prohibited agreement or activities such as tying agreement, predatory pricing, exclusive dealing concerning resupply and therefore to prevent other to compete in the market.

Ⅳ. Business Competition Supervisory Commission

The Law No. 5 of 1999 also provides an independent body free from the Government's management and control to enforce the Law No. 5 of 1999 and to regulate business competition and independent business practices. This agency is supposed to supervise the performance or the conduct of business actors by examining their agreement or their activities to prevent monopolistic practice or unfair competition. This commision established by Presidential Decree No. 75 of 1999 Concerning Business Competition Supervisory Commission. The commission in Indonesia is recognized as Komisi Pengawas Persaingan Usaha or KPPU. Practically, is in charge not only to supervise the trading activities but also functioned as a tribunal regarding with violation of the Law No. 5 of 1999. Therefore, the commission as the regulatory agency has administrative power and acts as quasi judicial power. The administrative power of Commission including:

a) Evaluating the agreement or the business activities which may result in occurrence of monopolistic practice or unfair competition

b) Evaluating the existence of dominant position or the improper use of dominant position of a certain business actor which may result in occurence of monopolistic practice or unfair competition

c) Providing advice and giving suggestion and consideration concerning the Government policy related to monopolistic practice and making directives or publication related to the Law No. 5 Year 1999

d) Issuing guide lines and policy statement regarding to competition practice according to the Law No. 5 of 1999

e) Assisting business actors and the public to comply with the Law No. 5 of 1999

The Commission also has authority to law enforcement (quasi judicial power) including:

a) Receiving report of the allegation that a certain business actor is conducting monopolistic practice or unfair competition

b) Coducting preliminary investigation, summoning the alleged business actor to attend the commision tribunal and deciding whether the alleged agreement or business activities ia a monopolistic practice or unfair competition

c) Issuing civil remedies such as:

1) Stipulation of cancellation of prohibited agreement

2) Order to the alleged business actor to discontinue the monopolistic activities

3) Order to the alleged busniess actor to discontinue misuse of dominant position in the market

d) Stipulation of cancellation of the legal entity decision to conduct merger or consideration of business entity

e) Order to pay compensation of loss caused of business agreement or business activities

f) Order to pay fines of up to (approximately) U $ 2.5 million

The Commission may seek criminal penalties for certain violations enumerated in Art. 48 of Law No. 5 of 1999 through submission to police investigation who may refer to the matter to the prosecutor authority. The criminal fines is up to U $ 10 million and prison sentences up to 6 months.

Ⅴ. The Role of the Court

The Law No. 5 Year 1999 gives right to the parties who suffer loss from the prohibited agreement or prohibited activities to report in writen to the Commission. The same right is also given to any person who knows that violation of Law No. 5 Year 1999 is occured. Accordingly, the Commission itself also may conduct examination whenever the commission find the occurence of monopolistic activity or unfair competition.

The proceeding to examinate the claim take place in the Commission site. Firstly, the preliminary examination conducted within 30 days after the receipt of report. The urgency of the preliminary examination is to determine wheter the Commission is obliged to take further examination. The Commission is required further examination to determine whether violation of Law No. 5 Year 1999 is occured or not within 30 days since the completion of further examination.

The implementation of the Commission decision must be conducted within 30 days since notified to the reported business actor. If the reported business actor failed to implement the Commission's decision voluntarily, this condition can be a sufficient evidence for the investigator to conduct the investigation of criminal violation of the the Law No. 5 of 1999 provisions. Business actor may submit objection to District Court within 14 days after receipt the notification of the Commission decision. The is Court required to give decision of objection within 30 days from the commencement of examination before the court. The business actor who object to the court decision may submit appeal to the Supreme Court as the highest judiciary body. The

Supreme Court must render the decision within 30 days of receipt of petition for appeal. If the decision has acquired final and binding force, the enforcement order for execution should be requested from the District Court.

The criminal provision examination is conducted in the District Court where the violation takes place. The violations concerning prohibited agreement or prohibited activities (such as monopolistic practices, market control or misuse of dominant position) are punishable with criminal penalties and fine and additional criminal sanction as well. The criminal fines is up to $ 10 million (approximately) and prison sentences up to 6 months. The additional criminal sanction includes:

a) Cancellation of business license

b) Prohibition to business actor to take position as director or commissioner of legal entity for certain time

c) Termination of specific business activities which gives rise to loss to other parties.

Conclusion

The nature of unfair business competition or monopolistic business practices provided in the Law No. 5 of 1999 covers prohibited agreement, prohibited activities and dominant position. An agreement and activities in trade are considered prohibited by rule of reason *if that agreement or business activities may result in monopolistic practices or unfair business competition*. The business activities assumed as monopolistic or unfair business subject to rule of reason approach include market division, cartels, trust and bid rigging. Other agreement or business activities are considered *per se illegal*. The business activities assumed as monopolistic or unfair business subject to per se illegal including price discrimination, exclusive dealing, tying agreement, reciprocal dealing, abuse of dominant market and cross share ownership.

Obviously, the Law No. 5 of 1999 was not proposed to foster economic growth through the government control, rather the Law itself mainly proposed to boost the fair business practice in Indonesia. The law itself does not deal with the international trade issues such as the chance for Indonesia to sell its products or services to China and the competing price of each products in domestic market. Therefore Indonesia experiences concerning trading with China within FTA framework is subject to the law No. 5 of 1999 in general basis only within domestic market. The competition conduct in trade between Indonesia and China along with the unbalanced market power issue is likely covers by the said law.

In the future, if Indonesia products cannot compete fairly with those from China, it is possibly that the business actors from China might gain dominant position in the market and take control of the market. Moreover, it is known that China's business actors tend to sell their product cheaper than other Asean countries in order to accumulate the export volume of goods to Indonesia. Such activities to supply goods by selling the goods at loss or setting price to a very low price rate might be violate the Law No. 5 of 1999 if restrain other competitor to compete in the relevant market to sell the same products or goods.

Indonesia and China need to provide a legal framework concerning the monopolistic practices or unfair competition in the FTA to improve the bilateral cooperation. It is necessary to have the legal framework that supports a competitive market in FTA between Indonesia and China to gain the mutual benefit in trade. There must be guarantees of genuine price competitive and access for Indonesia business actor to sell its product to China and likewise. Another important legal issue from the FTA among Indonesia and China including the consumer protection and intellectual property protection legal framework also would be necessary. It is time for both country to harmonize the business competition among ASEAN countries, particularly between China and Indonesia to promote the FTA.

中国—东盟自由贸易区相关的法律问题:基于印度尼西亚法官的视角

Ifa Sudewi，印尼雅加达中心地区法院副院长
Elyta Ras Ginting，印尼苏腊巴亚地区法院副院长
Joni，印尼茂物地区法院法官

内容摘要

中国—东盟自由贸易区的建立引发了印尼方面的担心，鉴于中国经济的迅速发展，以及印尼市场体系的不完善，亟待完善有关的法律制度以确保两国间建立自由公平的贸易关系。本文对印尼国内有关公平竞争的法律法规、相关的商业竞争监察委员会以及法院在其中的作用进行分析，指出印尼尚未建立完善的法律体系以处理双边贸易公平竞争问题，建议中印两国应在自由贸易区内部建立相应的法律框架以解决垄断与不公平竞争贸易行为，从而促进双边合作。

关键词:CAFTA;垄断行为;不公平竞争行为;禁止性贸易活动

目　次

中国—东盟自由贸易区规则的不足与完善之策

张晓君[*] 徐忆斌[**]

内容摘要

按照“框架协议十具体协议”的模式,中国—东盟自由贸易区基本形成了涉及货物贸易、服务贸易、与贸易有关的投资、贸易争端解决等领域的一系列规则体系。在WTO多边贸易体制的背景下,结合中国—东盟自由贸易区实施以来的具体情况,剖析对中国—东盟自由贸易区规则的不足进而提出相应的完善之策,以促进中国—东盟自由贸易区的健康发展。

关键词:中国—东盟自由贸易区;规则;缺陷;对策

目 次

---

* 张晓君,西南政法大学国际法学院副院长、教授,中国—东盟法律研究中心秘书长。

** 徐忆斌,西南政法大学国际法学院讲师,法学博士。

前　言

21世纪以来，区域经济一体化已经成为不可阻挡的趋势，成为经济全球化的重要内容，在一体化的浪潮中扮演着重要的角色。与此相应，各类区域经济组织纷纷建立，对全球经济的发展发挥着重要作用。作为当今经济最为活跃和发展迅速的新兴经济体，中国率先开启了与东南亚国家联盟的一体化进程，并以法律形式加以规范化和制度化。2002年11月4日，在第六次中国—东盟领导人会议上，中国与东盟领导人共同签署了《中国—东盟全面经济合作框架协议》，双方一致同意于2010年建成"中国—东盟自由贸易区"（下文简称CAFTA）。作为中国对外签订的第一个自由贸易区协定，并且是与一个区域组织签订的协定，该协议的意义是显而易见的，对日后参与其他的区域经济一体化起到了示范效应。

CAFTA法制建设思路采取的是一种"框架协议＋具体协议"的模式，即先以框架协议的方式在各缔约国之间确定共同目标，而后各方就具体事项进行谈判，并以具体协议将谈判结果纳入已有的法律框架，从而形成整体制度。2004年1月，中国与东盟双方启动了"早期收获计划"，600种农产品先行降低关税。同年11月，在第八次中国—东盟领导人会议上，中国和东盟签署了《中国—东盟全面经济合作框架协议货物贸易协议》（下文简称《货物贸易协议》），其包括了23个条款和3个附件。该协议的实施，标志着中国—东盟间的全面降低关税的进程开始启动，首批7445种商品的关税降到20％左右。2007年1月14日，中国与东盟签订了《中国—东盟全面经济合作框架协议服务贸易协议》（下文简称《服务贸易协议》），CAFTA向纵深开始发展，标志着区内服务贸易市场的开放。2009年8月，在泰国举行的第八次中国—东盟经济贸易部长会议上，中国与东盟签署了《中国—东盟全面经济合作框架协议投资协议》（下文简称《投资协议》），完成了CAFTA协议规定的区内主要领域的自由化法制建设。至此CAFTA基本具备了建构自由贸易区的法制条件。2010年1月1日，CAFTA如期建成。然而，尽管从宏观制度层面审视，CAFTA"框架协议＋具体协议"的模式已经初步具备，但是在内部和操作层面上，CAFTA有很多"细微"不足，特别是涉及制度的协调和执行力问题。

一、CAFTA 货物贸易规则的不足与完善之策

《货物贸易协议》是中国签订的首个区域货物贸易协定,也是中国与东盟间具有里程碑意义的协议,它的达成和实施,为全面推进自由贸易区的建设奠定了基础。它以 WTO 规则为基础,同时兼顾 CAFTA 自身的需要,着重体现对东盟四个新成员国老挝、缅甸、柬埔寨、越南的优惠待遇和特殊照顾,体现了自由贸易区灵活性的特点。[①] 具体而言,《货物贸易协议》具有以下特点:首先,协议的内容贴近 WTO 规则。"货物贸易协议"在条文的订立上以 GATT1994 为参照,有的条款甚至照搬后者条款。如"货物贸易协议"第 2 条"国内税和国内法的国民待遇"中,直接规定 GATT1994 第 3 条"国内税和国内法的国民待遇"作为其内容一部分。在非关税措施、贸易技术壁垒、卫生与植物卫生措施、补贴与反补贴措施、反倾销措施和知识产权等方面适用 WTO 的相应规定。[②] 在采取保障国际收支平衡措施时,则以 GATT1994 和《关于执行 GATT1994 国际收支条款谅解》为根据。其次,《货物贸易协议》突出了 CAFTA 自身的需要,如东盟承认中国市场经济地位,承诺对中国不适用《中国入世议定书》第 15 条(反倾销替代国定价)和第 16 条(特殊保障措施)以及《中国加入工作组报告书》第 242 段(纺织品特保条款)。又如中国在《〈中国—东盟全面经济合作框架协议〉修正议定书》中以"早期收获计划"给予东盟的农产品以关税优惠。在一般例外中,出于需要,双方将原料以及短缺产品列明其中。[③] 此外,对贸易的商品分不同的路径和不同的贸易模式:普通路径(Normal Track)中减让和消除关税的货物以附件一中的模式(modalities)进行;列在敏感路径(Sensitive Track)中减让和消除关税的货物以附件二的模式(modalities)进行。《货物贸易协议》符合 WTO 规则又有其区域特色,有助于协调多边贸易体制和区域体制,构建良好的区内企业公平和公正的贸易竞争环境,也对解决中国市场经济地位起到了很好的示范作用。就目前《货物贸易协议》的实施来看,主要面临如下的问题:

第一,短期减税力度较大,对中国农业造成压力。在 CAFTA 推进中,最早

---

① Stefano INAMA, The Association of South East Asian Nations People's Republic of China Free Trade Area: Negotiating Beyond Eternity with Little Trade Liberalization, *Journal of World Trade*, 2005,(3):560.

② 《中国—东盟自由贸易区货物贸易协定》第 7 条"WTO 纪律"。

③ 《中国—东盟自由贸易区货物贸易协定》第 12 条(I)(j)款。

实施的是“早期收获”安排，而在关税方面，有的是双方互免，但更多的则是单方减让，而且在这些农产品中，中国的竞争力也较弱。为了推进自由贸易区的建立，中国没有提出国内农产品实行特定产品和例外产品保护，中国现有的农民生产经营方式无法适应这种竞争，在国际市场竞争环境中将会处于不利地位。为加入世贸组织，中国已经对于农业进行了较大力度的结构调整，在此基础上，“早期收获”产品减税幅度过大，超过了某些区域农业的承受能力，会造成冲击，加大了农业结构调整的困难。

第二，贸易政策协调难度大，出口风险预计不足。中国和东盟在出口商品导向和产业结构上有很高的相似度，这无疑增加了双方之间政策协调的难度。只有在出口贸易政策方面进行紧密协调，才能避免因成员国对各自出口产品政策上的支持而造成的恶性竞争。同时，在 CAFTA 这样较为松散且成员间差异较明显的一体化制度安排中，缺乏统一规范的市场机制，投资贸易环境不稳定，经贸往来存在的风险较大。

第三，出口面临繁多的壁垒风险。通过《货物贸易协议》的安排，具有竞争优势的产品会由于关税的降低和取消而相应的增加出口总量。但是，出口的急速增加不可避免地会对进口国造成不小的压力，在降低和取消关税的情况下，一些成员国有可能会选择采用非关税壁垒的方式，比如提高农产品的质检标准，通过对进口商品实行严格的检验检疫制度，进而限制具有竞争优势产品向其出口，无疑这也是需要未雨绸缪的一项挑战。

第四、贸易导向趋同、产业结构重叠。中国与东盟都不以对方为最主要出口市场，在贸易结构上其两者呈现出导向趋同而非互补的特点，特别是其都倾向于以美欧为主要出口市场，同时由于出口的商品也都以劳动密集型产品和低技术层次的制成品为主，因此，虽然双边贸易迅速发展，但是自贸区的建立并没有大幅度减轻区内各方对区外市场的依赖，相反可能会抵消自贸区的集团优势。因此，如何扩大区内贸易互补性需求或者培育良好的对外贸易竞争机制是 CAFTA 面临的又一问题。

上述问题的解决，需要从内外两个方面进行解决。内部而言，即如何解决中国自身应对向东盟开放市场后带来的一系列冲击，笔者认为，市场开放以及自贸区的构建必然会造成体系内部的重新洗牌，影响和冲击是难免的，从长远看，这有利于竞争力的提高和产业的发展。但同时也应该看到，市场的包容力是强大的，各方产业都有其绝对或比较优势，如中国的市场，许多产业特色鲜明，在竞争博弈中仍具优势。虽然自贸区的许多制度都借鉴于世贸规则，但也有其地区特点，只要各方致力推动规则的执行，是可以处理好成员间的经贸关系的。外部而言,构建CAFTA的基本初衷和目标应是以维护地区的经济发展和政治关系为契机。从战略的高度看,通过区内紧密合作来转变经济增长模式,以本区域的市场内需来拉动区域经济整体增长,优化区域分工与资源配置,以减少对区外发达国家的过度依赖。如此也才能加深一体化的依赖度,更好地发挥自由贸易区的集团优势。通过内外两方面的不断加深和磨合,能够解决存在的问题,推动CAFTA下的货物贸易健康而有序地发展。

二、CAFTA投资规则的不足与完善之策

2002年签署的《中国—东盟全面经济合作框架协议》是CAFTA的基础性法律文件,其提出的"逐渐实现投资机制的自由化"的目标,为相互投资关系的协调指明了发展方向。但从现有的制度供给来看,《框架协议》中关于"投资"的规定较为原则和概括,内容不够具体。为此,必须尽快制定能为各方所接受的、综合性的投资协议,对中国与东盟之间相互投资的总体方案和具体事项作出统一的安排。2009年8月15日,中国与东盟签署了CAFTA下的《投资协议》。该协议共27个条款,目标在于促进东盟与中国之间投资流动,建立自由、便利、透明和具有竞争性的投资体制。主要涉及投资待遇、征收与损失补偿、转移和利润汇回、代位求偿、缔约方间争端解决、缔约方和投资者间争端解决、一般例外、安全例外等内容。应该说,《投资协议》在CAFTA范围内创建了统一的区域投资保护法制。同时,在保护外国投资者私益的同时也试图兼顾了东道国国家主权。与《货物贸易协定》相比,投资规则中的大部分内容都超出了WTO相关规则。在投资待遇方面,协议规定双方相互给予投资者最惠国待遇、国民待遇和公平待遇,促进投资便利化。但《投资协议》也并非一步到位旨在实现完全的投资自由化,而是规定了若干例外,实际上实行的是渐进式的投资自由化,与当今各国在投资领域的对外开放程度基本相称。对于投资争端的解决,《投资协议》规定了两种情况:第一种是缔约国政府之间的投资争端,要根据《投资协议》第13条解决,该条规定沿用《争端解决机制协议》的相关规定和程序。第二种情况是关于缔约国政府与另一缔约国私人之间的争端,要根据第14条第4款的规定,可以提交包括国际投资争端解决中心在内的多种可选择的仲裁机构仲裁。

作为CAFTA全面建成的标志性协议,各方期望其签署和生效能极大促进中国与东盟国家之间的相互投资,并妥善兼顾东道国的主权利益。但是不可否认的是,此项协定只有27个条款,作为一项区域经济合作框架下的投资规则甚为疏漏,同时对于其他的CAFTA内部成员之间已经达成的双边投资协定等也

未加考虑，因此实有必要根据“框架协议”中所确定的投资原则，参照 WTO《与贸易有关的投资措施协议》、《东盟投资区框架协议》以及中国与一些东盟国家间的双边投资协定的具体规定，并考虑到中国与东盟国家有关利用外资、对外投资的国内立法，从条约解释和制度比较的角度作出一定的澄清。

总体上，《投资协议》的投资自由化程度还不够高，仍存在较大的缺陷。这主要体现在：一是对投资者待遇实施的是准入后国民待遇，投资准入领域仍由各国国内法加以规定；二是对“履行要求”具体内容的缺失；三对中国实行的投资待遇问题。我国与东盟 8 国（除缅甸、柬埔寨）的双边投资协定都规定了最惠国待遇或者最惠国待遇和公平公正待遇，《东盟投资区框架协议》（AIA）规定了“在 2010 年前将国民待遇扩大到东盟投资者，在 2020 年前扩大到所有投资者，本协议下例外条款除外”，《投资协议》仍然实行中国在 BIT 采用的最惠国待遇，在投资待遇这个问题上没有进展，相对于 AIA 反而是一种倒退。[①]此外，《投资协议》还存在着诸如约束的国家行为范围过于狭窄、缺乏审慎措施条款、根本安全例外条款未受到必要的制度性约束等问题。[②]《投资协议》条文含混或过于简单，操作性不强。例如《投资协议》中多处使用“经必要修改”后适用本协议或纳入本协议等措辞，但是对于如何“修改”却没有更进一步的解释或说明；关于“不符措施”没有任何界定和描述；对于投资促进、投资便利化的规定可操作性有待加强。对此，需要加以改进和革新，《投资协议》的修改和后续谈判应扩大受约束的国家行为之范围，增设审慎措施条款，对根本安全例外条款予以必要的、程序性的制度约束。综观各层面的投资立法，外资准入自由化都受到了或多或少的限制，《投资协议》实施准入后国民待遇是现实的选择，但是也必须看到投资自由化不断深化与加强是投资规则不容争议的趋势。在此基础上，强化《投资协议》的可操作条款，通过条约解释或者在个案来具体化，以此不断完善。例如，通过添加附件的方式列举“不符措施”清单；“透明度”原则过于抽象、权利义务不明确，则可以通过将其分解为具体的原则或条款化来增强其可操作性。当然，这需要中国与东盟国家的共同努力，通过协商，选择出一个各方均能接受的方案，选择一种最优的制度安排，逐渐消除法律制度层面的障碍，以适应和促进区域投资自由化的发展。

---

① 丁丁等：《论中国—东盟自由贸易区的投资自由化和便利化》，载《国际商务——对外经济贸易大学学报》2005 年第 6 期。

② 参见魏艳茹：《〈中国—东盟投资协议〉：成就、不足与完善》，第四届“中国东盟法律合作与发展高层论坛”会议论文集。

晚近投资协定领域出现一些新的变化。比如,投资协定的内容和条款日益复杂,已经超出了传统投资保护协定的范围;投资者与东道国间的争端解决条款的日益详尽;东道国的监督和管制体制也更多地受到关注。同时,投资领域的潜在风险不断增加,投资者和东道国之间的争端案件迅速增多,有必要进一步改革投资者与东道国的国际仲裁机制,加强其公开性、透明性以及对国际仲裁员的纪律约束。就 CAFTA 投资争端解决制度而言,应在协定基础上加以进一步完善,构建符合本地区"和"和"合"的传统文化特色的争端解决机制,例如对于投资者与东道国间的争端,应该慎用协议规定的争端解决仲裁机制,充分利用磋商、交流、谈判等方式来解决分歧。

此外,中国与东盟国家间的相互投资额还比较低,特别是中国对东盟的 FDI 在数量上与东盟对中国投资相比还处于非常低的水平,未来如何进一步扩大双方之间的投资,特别是如何大力促进中国对东盟投资是一个需要关注并亟待解决的问题。近年来,中国政府积极鼓励企业"走出去"到东盟国家投资。CAFTA 的建成,为中国企业走出去提供了新的机遇。随着《投资协议》的实施,双方将相互给予投资者国民待遇、最惠国待遇和投资公平公正待遇,可以预见,中国与东盟相互投资额将会快速增长。政府应加强能力建设,搭建中国企业与东盟企业间沟通的平台,支持行业协会发挥更大的作用。同时办好诸如东盟博览会等各类展会促进交流合作。

三、CAFTA 服务贸易规则的不足与完善之策

2007 年 1 月中国与东盟签署了 CAFTA 下的《服务贸易协议》(下称《协议》),这也是中国与其他国家签署的首个关于区域服务贸易的协议。《协议》的签署标志着中国与东盟就服务贸易的交往活动的规模化和规范化的开始,为中国创造了一个货物贸易、服务贸易良性循环的法律环境。[①] 但毕竟 CAFTA 服务贸易制度建立时间短,存在诸多不完善之处。同时,区内的服务贸易发展也呈现出实力均等,程度不深以及互补性强的特点。一方面,东盟国家大都为发展中国家,经济发展水平相对落后,服务业发展都较缓慢:除在新加坡、马来西亚、泰国等新型工业化国家外,其他像柬埔寨、老挝、缅甸、越南等国家,服务业没有多大的发展。就中国而言,服务业发展水平也不高,甚至占全球的服务贸易份额的

---

① 参见张晓君:《中国—东盟〈服务贸易协定〉与中国服务业发展》,载《河北法学》2010 年 3 月。

比例还低于东盟各国。中国与东盟各国间的服务贸易大多集中在低端领域，如旅游、建筑、教育等，而在像金融、管理、咨询等服贸的高端部分，则更为落后。另一方面，中国与东盟在咨询、金融、教育、旅游、电子商务、人力资源开发、基础设施建设管理、城市规划等领域存在很大的合作空间。尤其是在旅游资源上，中国和东盟各有优势，互补性较强，中国拥有悠久的历史文化、优美的自然风光和特有的人文景观，而东盟国家则有神秘的热带雨林、迷人的岛屿风光和奇异的风俗习惯。目前，东盟10国均已成为中国公民出国旅游目的地国。中国与泰国、新加坡、菲律宾、越南、缅甸等东盟国家分别签署了政府旅游合作协定或旅游合作谅解备忘录。CAFTA 的建立必将推动双方旅游业的进一步发展。

总的来看，CAFTA 下以《服务贸易协议》为基础的制度，是与中国及东盟在服务贸易发展方面的特点联系起来的，但与其他区域服务贸易一体的制度实践相比较，仍存在着很多方面的问题与差距。

第一，市场准入程度不高。《框架协议》第1条明确了其目标是加强和增进各缔约方的经济、贸易和投资合作，为货物贸易和服务贸易提供便利的条件，以逐步实现货物贸易和服务贸易的自由化，并旨在缩小各缔约方发展水平的差距。《协议》进一步规定各成员方在 GATS 所做承诺的基础上，继续扩展服务贸易自由化的深度与广度。但就目前而言，CAFTA 区内市场开放的程度还不高，存在着很多限制。《协议》的承诺减让表采取的是"肯定清单"模式，与 NAFTA 采取的否定模式相比，具有很强的隐蔽性或灵活性，也使其透明度较低。CAFTA 各国的服务贸易起步晚，大大落后于欧盟和 NAFTA，因此，在一些涉及国家经济安全、新兴产业、幼稚产业上各国都实行了很多的限制，在很多领域还存在着不同程度的服务贸易壁垒。这些不同程度的贸易壁垒对中国和东盟之间的服务贸易建设增加了难度，也给服务提供者带来了不便，阻碍了服务贸易自由化的进程。

第二，资格认可体制不灵活。人力资本的充实无疑将提高服务的产量和质量，对服务提供者的资格认可制度正是反映了对服务贸易质量的维护，而服务贸易的发展反过来也会促升服务提供者的素养，由此形成良性的互动。因此，服务贸易人才的培养和资格认可制度的完善至关重要。为使服务提供者获得授权、许可或证明的标准或准则得以实施，《协议》规定一缔约方可承认在另一缔约方已获得的教育或经历、已满足的要求、或已给予的许可或证明。这给服务提供者的跨境流动提供了一定的方便，但由于不同服务行业的特异性，这样统一的标准并非能适用于每个服务贸易领域。因此，服务贸易领域加强分类标准确定和资格的认可，这对于 CAFTA 服务贸易人才的培养将起到有益的反作用，也将促进高级人才在区域内流动。目前,CAFTA 下服务贸易资格认可方面仍缺乏细化标准。

第三,具体承诺较为局限。CAFTA 内各成员国虽然大多为发展中国家,但是发展水平存在差距较大,特别是东盟新四国的发展水平相对落后。《协议》第17 条规定加强柬埔寨、老挝、缅甸和越南的参与。规定其他各国应采取具体承诺的方式,通过商业基础上的技术引进,加强柬埔寨、老挝、缅甸和越南国内服务的能力、效率和竞争力;促进该四国进入销售渠道及信息网络;对它们有出口利益的服务部门的市场准入和服务提供方便,实现自由化;且对该四国展现适当的灵活性,允许它们开放较少的部门和较少的交易种类,并按照它们各自的发展情况逐步扩大市场准入。反观 NAFTA,美国和加拿大给予墨西哥以差别待遇,这是由三国在经济发展水平上的悬殊所造成的,如在三国之间实行部分商品不同关税率和差别化的取消贸易壁垒的措施,正是因为这些差别待遇减少了自贸区内三国的摩擦和冲突。相比较而言,CAFTA 下服务贸易的具体承诺未深入和开放,提供的开放程度较为局限。此外,由于 CAFTA 的发展中国家色彩较浓,广泛存在着国家经济安全、保护幼稚产业与开放服务业市场的矛盾,因此,如何解决好这些矛盾对于自由贸易区的发展是非常重要的,但也是一个极为棘手的问题。

对于以上这些问题,笔者认为,CAFTA 内的市场准入开放程度还不高,与欧盟和 NAFTA 的开放程度不可同日而语。因此,各国应致力于逐步减少服务贸易壁垒,积极地进行开放服务贸易部门的谈判,通过谈判不断地扩大市场准入的范围。由于 CAFTA 作为最大的发展中国家组成的自贸区,必须从中国与东盟各国的服务业的实际出发,应要坚持逐步开放的方式。所以,自贸区允许成员国对涉及国家经济安全、幼稚产业和一些关键性服务行业进行保护。[①] 就是说,要促进区内服务贸易的发展,就必须正确地处理自由化和逐步开放的关系。这也体现了对这些相对发展滞后国家的优惠,与 NAFTA 的差别待遇有异曲同工之处。但应明确这种差别待遇原则存在的领域及其可行措施。在 CAFTA 区内实行切实可行的差别待遇有利于提高经济上处于落后水平的缔约国的积极性,实现互利互惠,从推动自由贸易区的发展。此外,中国和东盟各成员国应建立或指定类似于《货物贸易协议》项下的组织协调机构,以监督和促进《协议》的实施,增强服务贸易的机制性。《服务贸易协议》已逐步减少服务贸易的市场准入的限制,为中国与东盟服务贸易提供了制度性的保障,这一区域法律制度的安排必将

① 参见《服务贸易协议》第 23 条关于服务贸易逐步自由化的规定。

对中国和东盟乃至世界经济的发展产生深远的影响。因此，应把握好这一历史契机，采取措施切实落实这一法律制度，形成中国和东盟在服务贸易领域的联动效应，在 CAFTA 的建设中发挥积极的推动作用。[①]

四、CAFTA 争端解决规则的不足与完善之策

CAFTA《全面经济合作框架协议》下创建的争端解决机制，为 CAFTA 的运行提供了强有力保障，成为了其生存和发展的安全阀，对促进双边经贸关系的发展具有重大的意义。争端解决机制的不断完善，是自贸区走向成熟的标志。2004 年 11 月中国与东盟签署的自由贸易区框架下的《争端解决协议》就是落实《框架协议》的重要步骤和措施。《争端解决协议》包含了 18 个条款和一个附件，它对争端适用的范围，磋商程序，调停和调解，仲裁庭的设置、职能、组成和程序，仲裁的执行、补偿和中止减让作了一系列的规定，创设了富有自己特色的争端解决机制，为 CAFTA 提供了必要的法律基础和保障，是自由贸易区赖以生存和发展的基本制度安排。作为一个新的机制，加上受亚洲传统文化的影响，争端解决制度存在着的问题和缺陷是显而易见的。

第一，争端主体的局限性。在当今的国际经济交往中，实践主体主要还是私人企业。CAFTA《争端解决协议》在序言中明确指出，争端当事方仅指东盟成员国和中国，也就是说，只有该自由贸易区的成员国政府才能作为争端主体提起申诉，企业和个人都被排除在争端主体之外。这样的主体范围限制在一定程度上约束了私人性质的投资者的投资积极性。[②]

第二，仲裁员遴选的拖沓性。《争端解决协议》明确规定了仲裁员应当是熟知法律、国际贸易、国际经贸争议解决等方面知识的专家，但却没有为当事人提供仲裁员名册。NAFTA 以及国际上主要的仲裁机构都为争端当事人提供了仲裁专家名册，以便利当事人从中挑选自己认为合适的仲裁员。如果不提供仲裁员名册，就有可能使仲裁庭的成员不受名册的人选限制，使争端方在选择仲裁员

---

① 参见张晓君:《中国—东盟〈服务贸易协定〉与中国服务业发展》，载《河北法学》2010 年 3 月。

② 在此方面，根据之后制定的《投资协议》第 14 条第 4 款的规定，可以提交包括国际投资争端解决中心在内的多种可选择的仲裁机构仲裁。因此，CAFTA 投资争端已经涉及关于缔约国政府与另一缔约国私人之间的争端。但是具体而言，在货物、服务等领域，私人仍然不能够享受到此等争端解决的权利。

时由于人选范围太广而拖延时间或者影响了协议的达成,从而影响 CAFTA 下争端解决机制的效率。

第三,裁决公正性缺乏保障。《争端解决协议》中规定了仲裁这种具有约束力的争端解决方法,并且规定裁决具有最终的法律约束力。由于缺少相应的纠正或复核程序,可能会因此产生不公正的结果,并由此引发更大的争端,会产生诸如以下的问题:仲裁庭裁决结果由于缺少了一定的监督有时会出现不尽合理的情况,如因仲裁庭组成的不当或明显超越权限,裁决赖以成立的理由不清等而使裁决不公正时,对于仲裁庭作出的裁决是应继续维持其权威性还是应如何处理。而在 WTO 中争端任一方如对专家组报告所涉及的法律问题及专家组所作的法律解释有异议,可向上诉机构上诉,以求得公正的判决。

第四,争端机构稳定性欠缺。《争端解决协议》虽然规定中国与东盟间的经贸争端可以依《争端解决协议》解决,该协议对执行程序也作了一系列的规定,但由于 CAFTA 没设立一个专门负责审议和处理法律问题和通过司法手段解决成员国争端的机构,使得争端解决程序缺乏可操作性,影响到了 CAFTA 规则的执行力。而 WTO 规则的执行力较强,与 WTO 设立有专门争端解决机构有关。随着 CAFTA 建设步伐的加快,区内经贸交往的密切,引发的争端必然增多,因此,缺少相对稳定的常设争端解决机构,不利于有效地运行争端解决机制,不利于自由贸易区的发展。

第五,裁决措施较为粗糙。《争端解决协议》在第 13 条中规定了赔偿、减让或利益的中止,但是没有明确惩罚的幅度和执行机制。WTO 及 NAFTA 要求惩罚水平应与利益损害或丧失的水平相当。WTO《关于争端解决规则与程序的谅解》(DSU)第 22 条第 6 款还规定,被申诉方如果认为申诉方所提议的惩罚水平违背了水平相当原则的,可以提请仲裁;NAFTA 协定第 20 章和第 19 章也都规定了被申诉方认为惩罚水平明显过高,超出合理限度时有权提出异议,请求专门小组对此进行裁决。

总之,CAFTA 争端解决机制中没有常设的争端解决机构,仅建立临时的仲裁庭,当争议解决完毕后,临时仲裁庭自行解散。没有常设的仲裁庭对于争端解决机制来说是致命的缺陷。常设的争端解决机构能够提供仲裁的效率,保持前后仲裁的一致性等,因此应建立常设的仲裁庭。此外,中国—东盟自贸区偏重于政治方式的解决模式也不利于快速的解决纠纷,与 NAFTA 的主要运用仲裁的方式,并且根据不同的争端类别建立不同的争端解决做法相差较大。

对于如何完善 CAFTA 下的争端解决程序,有学者认为,需要建立有私人主体参与的中国—东盟商事纠纷解决机制,通过该机制可以打破西方世界在商事仲裁领域内的垄断局面,减少解决商事纠纷的成本,提高中国与东盟各国之间的商贸效率。[①] 而围绕争端的仲裁规则,及在选择争端解决机构过程中避免冲突的问题,有学者建议,应成立一个由独立的非政府法律和仲裁专家组成的轮值委员会,由这个组织的负责人指定仲裁庭主席;在确定第三方与争端是否有"实质利益"关系时,应进行客观而不是主观的解释。如果现有行为的结果会对第三方产生影响,可以认为涉及第三方的实质利益;鼓励各成员国在同时涉及 WTO 和自由贸易区义务的争端时,首先使用自由贸易区争端解决机制,而不是求助于更为激烈的 WTO 争端解决机制。[②] 就现行的争端解决模式而言,CAFTA 争端解决机制采取的是磋商到仲裁的模式,这个模式是介于传统的模式和司法之间的模式,没有上诉机构,仲裁庭只具有临时性。迄今为止,还没有一件争端案提交,这与争端机制程序不严谨、效果不确定等缺陷有关。因此,需要进一步完善 CAFTA 争端解决机制,使之更具执行力,在中国与东盟经济发展一体化的进程中发挥其应有的作用。

---

① 参见沈四宝:《论中国—东盟商事争议解决机制的构想和建议》,第四届"中国东盟法律合作与发展高层论坛"会议综述。

② See Professor Dr. Colin Yee Cheng ONG, Dispute Settlement Mechanism For Cafta: Any Room For Future Refinement?, 第四届"中国东盟法律合作与发展高层论坛"会议综述。

The Flaws and Countermeasures in Rules of CAFTA

Zhang Xiaojun Xu Yibin*

Abstract

According to the pattern of Framework Agreement-Specific Agreement, China-ASEAN Free Trade Zone (CAFTA) established a series of rules involved in trade in goods and services, trade-related investment and trade-dispute settlement. In light of specific conditions since CAFTA founded and WTO rules, it detailed the flaws in rules and proposed the countermeasures.

Keywords: CAFTA; Rules; Flaws; Countermeasures

Content

- Introduction
- The Flaws and Countermeasures in Rules of CAFTA involved in Trade of Goods
- The Flaws and Countermeasures in Rules of CAFTA Involved in Trade-related Investment
- The Flaws and Countermeasures in Rules of CAFTA involved in Trade of Service
- The Flaws and Countermeasures in Rules of CAFTA involved in Trade-dispute Settlement

---

* Zhang Xiaojun, vice dean of International Law School of Southwest University of Politics and Law, Dr. &Prof. of Law, the secretary—general of China—ASEAN Law Research Center;

Xu Yibin, teacher of International Law School of Southwest University of Politics and Law, P. H. ,D.

从CAFTA到东亚共同体：中国的区域经济一体化之路及其法律构建

何 力*

内容摘要

东盟自由贸易区是区域经济一体化最成功的例子之一，得到了全世界的普遍关注和尊重。中国自改革开放后开始了区域经济一体化进程，21世纪初期成功地和东盟建立了中国东盟自由贸易区，为双方发展贸易和投资等经济交往创造了最佳外部条件。CAFTA的法律框架以CAFTA协定为核心，结合其项下的《货物贸易协定》、《服务贸易协定》、《投资协定》和《争端解决机制协定》，构成了一个有宪法性规定、包含实体法和程序法在内的比较完整的法律体系。CAFTA的成功推动了日韩与东盟的自由贸易区的成立，并向包括东南亚和东北亚在内的东亚自由贸易区发展，最后有可能建成接近欧盟模式的东亚共同体。其法律制度的设计以现今的CAFTA法律制度为出发点，然后是建立NAFTA模式的东亚自由贸易区法律机制，最后升格到欧洲共同市场模式的法律机制。

关键词：CAFTA；东亚共同体；区域经济一体化；法律构建

目 次

---

* 何力，复旦大学法学院教授，复旦大学法学院东亚与日本法研究中心主任，中国—东盟法律研究中心研究员。

- 中国参与区域经济一体化与 CAFTA 的建立
- CAFTA 的法律框架构造
- 以东盟为核心的东亚区域经济一体化之构想
- 东亚自由贸易区及东亚共同体的法律制度设计

一、区域经济一体化与东南亚区域经济一体化的成功

经济全球化和经济区域化是战后国际经济发展的两大趋势。经济区域化也叫区域经济一体化,是指地理相邻的特定区域的国家或经济体,通过契约或协定,促使资本、技术、劳动、信息、劳务和商品的自由流动和有效配置,为追求共同的经济利益而实行的经济合作或经济联合。在贸易方面,经济全球化体现为 GATT-WTO 多边贸易体制,而区域经济一体化则体现了国际经济格局的多极化发展。[①] 区域经济一体化具有贸易转化效应和贸易创造效应。前者基于差别待遇导致其与域外的贸易转化为域内贸易,某种程度上具有保护主义色彩。但后者增加了贸易总量,促进国际分工,通过国际经济再配置,直接或间接给域外经济体带来利益,从而也能与 GATT-WTO 体制共存。GATT 第 24 条以及 GATS 第 7 条是协调区域经济一体化和多边贸易体制的法律依据。

区域经济一体化的远因是第二次世界大战前的团块经济(bloc economy)。20 世纪 20 年代末开始的世界性经济大萧条发生后,各国相继放弃金本位制,自由贸易体制崩溃,一些国家与其主要殖民地或经济势力范围地域结成团块经济,主要有英镑经济团块、法郎经济团块、美元经济团块以及日元经济团块。相互对立的团块经济使得国际经济联系被彻底隔断,这也是诱发第二次世界大战的经济要因之一。鉴于这次沉重的历史教训,战后各国摒弃了团块经济的经济隔断和对立,自发地开始区域性经济合作。20 世纪 50 年代,欧洲经济共同体和苏联东欧国家建立的经济互助委员会代表了经济区域化的草创时期。60 年代到 70 年代,欧洲共同体的成功,使得区域经济一体化开始蔓延到拉丁美洲、非洲和亚洲某些区域,大有全面开花之势。80 年代到 90 年代

① 王雨本:《WTO 之外的国际经济组织》,人民法院出版社 2002 年版。

初期，欧洲以及若干区域经济一体化组织开始大幅度提高经济一体化的层次，出现了经济联盟和货币联盟，比如欧洲联盟和西非国家共同体等的出现。90年代中期以来，形成了WTO与几大区域经济一体化集团并存的国际经济大格局，比如欧盟(EU)、北美自由贸易区(NAFTA)、东南亚国家联盟(ASEAN，以下简称东盟)、拉丁美洲的南方共同市场(MERCOSUR)等。

东盟成立于1967年，创始成员国有印度尼西亚、马来西亚、菲律宾、新加坡和泰国五国。它本来是作为美国冷战世界战略的一环而建立起来的政治组织。但是从20世纪70年代末以来，其政治和冷战色彩渐渐淡化，其经济部长会议主导的经济合作职能逐步强化。1984年文莱独立后加入，与先前五国构成东盟6个老成员国。1995年到1999年，越南、缅甸、老挝、柬埔寨相继加入，成为东盟4个新成员国。

1992年10月，东盟经济部长会议通过了《有效普惠关税协定》，确定从1993年到2008年，以15年为期建立东盟自由贸易区，逐步将关税税率降到5%以下，完全取消成员国间的非关税委员会。为此成立了东盟自由贸易区理事会作为东盟自由贸易区的专门机构。之后又在1994年和1998年先后决定将时间表提前6年，并在1999年第13次东盟自由贸易区理事会上确定最终目标为实现零关税，具体日程是，老成员国的最后期限为2016年，新成员国的最后期限为2018年。同年11月又进一步分别提前为2010年和2015年。

东盟自由贸易区的成立和发展引起了全世界的普遍关注。它成功地完成了从意识形态型国际组织向脱意识形态的经济贸易型国际组织转化。东南亚地区凭借经济的高速增长在世界舞台上增强了其发言权，东南亚国家的整体经济实力大大加强。其中新加坡成功地跻身于发达国家的经合组织之列，泰国、马来西亚和印度尼西亚也曾经是东亚经济高速发展奇迹的主角。在实现经济高速发展的过程中，东南亚国家联盟的各成员国一直在认真考虑和探讨将东盟转化为紧密型区域性经济一体化组织，以使在世界经济贸易中占有一席之地。[①]

二、中国参与区域经济一体化与CAFTA的建立

中国自改革开放，逐步融入经济全球化潮流后，曾长期以来游离于区域经济一体化之外。中国地处东亚地区，历来是区域经济一体化方面的真空地带，

① 《东协迈向零关税目标》，载《亚洲周刊》2002年第1期。

缺乏区域经济一体化的传统和环境。然而,在全球性的区域经济一体化潮流下,一个国家单打独斗已经不是最好的选择。中国如果不参与到区域经济一体化之中,单纯依靠 WTO 的多边贸易体制,是很难维护自己的国际贸易乃至经济利益的。[①]

中国参与区域经济一体化最早的举动是 2001 年加入《曼谷协定》。该协定全称为《亚太经社委员会发展中成员之间贸易谈判第一协定》(*First Agreement on Trade Negotiations among Developing Member Countries of the Economic and Social Commission*),是在联合国亚太经社委员会主导和推动下于 1975 年在泰国曼谷签署的,对于成员国之间贸易进行的优惠安排。最初有印度、韩国、孟加拉国、斯里兰卡、老挝、泰国、菲律宾 7 个国家签署,但是泰国和菲律宾没有完成协定核定程序,因此该协议首先在 5 个成员国生效。后来巴布亚新几内亚也签署了协定,但也没有完成核准程序。中国于 1994 年申请,2000 年 4 月签署协定,2001 年 5 月 23 日起正式成为该协定的成员国。这是中国参加的第一个具有实质性贸易安排的区域性贸易协定。该协定就 663 项 HS 税号的产品实行优惠关税,中国与协定原成员国之间达成了其中的 634 项产品的关税减让。不过,该协定总体上所涵盖的产品并不多,对于中国参与区域性经济一体化并不具有全面意义。[②]

中国—东盟自由贸易区(CAFTA)的创建是中国参与区域经济一体化的第一个具有重大意义的举动。中国与东盟从 1991 年就开始正式对话。1997 年中国领导人出席首次中国—东盟领导人会议,发表了《中国—东盟联合宣言》,确定了面向 21 世纪的中国—东盟睦邻互信合作伙伴关系。在第五届中国—东盟领导人会议上,双方同意于 10 年内建立 CAFTA,并授权中国与东盟各国经济部长和高管尽快开始谈判。为了支持东盟一体化进程,中国宣布,将率先向东盟三个最不发达国家老挝、缅甸和柬埔寨提供特惠关税待遇。

2002 年 11 月,在第六次中国—东盟领导人会议上,中国与东盟领导人共同签署了《中国东盟全面经济合作框架协议》(CAFTA 协议),决定到 2010 年 1 月 1 日建立 CAFTA。这标志着 CAFTA 建设的全面启动。

2004 年 1 月,中国与东盟双方启动了"早期收获计划",600 种农产品先行降低关税。同年 11 月,在第 8 次中国与东盟领导人会议上,中国和东盟签署

---

① 徐奇渊、刘力臻:《中国参与国际区域经济一体化问题文献综述》,载《开发研究》2006 年第 1 期。

② 何力:《国际经济法论》,上海人民出版社 2002 年版,第 23 页。

了CAFTA项下的《货物贸易协定》。它包括23个条款和3个附件。该协定的实施，标志着中国—东盟间的全面降低关税的进程开始启动。首批7445种商品的关税降到20%左右。2007年1月，中国与东盟签署了CAFTA项下的《服务贸易协议》，开始了CAFTA向纵深发展。2009年8月，在泰国举行的第八次中国—东盟经济贸易部长会议上，中国和东盟签署了CAFTA项下的《投资协议》，至此完成了CAFTA协议规定的CAFTA的主要领域的建设。在此基础之上，2010年1月1日，CAFTA如期全面建成。中国与东盟6个老成员之间超过90%的产品实行零关税。中国对东盟的平均关税从自由贸易区建设之前的9.8%降至0.1%，东盟6个老成员对中国的平均关税率也从之前的12.8%降至0.6%。到2015年，中国与东盟4个新成员之间的贸易自由化水平也将达到同样水平。双方的服务业也将进一步向对方开放，投资环境大大改善。[①]

显然，CAFTA是中国倾注了全部精力精心打造和参与的区域经济一体化。中国的区域经济一体化无疑是以此为核心，围绕着CAFTA而展开的。除此之外，中国还参与了其他一些区域的经济一体化活动。

中国内地和香港之间、中国内地与澳门之间于2003年分别签署了两部《CEPA(关于建立更紧密经贸关系的安排)》，中国大陆和台湾之间于2010年签署了《海峡两岸经济合作框架协议》(ECTA)。这三部协议具有自由贸易性质，但是由于香港、澳门、台湾是中国境内的三个单独关税区，还没有达到区域经济一体化层次。

在APEC(亚太经合组织)框架内，2004年APEC工商咨询理事会(ABAC)提出建议，从2007年开始创建由APEC现有21个成员组成的亚太自由贸易区(Free Trade Area of the Asia-Pacific，FTAAP)，得到了美国等国政府的支持，并且开始了实务性谈判，目标在于实现零关税和消除非关税壁垒的完全贸易自由化。

此外还有《环太平洋战略性经济合作协定》(*Trans-Pacific Strategic Economic Partnership Agreement* ，TPP)，简称《环太平洋经济协定》，目标在于到2015年彻底废除除了极少特别保留商品外一切工农业商品关税，2006年5月已有新加坡、文莱、智利、新西兰批准协定并已生效。澳大利亚、秘鲁、美国、

---

① 《综述:中国—东盟自贸区推动区域经济一体化新航程》，中国新闻网，http://www.chinanews.com.cn/cj/cj-gncj/news/2010/01-08/2060544.shtml，访问日期:2010年10月29日。

越南、马来西亚、哥伦比亚、加拿大、日本和中国都有积极参加谈判,将此计划向前推进的意向。[①]

三、CAFTA的法律框架构造

CAFTA已经开始运行,相关法律框架已经形成,有必要从宪法及国际法、贸易法及投资法等实体法、争端解决机制等程序法三个方面对其构造进行分析。

关于宪法及国际法方面,要确定CAFTA协定的宪法性文件的法律性质,必须维护其最高效力。它主要调整以下几个方面的法律关系。

首先,规定有关CAFTA的宗旨、基本权限、组织机构,为CAFTA自身运行的基本法律依据。CAFTA项下的各项CAFTA协定,包括《货物贸易协定》、《服务贸易协定》、《投资协定》、《争端解决机制协定》及其具体运作规则,都要与CAFTA共同构成CAFTA法律体系,必须要与CAFTA的规定一致。如果其规定的具体运作规则和实践与CAFTA的规定发生冲突,则应该服从CAFTA的规定。

其次,与WTO及其规则的相互关系。中国以及东盟大部分国家是WTO的成员,因此CAFTA必须要符合WTO关于区域经济一体化的相关规定,不能与之相冲突。[②] CAFTA还必须对其项下所有的协定和法律文件是否符合WTO规则全面负责。

再次,与缔约国法律的关系。作为一部满足《维也纳条约法公约》要件的国际条约,CAFTA的效力必须在其各个缔约国国内得到尊重。缔约国有义务保证CAFTA的效力在国内得到实施。现阶段的CAFTA还没有取得欧盟那样的超国家效力,因此CAFTA主要是通过缔约国制定国内法实现其国内效力。

最后,与《东盟自由贸易协定》之间的关系。东盟成员国同时也是CAFTA的缔约国,对其而言就存在着当两部协定发生冲突时到底应该以哪一部协定优先的问题。CAFTA虽然中国为一方,只有一国,东盟一方却有10个国家,但是本质上应该是双边自由贸易协定,即东盟一方为一个整体。从这点

---

① Trans-Pacific Strategic Economic Partnership. Wikipedia, http://en.wikipedia.org/wiki/Trans-Pacific_Strategic_Economic_Partnership,访问日期:2010年10月29日。

② 即GATT第24条,GATS第7条。

看，当两部协定发生冲突时，东盟国家可以优先遵从东盟自由贸易协定。但是国际法上看，这两部自由贸易协定根据《维也纳条约法公约》和《WTO 协定》都属于同一序列国际条约，根据“后法非前法”原则，CAFTA 的效力应该优于东盟自由贸易协定。当然在实务中一旦出现了冲突的可能性，东盟国家有义务通过条约解释或者其他方式回避这样的事态发生。

在贸易法、投资法等实体法方面，要具体解决 CAFTA 项下的《货物贸易协定》、《服务贸易协定》、《投资协定》的具体运作相关问题。

首先，2005 年 7 月 1 日开始实施《货物贸易协定》，共有 23 个条款和 3 个附件。该协定规定，从 2005 年 7 月 20 日起，中国与东盟大部分货物逐步削减关税，涉及约 7000 个税目的商品，包括早期收获计划的商品。到 2010 年 1 月 1 日，中国与东盟 6 个老成员国实现零关税，东盟 4 个新成员国到 2015 年实现零关税。各成员国可以提出有限的敏感产品清单，作为一刀切的零关税目标的例外。在非关税措施方面，实行中国—东盟原产地规则，各缔约国制定相应的海关法规具体实施该原产地规则，凭缔约国签发的原产地证书享受优惠关税。积极实行中国—东盟海关国际合作，实行通关便利化。[①] 在保障措施、数量限制和非关税壁垒等方面都有具体规定。东盟作为一个整体承认中国的市场经济地位。

其次，2007 年 7 月 1 日开始实施《服务贸易协定》。该协定规定了双方在服务贸易方面的义务，基本参照了 GATS 的文本，共有四个部分，33 个条款和 1 个附件。附件列举了中国和东盟十国的具体减让承诺表。根据渐进自由化条款，双方还要进行第二轮服务贸易减让谈判。

最后，2009 年 8 月 15 日签署了《投资协定》。该协定 27 个条款，涉及投资待遇、透明度、投资促进与便利等内容。其中大部分规定都超出了 WTO 的相关规则的范围。在投资待遇方面，协定规定双方相互给予投资者国民待遇、最惠国待遇和投资公平待遇，为双方投资者创造一个自由、便利、透明及公平的投资环境，为其提供充分的法律保护，促进双方投资便利化。投资协定并非一步到位旨在实现完全的投资自由化。其中在最惠国待遇等方面规定了若干例外，实际上实行的是渐进式的投资自由化，与当今各国在投资领域的对外开放程度基本相称。

---

① 《中国—东盟海关合作概况》，第六届中国—东盟博览会海关与商界合作主题论坛网站(http://www.customs.gov.cn/tabid/34886/Default.aspx)，访问日期：2010 年 1 月 30 日。

在程序法方面，以 2005 年 7 月 20 日签署的《争端解决机制协议》为核心，还有《投资协定》中关于投资事项的争端解决机制的规定。

《争端解决机制协议》主要用于贸易争端的解决，参照了 WTO 的 DSU，有 18 个条款和 1 个附件。由于不设常设性争端解决机构，所以争端解决采取仲裁的方式，该协议对仲裁的前置程序、仲裁庭的设立、组成、职能、程序及其中止与终止、补偿和中止减让或利益等问题都做出了具体规定。

《投资协定》规定了两种情况。第一种是缔约国政府之间的投资争端，要根据《投资协议》第 13 条解决。该条规定沿用《争端解决机制协议》的相关规定和程序。第二种情况是关于缔约国政府与另一缔约国私人之间的争端，根据第 14 条第 4 款的规定，可以提交包括国际投资争端解决中心在内的多种可选择的仲裁机构仲裁。

CAFTA 并无关于不同缔约国私人之间的投资争端的规定。按照传统的做法，是将此类争端留给国内法解决。[①]

通过以上三个方面可以看出，CAFTA 已经建立了包括宪法性规定、实体法和程序法在内的比较完整的法律体系。

四、以东盟为核心的东亚区域经济一体化之构想

这里所说的东亚是一个广域的地理概念，即包括中国、日本、蒙古、朝鲜半岛在内的东北亚和包括东盟国家在内的东南亚。这一区域自战后以来，从日本经济复苏和高速增长开始，历经亚洲四小龙的兴起、泰国和印尼的经济勃兴、中国改革开放后的经济腾飞、越南等国的后起直追等几波经济增长的浪潮，已经成为今天世界经济成长的中心，俨然与北美和欧盟一并构成当今世界经济的三极。美国、加拿大和墨西哥组成的 NAFTA 拥有金融中心纽约、强大的高科技和信息技术产业，还有巨大的市场。经济规模与其相当的欧盟以无国界的经济联合为优势，形成了世界最大的单一市场。东亚地区日本、中国、韩国以及东盟则以制造业见长。

从区域经济一体化的角度看这三极，北美的 NAFTA、欧洲的欧盟都有成熟的区域经济一体化模式，而东亚地区的日本、中国和韩国并没有相互结成经济一体化组织，东南亚国家虽有经济一体化组织，但其经济规模在东亚乃至世

---

① 凌斌、潘海清、张莎：《中国—东盟自由贸易区投资争端解决机制构建浅析》，载《法制与经济》2010 年 2 月上旬刊。

界上的影响都有限。东亚地区经济一体化不发达，经济统合程度较低的状况大大减损了其在国际经济事务乃至法律规则上的话语权，不得不接受欧美主导的国际经济游戏规则，其制造业和出口主导经济的特殊要求在这个游戏规则中得不到充分的反映。这种状态其不利于维护东亚地区各国的正当经济利益。因此，东亚地区像欧盟、NAFTA 那样早日实现东亚区域经济一体化，统合成一个有力的整体，已成为当务之急。东亚地区的经济实力和经济的相互依存和互补的性质也决定了有必要尽早实现东亚区域经济一体化。

不过，东亚地区国际关系的现状并不能够顺利导致东亚区域经济一体化。中国与日本、韩国与日本存在着领土争端，中韩两国和日本之间还存在着历史认识等种种问题。这些首先就阻碍了东亚最大的三个经济大国相互结成东北亚经济一体化组织。

但是 CAFTA 的建立，为东亚区域经济一体化开辟了一个新的思路。那就是以东盟作为东亚经济一体化的平台，第一步是东盟分别和东北亚三个国家缔结自由贸易协定，分别形成三个“10＋1 模式”的自由贸易区，即 CAFTA、日本—东盟自由贸易区和韩国—东盟自由贸易区。第二步是待三个自由贸易区发展稳固之后，再由东盟牵头成立东亚自由贸易区，即“10＋3 模式”。第三步是将该自由贸易区逐步深化，以欧盟为榜样，建成高度经济一体化的东亚经济共同体。这一构想的合理性可以分别从东盟、中国以及其他东北亚国家的角度上进行分析。①

首先从东盟角度看。东盟固然有着良好的连带关系，发展也很顺利，目前正准备到 2015 年将东南亚国家联盟升格至东南亚共同体。但是也必须看到，东盟自由贸易区属于垂直型经济一体化，即成员国之间经济和社会发展水平差距比较大，包括最不发达国家在内的发展中国家与像新加坡那样的发达国家同在，因而经济合作和交往在一些国家之间难以向深度发展。其成员国之间的贸易和投资额在总贸易额和总投资额中所占的比例也有限。② 而相比之下，中国、日本、韩国与很多东盟成员之间的双边贸易量和投资额很多都远远大于东盟国家之间的贸易量和投资额。因而，与中国、日本、韩国发展双边贸易，建立“10＋1 模式”的自由贸易区能够获得比东盟内部更好的经济效果，即

---

① 余振、沈铭辉、吴莹：《非对称依赖与中国参与亚太区域经济一体化路径选择》，载《亚太经济》2010 年第 3 期。

② 许文骊、李莉：《建立中国—东盟自由贸易区之利弊分析》，载《西南民族大学学报》（人文社科版）2005 年第 4 期。

便东盟打算提高其经济一体化水平,其效果也是有限的。将东盟的经济一体化发展上升到东亚经济一体化,更能发挥东盟一体化的实际效果;即使建立了东亚经济共同体也不会减损东南亚共同体的效果。荷兰、比利时和卢森堡三国就先于欧洲共同体建立了荷比卢关税同盟,也曾为欧共体的发展起到了一定的促进作用,这就是一个正面的例子。

其次从中国的角度看,中国经济的高速发展需要更大的海外市场。在金融危机后欧美保护主义日渐复燃的情况下,受金融危机打击相对较小,在贸易、技术上具有互惠互补性质的中日、中韩经济关系有必要进一步深化,这是扩大自由贸易区的目标。由于历史、政治等种种原因,中国与日本等国直接建立自由贸易区比较困难。因而以东盟为媒介,先通过东盟与东亚三国单独的"10+1模式"进行合作,然后在此基础上扩大到"10+3模式"合作,建立包括东南亚和东北亚在内的东亚自由贸易区,对于中国来说具有深远的意义。中国总理温家宝在2010年10月29日第十三次东盟与中日韩(10+3)领导人会议的讲话中说,"要坚持以'10+3'为主渠道,推进东亚自贸区建设"。[①] 这正式勾画出了中国意在通过东盟平台实现东亚自由贸易区的路线图。

对于日本和东亚整体来说,日本国内政局因领土问题、历史问题等时时影响其与邻国关系,难以直接与中国等国启动东亚自由贸易区建设。然而在经济方面,随着中国经济总量取代日本成为世界第二位,日本与中国的贸易往来已经超过日本与美国,日本经济更加离不开中国,更有必要通过自由贸易协定来巩固和促进中日经济交往。由于中日直接签署双边自由贸易协定难以实现,能够通过东盟的"10+3"机制建立东亚自由贸易区,无疑是最佳选择。其好处在于可以避免中日之间的各种非经济领域的争端,在东盟的政治包容力下妥善处理中日经济关系。只要中日两国能够在具有处理与任何国家或国家集团关系能力和地位的东盟的中介下,在同一个自由贸易区内扩大交往和加深相互理解,反过来也能为中日两国的历史和解打下坚实的基础。在东亚,只有中日实现真正的和解,才能建立起欧盟那样的东亚共同体。这对于整个东亚来说都是福音,其经济效应的相乘效果将会扩及全世界。一个经济上相互统合的东亚大市场是完全可以和欧盟、北美自由贸易区相匹敌的超级经济体。从其发展潜力来看,经济总量也可能会超过欧盟或北美自由贸易区。这样,东亚国家就能在国际经济舞台上,在国际经济规则的制定和运用方面发出自己

① 温家宝:《加强"10+3"合作社东亚振兴必由之路》,中国新闻网,http://www.chinanews.com.cn/gn/2010/10-29/2622658.shtml,访问日期:2010年10月29日。

的声音，这个声音是不能受到欧盟和北美漠视的。只有这样，才能彻底扭转东亚国家在参与制定国际经济法律规则方面与其经济规模和地位不相称的弱势状态。

至于东亚自由贸易区的实施范围应该有多大也是必须要考虑的事情。现在的“10＋3模式”固然是一个理想的范围。但是东盟还有“10＋6”，即加上澳大利亚、新西兰、印度，还有亚欧论坛。东盟本身也有可能扩大，接纳东帝汶和巴布亚新几内亚。日本自鸠山前首相重提东亚共同体时也有“10＋6”构想，后来又因考虑到日美关系，还想把美国也拉进来。笔者的观点是，由于东亚自由贸易区的构想是建立在东盟平台上，因此东盟扩大应该是东亚自由贸易区自然的范围。但是范围不宜扩大到澳大利亚、新西兰和印度。这是因为它们已经不是传统意义上的东亚范围了。如果可以扩大到印度，那么南亚各国是否也该包括进来呢？如果可以扩大到澳大利亚和新西兰，那么是否可以扩大到南太平洋各国呢？与这些国家之间完全可以通过东亚自由贸易区与其建立双边经济合作的方式，或者签订双边自由贸易协定来实施更紧密合作。至于美国，它本身就是北美自由贸易区的核心。如果包括了美国，就失去了东亚的地域特性，在国际经济规则和事务中就会大大淡化东亚的特殊利益和诉求。而如果未来的朝鲜和蒙古的经济适合参与东亚自由贸易区，只要条件具备，当然也是在东亚自由贸易区的范围内。

五、东亚自由贸易区及东亚共同体的法律制度设计

上述的从CAFTA经东亚自由贸易区过渡，最后建成东亚共同体的三个步骤也必须要有一个法律制度的设计。一个自由贸易区乃至经济共同体如果没有有力的法律机制配套，其运行和维持将会遇到巨大的困难，就有可能招致失败。

第一阶段是中国、日本和韩国分别与东盟建立双边自由贸易区。在中日韩三国中，中国走在前面，已经先于日韩建成了自由贸易区，并有相应的法律制度配套。这为日韩两国在建立各自与东盟的自由贸易区及其法律制度提供了现成的模板。它们或多或少吸收CAFTA法律制度的内容后，可以根据自己的经济实情作出若干修订后建立其各自的法律制度。一般而言，日韩两国实行高度的农业保护主义政策，意在将大量农产品纳入敏感产品清单中。

第二阶段是在中日韩三国都各自与东盟建立自由贸易区的基础之上设

计其相关法律制度。中国与东盟比较顺利地达成相关协议，率先建立了CAFTA法律机制，这必然会极大地影响到后来的日韩与东盟的自由贸易区法律制度的创设。[①] 而日韩与东盟之间在农产品保护措施方面的分歧及其解决方案是基于日韩特殊国情形成。在未来的统一的东亚自由贸易区法律制度设计上，中国和除新加坡外的所有东盟国家都有较大的农业出口贸易，因此日韩的农业保护措施并无普遍性。因此，CAFTA的相关法律制度可以作为未来东亚自由贸易区法律制度的蓝本。在这里还要注意尊重东盟国家的一体性。我们应该看到，鉴于东亚地区政治、社会和国际关系的现实，从CAFTA到东亚自由贸易区的整个进程都是以东盟为基础平台。因此，即使未来的东亚自由贸易区及其法律制度得以建立，都可以容纳东盟各国作为一个整体在自由贸易区内的存在。如果东盟国家有这样的诉求，应该在其法律制度的设计上充分考虑到这一现实，从国际组织法和国际条约法层面上妥善处理东亚自由贸易区及其法律规则与成员国之间、与东盟之间的各种关系，在东亚自由贸易区及其法律框架下东盟有关法律规则与成员国之间的关系。[②]

第三阶段是东亚自由贸易区深化发展的结果即东亚共同体。虽然成员国也许还是那些，空间地域范围可能并没有扩大，但是其法律制度的设计必须有所变化。区域经济一体化的法律机制根据一体化程度的高低各有不同。一体化程度最低的是优惠的贸易安排，然后依次是自由贸易区、关税同盟、共同市场、经济同盟和完全经济一体化。CAFTA为典型的自由贸易区，与NAFTA具有同样性质。以CAFTA为蓝本建立的未来的东亚自由贸易区也应该不超过这个程度，因此其相关法律制度可以参照NAFTA的做法。而东亚共同体既然是东亚自由贸易区的升级版，当然至少会超过关税同盟阶段。从现阶段的CAFTA就包含了投资措施和服务贸易来看，进一步提高到实现生产要素商品、人员、资本和服务全面自由流动的共同市场的水准上完全可以做到的。在这方面，欧盟的发展历程及其建立相关的法

---

① 日本・ASEAN包括的経済連携協定．ウィキペディア日本語版．http://ja.wikipedia.org/wiki/%E6%97%A5%E6%9C%AC%E3%83%BBASEAN%E5%8C%85%E6%8B%AC%E7%9A%84%E7%B5%8C%E6%B8%88%E9%80%A3%E6%90%BA%E5%8D%94%E5%AE%9A．访问日期：2010年10月30日。

② 陈卫东：《东亚地区建立自由贸易区的法律框架初探》，载《辽宁大学学报》(哲学社会科学版)2006年第5期。

律机制的经验值得借鉴。1958 年欧洲经济共同体运行，1968 年欧洲共同体关税同盟建成，接着开始了共同市场的建设，然后建成包括货币联盟在内的欧洲联盟，整个过程都伴以欧洲共同体法乃至欧盟法的制度设计和支持，成为世界各个区域经济一体化实践不可多得的样板。未来的东亚共同体的法律制度设计是可以参照欧盟法的，具体而言就是欧洲共同体法的共同市场阶段的法律制度。

From CAFTA to East Asian Community: the Path of Regional Economic Unification of China and Its Legal Constructions

He Li*

Abstract

AFTA, concerned and researched in globally, is treated as one of the most successful models in regional economic unification. Since the reform and opening-up policy, China has initiated the process of regional economic unification. And it has established the CAFTA with ASEAN since 21th century which provides the best external conditions for the bilateral development of trade and investment. The treaty of CAFTA can be seen as the core of the legal framework of CAFTA, under which are Agreement on Trade in Goods, Agreement on Trade in Services, Investment Agreement and Agreement on Dispute Settlement Mechanisms and all these compose as an integral legal system. And this legal system consists of the constitutional provisions, substantive law and procedural law. The success of CAFTA has moved Japan and South Korea to establish their FTAs with ASEAN, and it will lead to the goal of East Asia Free Trade Area which may ultimately upgrade to East Asian Community in the light of the mode of European Union. The current legal system of CAFTA can be trusted as the cornerstone of East Asian Community's. Then the next step is to build the legal system of East Asia Free Trade Area like NAFTA and the ultimate objective is to shift it into the highest level of legal system as European Common Market.

* He Li, professor of Law School in Fudan University, director of the East Asia and Japanese Law Research Center in Fudan University, researcher of the China-ASEAN Legal Research Center.

Keywords: CAFTA; East Asian Community; Regional Economic Unification; Legal Construction

Content

中国—东盟相处的法律准则
——和平共处五项原则的传播与发展

王玫黎*

内容摘要

随着中国签署《东南亚友好合作条约》以及中国—东盟自由贸易区的建立,中国—东盟关系迈向了一个新的高度。国家之间不可避免会产生各种分歧和冲突,中国—东盟相处仍可依据和平共处五项原则。和平共处五项原则作为国际法的基本原则,它的产生和传播源于亚洲国家,也同样可以作为处理中国—东盟关系的法律准则。

关键词:中国—东盟;和平共处五项原则;亚非会议;万隆精神

目　次

---

* 王玫黎,西南政法大学国际法学院教授,法学博士,中国—东盟法律研究中心咨询委员,主要从事国际法的研究和教学。

1954年由亚洲的中国、印度、缅甸三国共同倡导的和平共处五项原则已走过半个多世纪的风雨历程，成为了指导各国事务的国际法基本原则。同样，伴随着中国与十个亚洲国家组成的东南亚国家联盟[①]关系的增进与发展，[②]和平共处五项原则仍然将发挥其巨大的影响，作为处理中国—东盟关系的法律准则。理清与思索这一问题，不仅对于认清和平共处五项原则在国际法和国际关系中的地位很有必要，而且对于建立新型的地区关系，推动国家间和平与发展也有很大的指导意义。

在中国的外交政策和国际法理论中，没有哪一项理论能与和平共处五项原则相提并论。在国际法的基本原则中，也没有什么能有和平共处五项原则那样兼具科学和时代的特点。尽管国际关系经历了各种风云变幻，和平共处五项原则却经受住了严峻的考验，显示出强大的生命力，并且日益深入人心，被越来越多的国家所接受，亦越来越成为当代国际关系中公认的基本和普遍的原则[③]。它的创立，促进了人类社会的进步，推进了国际法的向前发展。

一、亚洲国家合力造就了一个新原则的产生

和平共处五项原则的提出是时代的要求和产物。和平共处五项原则首先在亚洲提出绝非偶然。第二次世界大战以后，民族独立运动的风暴席卷全世界。从40年代后期到50年代，亚洲是这个风暴的中心。中国周边有相当一部分新独立的民族主义国家，如印度、缅甸、锡兰、巴基斯坦等。这些国家虽然与中国有着不同的社会制度和意识形态，但在重大国际问题上表现出与美国不同的立场，愿意突破美国对华禁运政策，与中国开展贸易，发展关系。在此

① 东南亚国家联盟(Association of Southeast Asian Nations)，简称东盟，其前身是由马来西亚、菲律宾和泰国3国于1961年7月31日在曼谷成立的东南亚联盟。1967年8月，印度尼西亚、泰国、新加坡、菲律宾4国外长和马来西亚副总理在曼谷举行会议，发表了《东南亚国家联盟成立宣言》(即《曼谷宣言》)，正式宣告东盟的成立。

② 在2003年10月举行的第9届东盟首脑会议上，东盟修改了该条约，明确其向东南亚以外地区开放的性质。2003年10月，中国作为该地区以外的大国第一个加入条约，签署了《东南亚友好合作条约》(*Treaty of Amity and Cooperation in Southeast Asian*)，为中国—东盟关系的进一步合作与深化创造了新契机。

③ 王铁崖:《国际法引论》，北京大学出版社1998年版，第226页。

背景下，中国将和平共处思想具体化为五项原则。[①] 获得独立的国家迫切需要和平稳定的国际环境和建立新型平等的国际关系，同所有国家和平共处，以维护国家主权，振兴民族经济，建设自己的国家。和平共处五项原则，就是在这样的时代背景下产生的，它一问世便在国际上受到广泛的支持与欢迎。

虽然和平共处思想最早是由列宁提出来的。[②] 但和平共处五项原则作为一项国际法基本原则的产生却与我国当时复杂的国际局势有关。一方面中国同当时刚刚建立的一大批独立国家，由于长期遭受帝国主义和殖民主义的侵略，经济、文化都比较落后，作为国际政治舞台上的新生力量，维护和巩固已经取得的政治独立成为这些国家的当务之急，它们迫切需要有一个和平环境发展民族经济，它们在相互关系中都有互相尊重主权和独立、互不干涉侵犯、以平等地位开展经济合作的共同要求；同时，战后随着老牌帝国主义的衰落，新的超级大国走上了国际政治舞台，开始形成新的两极对峙。他们对于一大批新独立国家的建立并不甘心，于是采取经济压迫、军事威胁、政治讹诈甚至直接入侵等一切手段，直接威胁着许多国家的主权和领土完整。美国除了极力阻止我国在联合国合法席位的恢复之外，还梦想一举消灭朝鲜，然后以朝鲜为跳板进犯中国。在朝鲜战争中，美国操纵第五届联合国大会，通过了中朝为“侵略者”的决议，打着联合国的旗号，拼凑有 15 个国家参加的侵略军开赴朝鲜作战，并对朝中实行制裁和禁运。另外，美国继续侵占我国领土台湾，并同蒋介石政权订立《共同防御条约》，干涉我国内政，破坏我国领土主权和独立。美国这一行为严重地践踏了国际法原则，遭到全世界大多数爱好和平的国家和人民的谴责。

广大人民渴望着一种新型的处理国际关系的原则，和平共处五项原则正是基于这种要求而产生了，它是中国、印度这两个刚独立的国家于 1953—1954 年就中国西藏关系问题谈判时，由中国首先提出的。最早体现在 1954 年 4 月 29 日中印达成的《关于中国西藏地方和印度之间的通商和交通协定》

---

① 蔡武：《在和平共处五项原则国际研讨会上的发言》，载《南亚研究》2004 年第 2 期。

② 在俄国十月革命胜利后，列宁曾运用马克思主义关于社会主义革命只有在几个资本主义国家同时胜利才能成功的设想，大力支持德国、匈牙利等欧洲国家的社会主义革命，但遭到失败。不久，俄国内战爆发，面临资本主义世界包围的苏俄政权经受着严峻的生存危机。列宁的和平共处思想是受当时的国际国内形势所迫、针对资本主义国家而提出的，是一种权宜之计。但列宁的和平共处思想却为后来和平共处五项原则的提出奠定了理论基础。

的序言中。该序言所列举的五项原则是：互相尊重领土主权、互不侵犯、互不干涉内政、平等互惠、和平共处。1954 年 6 月，周恩来总理应邀访问印度和缅甸，先后同印度总理尼赫鲁、缅甸总理吴努举行会谈。6 月 27 日，尼赫鲁在欢迎周恩来的宴会上谈到："这些原则不但对我们两国适用，而且对其他国家也适用，对其他国家来说，这些原则可以作为一个榜样。"1954 年 6 月 28 日中印两国政府发表联合声明，重申了这五项原则，并将"平等互惠"改为"平等互利"。[①] 6 月 29 日，中缅两国政府发表了联合声明，再度确认了这五项原则是指导两国关系的准则。1954 年 8 月 11 日，周恩来总理在中央人民政府委员会会议上所作的外交工作报告中，第一次称这些原则为和平共处五项原则。和平共处五项原则从此成为中国处理同世界各国关系和国际事务的基本准则。

1954 年 6 月，中印、中缅总理在《联合声明》中确认和平共处五项原则为国际关系的指导原则，这些原则不仅适用于国家之间，而且适用于一般国际关系。和平共处五项原则在 1954 年中印中缅协定缔结之后立即得到巨大的声誉。它被规定在许多双边和多边的条约和协定等国际法律文件之中，包括政府声明和国际组织决议，并出现在许多记者招待会、政治家的演讲中等等。据统计，从 1954 年开始到现在，这类文件可能已达到 200 件。可以肯定地说，和平共处五项原则已为世界各大洲许多国家所接受。[②] 在东南亚国家联盟中，中缅在 1954 年 6 月 29 日发表的联合声明载明了和平共处五项原则，1955 年的中国与印度尼西亚发表的联合声明和 1956 年中国柬埔寨联合声明均重申了这一基本原则。可以说，和平共处五项原则的产生与发展有赖于亚洲国家的共同努力。

二、亚非会议十项原则传播了和平共处五项原则

1955 年 4 月 18—24 日在印度尼西亚爪哇首府万隆市召开的有 29 个国家参加的亚非会议（又称万隆会议），是亚非国家共同声讨殖民主义，探讨相互间合作与发展的大会，也是第一次将西方大国特别是前殖民主义国家排除在外，由亚非新兴国家自主举行的国际性会议。会议发表了著名的《关于促进世

① 同年 10 月 12 日，中苏两国政府发表联合声明，将"互相尊重领土主权"改为"互相尊重主权和领土完整"。

② 王铁崖：《国际法引论》，北京大学出版社 1998 年版，第 228 页。

界和平与合作的宣言》,产生了"万隆精神",为建立新型国际关系提供了理论依据,使之成为一个得到国际社会普遍承认的准则。

《亚非会议最后公报》确定了"促进世界和平和合作的十项原则",其中许多原则无论是在措辞上,还是在实质上都与五项原则相一致,可以说,亚非会议对五项原则的传播和推广起到了巨大作用。《宣言》提出的十项国际关系原则是对和平共处五项原则的引申和发展。其十项原则具体包括:(1)尊重基本人权及联合国宪章的宗旨和原则;(2)尊重一切国家的主权和领土完整;(3)承认一切种族的平等和一切大小国家的平等;(4)不干预或不干涉他国内政;(5)尊重每一国家按照联合国宪章单独地或集体地进行自卫的权利;(6)不使用集体防御的安排来为任何一个大国的特殊利益服务,任何国家不对其他国家施加压力;(7)不以侵略行为或侵略威胁、或使用武力来侵犯任何国家的领土完整或政治独立;(8)按照联合国宪章通过例如谈判、调停、仲裁或司法解决等和平方法,以及有关方面自己选择的任何其他和平方法来解决一切国际争端;(9)促进相互的利益和合作;(10)尊重正义和国际义务。这十项原则包括了和平共处五项原则的全部内容:第二项原则包含了和平共处五项原则的第一项"互相尊重主权和领土完整"的内容,第三项原则表达的是和平共处五项原则的第四项"平等互利"原则的含义,第四项是和平共处五项原则的第三项"互不干涉内政",第五项和第七项是和平共处五项原则的第二项"互不侵犯"原则,第八项第九项是和平共处五项原则的第五项"和平共处"原则。这十项原则比起五项原则,看似内容更加广泛,但实际是在五项原则的基础上引申和发展起来的。在亚非会议上,和平共处五项原则被写入会议公报,成为"万隆精神"的主要组成部分,并从亚洲走向世界。① 正如费正清所说:"在二十世纪五十年代中期,中国外交政策奉行的是和平共处路线,亦可称'万隆路线'。中国的威望稳定上升,影响日益加强,在一段时间内,中国似乎正成为世界新独立国家的旗帜。"② 1967年8月8日于曼谷成立的东盟,实际上一直是以亚非会议十项原则作为处理成员国关系的准则。正如邓小平同志在会见外国元首时指出:"运用和平共处五项原则,甚至可以消除国际争端中的一些热点、爆发点。我特别推荐50年代由我们亚洲人提倡的和平共处五项原则,作为今后国际政治新秩序的准则"、"处理国与国之间的关系,和平共处五项原则是最好的方式。其他方式,如'大家庭'方式,'集团政治'方式,'势力范围'方式,都会带来

① 李杰:《对新中国60年外交的思考》,载《国际问题研究》2009年第5期。

② 费正清:《剑桥中华人民共和国史(1949—1965)》,上海人民出版社1990年版。

矛盾，激化国际局势。总结国际关系的实践，最具有强大生命力的就是和平共处五项原则。”①

2006年10月30日，中国和东盟成员国的国家元首、政府首脑会聚中国南宁，举行纪念中国—东盟建立对话关系15周年峰会。在发表的联合声明中的第6条特别强调：“我们认为，中国—东盟对话关系在过去15年取得成果是因为双方恪守《东南亚友好合作条约》所体现的原则，和平共处五项原则，万隆亚非会议十项原则，《联合国宪章》的宗旨和原则以及其他相关的国际法、条约和公约。中国—东盟关系将继续以这些原则为指导。”由此得知，“和平共处五项原则”始终是中国与东盟国家关系发展、和谐相处的基本原则，绝对不会动摇。②

三、中国—东盟以和平共处五项原则为重要的指导思想

1976年，东盟五国政府首脑签署了《东南亚友好合作条约》，这一条约主要是将现代国际法基本原则转化为地区内成员的行为准则，该条约规定的六项基本原则是各成员国处理彼此关系的法律指导，成为整合该地区的法律基础。其中第2条规定，在处理国与国之间的关系时，缔约国将遵循以下基本原则：(1)各国相互尊重彼此的独立、主权、平等、领土完整和民族特性；(2)每个国家都有维护其民族生存、反对外来干涉、颠覆和强制的权力；(3)互不干涉内政；(4)用和平方式解决分歧和争端；(5)不以武力相威胁或使用武力；(6)在缔约国间进行有效的合作。《东南亚友好合作条约》规定的原则适用于中国，中国加入该条约使双方为进一步发展友好关系做出了条约式的规范而突破了以往的宣言这种文件的层次。而纵观内容不难发现，这六项原则与和平共处五项原则有着密切关系，几乎是五项原则的另一个版本。

为了进一步加强合作，促进一体化进程，2007年11月20日，东盟各国领导人在新加坡签署了《东盟宪章》(全称《东南亚国家联盟宪章》，Charter of the Association of Southeast Asian Nations。)该《宪章》于2008年12月16日生效，这是东盟成立40年来第一份对各成员国具有普遍法律约束力的文件，在东盟一体化进程中具有里程碑意义。在有关基本原则上规定继续坚持

① 《邓小平文选》第三卷，人民出版社1993年版，第96页。

② 《东盟宪章影响中国和平共处五项原则吗》，中评社，http://www.stnn.cc/pol_op/200702/t20070201_453700.html，访问日期：2010年10月1日。

不干涉内政的基本原则;尊重各成员国的独立、主权、平等、领土完整和民族特性;坚持以和平手段解决纷争;不干涉成员国内政。同样这种措辞与和平共处五项原则是同出一辙的。

长期以来,东盟组织是以"和平共处五项原则"为重要指导思想的。如今万隆会议的精神仍然发挥着作用,当前在国际事务特别是亚太地区事务中发挥着重要作用的东盟虽然是在万隆会议 12 年后才成立的,但它的崛起无疑直接和间接地得益于万隆会议的影响和"万隆精神"的哺育。[①] 东盟一些成员国如印尼政府历来主张以和平共处五项原则为基础,处理国与国之间的关系。[②] 一些外交官也表示"不仅万隆会议是以和平共处五项原则为基础的,而且不结盟运动的基础也是这些原则。联合国宪章里也包含着和平共处五项原则精神。和平共处五项原则是东盟坚持的原则,东南亚和平友好条约就包含了这些原则。"[③]

和平共处五项原则已经走过了五十余年的风雨历程,它逐渐深入人心,为各国反复采用,成为公认的国际法准则,促进国际法向前发展。[④] 它顺应了和平、发展的时代潮流,集中反映了世界各国人民的共同愿望和根本利益,它宛如一盏明灯,指明了处理国际关系的正确途径,促进了各国和睦相处,具有强大的生命力。[⑤] 受到许多国家包括东盟在内的广大发展中国家的热烈欢迎。我们有理由相信:和平共处五项原则并没有过时,在处理中国—东盟关系上,将来必定会发出更加夺目的光彩,我们愿意同东盟各国一道,在和平共处五项原则基础上建立国际新秩序,维护世界和平,获得共同发展,促进人类进步。

---

① 王世录:《万隆会议与东盟的崛起——万隆会议召开五十周年纪念》,载《东南亚》2005 年第 1 期。

② 汤平山:《印度尼西亚》,当代世界出版社 1998 年版。

③ 张云飞:《缅甸外交官:和平共处五项原则是久经考验的原则》,http://news.sohu.com/20050418/n225232815.shtml,访问日期:2010 年 10 月 10 日。

④ Wang Meili , Promoting the development of contemporary international law, PANCHSHEEL and the Future:Persectives On INDIA-CHINA Relations, Edited by C. V. Ranganathan. 2005.

⑤ 一丁:《国际舞台上的一盏明灯——纪念和平共处五项原则诞生四十周年》,载《世界知识》1994 年第 12 期。

Legal Guidelines for the Relationship Between China and ASEAN

——Dissemination and Development of Five Principles of Peaceful Coexistence

Wang Meili *

Abstract

With China signed the Treaty of Amity and Cooperation in Southeast Asia and the establishment of China-ASEAN Free Trade Area, China-ASEAN relations had reached a new level. A variety of differences and conflicts occur inevitably among countries, China-ASEAN can still get along with each other in accordance with the Five Principles of Peaceful Coexistence. The Five Principles of Peaceful Coexistence, as the basic principles of the international law, was generated and spread in Asian countries. It can be the legal guidelines for China-ASEAN relations as well.

Keywords: China-ASEAN; Five Principles of Peaceful Coexistence; Asian-African Conference; Bandung Spirit

Content

* Professor of Southwest University of Political Science and Law, cosultative member of the China-ASEAN Legal Research Center, PH. D, mainly engaging in the research and teachy of international Law.

中国—东盟FTA模式评析*

杨丽艳**

内容摘要

中国—东盟FTA已经启动,从模式角度来对其进行具体效应的评估是可行的。中国—东盟FTA模式属于FTA传统模式,或者说是浅层次模式:规制的范围有限,区域合作的一体化程度不高。究其原因可能是CAFTA是一个转型国家与一个经济一体化程度并不高的区域组织组成的自由贸易区,各成员国的国情可能还不足以应付"深层一体化"。这样的"浅层一体化"模式将带来不利的影响。

关键词:中国—东盟;FTA;模式

目　次

---

* 该文是国家民委项目2010年(编号为GM-2010-055)欧洲经济一体化进程中的区域认同与民族主义研究——欧盟法视角(2010-8-2011-3);广西人文社会科学发展研究中心"科学研究工程"2010年度第一期资助课题:FTAs的投资争端条款研究——以中国—东盟(CAFTA)为例的系列论文之一。

** 杨丽艳,广西师范大学法学院国际法学教授,法学博士,中国—东盟法律研究中心咨询委员。

中国—东盟 FTA 已经开始建成运作，但是它的具体效应恐怕还需要时间来检验。选择从模式角度来进行评析，或许也是一个评估角度。通过评估，可以为我国更有质量地和更有效地实施自由贸易区战略提供一个思考角度。

一、自由贸易区的定义

(一)经济学的定义

自由贸易区这一概念最初来源于经济学，是指：在贸易区内，各成员国取消了它们之间的贸易壁垒，但各自对外部世界进行贸易仍保留贸易壁垒。[①]根据该定义，我们也可以说自由贸易区是指对内(区域内)各成员国之间统一消除关税和其他贸易限制措施，对外(区域外)即对非成员国的贸易实施不同的关税制度和贸易规章的集团。

(二)GATT/WTO 的定义

《1947 年关税与贸易总协定》第 24 条以及世界贸易组织的《关于解释 1994 年关税与贸易总协定第 24 条谅解》中规定：自由贸易区(a free-trade area，24 条 8 款 b)被定义为："两个或两个以上的一组关税领土中，对成员领土之间实质上所有有关产自此类领土产品的贸易取消关税和其他限制性贸易法规(如必要，按照第 11 条、第 12 条、第 13 条、第 14 条、第 15 条和第 20 条下允许的关税和其他限制性贸易法规除外)"。

① 伍贻康、周建平：《区域性国际经济一体化的比较》，经济科学出版社 1994 年版，第 19 页。

二、FTA模式

(一)从法律效力角度分析

1. 高度经济一体化的超国家因素的以硬法机制为主的欧盟[①]模式。它的模式由欧盟法[②]和欧盟的多个超国家机构(行政、立法以及执法等几个方面)[③]构成。

2. 南北经济合作型的混合软、硬法机制的模式——北美自由贸易区。

《北美自由贸易协定》经过美加墨三国议会批准后,于1994年1月1日正式生效。根据该协议,缔约国将在15年内逐步削减直至取消所有货物贸易关税,取消货物和服务贸易、对外投资的非关税壁垒,实现商品、服务、投资资本的自由流动。

---

① 目前人们普遍地将"欧洲共同体"或"欧共体"称之为"欧洲联盟"或"欧盟",但是这两个名称具有不同的含义。从严格的法律意义上讲,尽管欧盟在组织结构上实现了一体化,原来的三个共同体各自仍然是独立的法律人格者,而欧盟并不具有法律人格,欧盟是在三个共同体的基础上建立起来的,但它并不能取代三个共同体,三个共同体是欧盟三大支柱之一(另两个支柱分别是共同体的外交与安全政策和司法与民政合作)。因此,《建立世界贸易组织协定》明文规定享有正式成员资格的是"欧洲共同体",而不是欧洲联盟。所以,在阐述欧共体的对外经贸关系包括它与WTO组织的关系时,不可用欧盟替代。见曾令良:《欧共体及其成员在WTO中的双重地位及其对中国的影响》,载《法学评论》1998年第1期。笔者认为在阐述经济一体化时也应以欧共体为主。但是自从2009年《里斯本协议》生效后,欧盟具有了法律人格。

② 欧盟法主要由欧盟与成员国签订的基础性条约(包括《欧洲煤钢共同体条约》、《欧洲经济共同体条约》、《欧洲原子能共同体条约》、《单一欧洲法令》、《欧洲联盟条约》以及《里斯本条约》等构成)、欧盟与第三国或国际组织签订的条约和欧盟通过的条例、指令和决定组成。

③ (1)欧洲理事会(European Council),即首脑会议,欧盟的最高权力机构;(2)欧盟委员会(Commission of European Union),是欧洲联盟的常设机构和执行机构;(3)欧洲议会(European Parliament),是欧盟的立法、监督和咨询机构,其地位和作用及参与决策的权力正在逐步扩大;(4)外交署;(5)欧洲中央银行(European Central Bank),简称ECB或欧洲央行;(6)法院:包括欧洲各大共同体法院(Court of Justice of the European Communities)和原讼法院(Court of First Instance),后更名为普通法院(General Court),欧盟法院(Court of Justice of the European Union)更名为欧洲法院(Court of Justice)时,同时欧洲法院新近还包括了欧盟行政法庭(The European Union Civil Service Tribunal)。

3. 南南经济合作型的以软法机制为主的模式——东盟自由贸易区以及拉美。东盟(Association of Southeast Asian Nations,英文缩写为 ASEAN)自由贸易区(ASEAN Free Trade Area,英文缩写为 AFTA)被认为是南南经济合作型的以软法机制为主的模式,理由有如下几方面:一是成员国几乎都是发展中国家;二是组织机构都为成员国平等合作式的,并未有超国家因素的机构;三是以不干涉内政为主要内容的"东盟方式"(ASEAN Way)为其主要运作机制;四是争端解决机构采取的是协商方式为主的软法机制。

4. 南北经济松散合作型的软法机制模式——亚洲及太平洋经济合作组织。

(二)时间角度:传统和新型的 FTA

1. 传统的 FTA:轴辐(HUB AND SPOKE)强调成员方的邻里地理关系结成为 FTA。同时在缔结条约方面,主要侧重于经济贸易,如货物、服务、投资以及争端解决。中国—东盟自由贸易区就主要是以这些内容为主。

2. 新型 FTA:并不一定基于地理关系;国家之间的 FTA 也不基于原有的一体化基础的程度;FTA 协定往往是基于 WTO 规则具有合法性,但是其内容则是依据成员方的意愿,有的范围与 WTO 相一致,有的属于 WTO 增项(WTO PLUS),如服务贸易,投资协定,政府采购,知识产权,社会事项,海关便利化,环境、劳工以及争端解决。

(三)WTO 增项与新型 FTA 模式及其对于 FTA 传统模式的挑战

1. WTO 增项与新型 FTA 模式

WTO 增项是指包括投资措施的国民待遇[①],竞争政策、政府采购、劳工和环境,在优惠贸易协定(PTA)下的服务贸易和知识产权保护,以及原产地规则。[②] 当 WTO PLUS 事项被包括在 FTA(也有人称为 PTA)时,也就是第三浪的 PTA(THIRD WAVE),具有这些内容的 FTA 也被称为深层一体化。这些也被笔者认为是对于只注重于传统 FTA 模式的挑战。

---

① Julia Ya QIN "WTO-Plus" Obligations and Their Implications for the World Trade Organization Legal System An Appraisal of the China Accession Protocol. *Journal of World Trade*, 2003, Vol. 37, No. 3, pp. 483～522. 2003 Kluwer Law International. Printed in The Netherlands.

② Andrew L. Stoler . The Future of "WTO-Plus" Provisions in Preferential Trade Agreements. 2010 International Trade Law Symposium ,Canberra, September 10, 2010 .

2.新型 FTA 模式及其对于 FTA 传统模式的挑战

新型 FTA 模式下规制范围增多,给传统的 FTA 模式带来了诸多挑战,比如对于成员国国内的法制和法治要求渐高,而且对于成员国相合作的法律协调、争端解决机制的设计、成员方价值取向的协调等方面都提出了更高的要求。

三、中国—东盟自由贸易区的模式类别及其分析

(一)中国—东盟自由贸易区的模式

中国—东盟自由贸易区的模式基本属于上述 FTA 传统模式。理由如下:

第一,规制的范围有限:如中国—东盟自由贸易区的条约到目前为止已经签署的有 6 个:2002 年 11 月签署《中国—东盟全面经济合作框架协议》;2003 年 10 月签署了《关于修订中国—东盟全面经济合作框架协议的议定书》,即早期收获计划[①],根据这一计划,中国与东盟成员国的 600 种农产品关税在 2004 年降到 10%以下,2005 年降到 5%以下,2006 年实现零关税;同时,还与泰国签署了《中华人民共和国与泰王国政府关于在(中国—东盟全面经济合作框架协议)"早期收获"方案下加速取消关税的协议》。根据此协议,中泰两国从 2003 年 10 月 1 日起对 188 种蔬果提前实现零关税;2004 年 11 月《中国—东盟全面经济合作框架协议货物贸易协定》,《中国—东盟全面经济合作框架协议争端解决机制协定》又相继签署,它们于 2005 年 7 月 20 日正式生效;2007 年 1 月,双方又签署了《中国—东盟全面经济合作框架协议服务贸易协议》,并于当年 7 月实施;2009 年 8 月 15 日签署了《中国—东盟全面经济合作框架协议投资协议》。2011 年 1 月 1 日,中国与东盟将依据上述系列协定全面建成中国—东盟自贸区。

第二,这些协议所造就的本区域合作的一体化程度不高,属于"浅一体化"(SHALLOW INTEGRATION),与其对应的是因为新区域主义(New Regionalism)指导下的深层一体化(Deep integration)。新区域主义,是国际关系学界的术语,是相对于老区域主义而言,包括六个特征:一是治理与政府(Governance vs. government)的区别,即设立了前景和目标以及实施它们的政策;二是进程与结构(Process vs. structure)的区别,即治理强调进程而不是结构;三是开放还是封闭(Open vs. Closed),即相对于老区域主义的关注

---

① Early Harvest Program, EHP。它最早被规定在《中国—东盟全面经济合作框架协议》中的第 6 款中。

边界和司法权因素，新区域主义则以发展、服务贸易输出、就业市场和污染堆积等在一个区域内的跨国界为强调因素；四是合作与对等协调(Collaboration vs. coordination)，即合作强调在平等基础上自愿签署协定，憎恨权力核心，旧区域主义则是隐含着权力核心(hierarchy)在区域内的具有权力的授权机构可以有权在其区域的疆界内的各种政府机构中决定各种资源的分配；五是信任与责任(Trust vs. Accountability)的区别，即老区域主义将对等协调责任捆绑在一起，而新区域主义是将信任作为区域内利益的一个有拘束力的相关因素作为谈判因素；六是授权或权力下放和权力(Trust vs. Accountability)的区别：老区域主义强调集权，这是一个零和游戏，新区域主义从授权中获取权力，所授的权力一部分来自于区域内邻居或联盟的决定或决策，或者在公共领域内的盈利或非盈利的团体的治理决定。① 在这六个特征的要求或指导下，RTAs 呈现出深度一体化：如产品处理和市场规制的规定(例如产品标准，竞争政策，劳力和环境)和财产所有权(知识产权保护，其他的无形财产，以及物化的投资和资金投资)以及服务贸易的规制和政策；在服务行业中的国外投资，贸易和人权，竞争规则，RTAs 协定里的持续性发展等。这在上述的 NAFTA、EU 等案例里已经做了相应的分析。但是在 CAFTA 里体现得不是很突出。尤其是知识产权保护、服务行业中的国外投资，贸易和人权，竞争规则，RTAs 协定里的持续性发展、以及靠消除和减少阻碍贸易发展的边界以外的规则以便利于贸易的涉及政治、机构等方面的措施(也是上述所称的 WTO PLUS ISSUES)。因此可以得出结论：CAFTA 目前仍处在浅层次(shallow integration)的区域经济一体化进程中。

(二)中国—东盟自由贸易区的“浅层一体化”模式的原因和影响分析

1. 中国—东盟自由贸易区的“浅层一体化”模式的原因

第一，CAFTA 是一个转型国家与一个经济一体化程度并不高的区域组织组成的自由贸易区，这样的成员方对结成的 FTA 模式是有影响的。我国虽然在建设社会主义市场经济，但是距离法治经济体制还是有距离的，也仍是一个发展中国家。东盟是东南亚国家联盟(Association of Southeast Asian Nations，简称 ASEAN)的简称，有 10 个成员国：文莱、印度尼西亚、马来西亚、菲律宾、新加坡、泰国、柬埔寨、老挝、缅甸和越南，其中，前 6 个国家加入东盟的

① Allan Wallis, The New Regionalism. http://www.munimall.net/eos/2002/wallis_regionalism.nclk.

时间比较早,是东盟的老成员,经济相对发达,后 4 个国家是东盟新成员。由于 ASEAN 仍是一个一体化程度不高的区域组织,10 个成员国的经济政策并不一致,关税也不一致,因此我国在与 ASEAN 谈判建立自由贸易区的时候,仍然只能是我国对十个国家的自由贸易措施谈判,尽管在自由贸易区的谈判和相应机构是我国的商务部和东盟经济高官会(简称 SEOM),以及中国—东盟贸易谈判委员会(以下简称"中国—东盟 TNC")。中国—东盟 TNC 和上述所有机构应通过中国对外贸易经济合作部(以下简称"中国外经贸部"现在为商务部)与东盟经济高官会(简称 SEOM),定期向中国外经贸部部长和东盟经济部长会议(简称 AEM)汇报其谈判进度及成果,①但是东盟本身的一体化超国家机构并不多,远不如欧盟,许多事务的决策仍然以各个成员国家各自为主。比如在每一个成员国国内设立的东盟国家秘书处,东盟经济部长会议(简称 AEM)也是由所有成员国的经济部长们组成的。② 这对于我国来说,当然会增加各种成本和难度。而缔约双方基本是发展中国家,由这些国家组成的 FTA,有人作了分析,正如同表 1 分析:

表 1 RTA 成员发展水平③(Level of development of RTA members)

	Type of integration 一体化类型	Type of integration 一体化类型
Level of Development	Shallow	Deep
1. North-North	yes	yes
2. North-South	yes	some deep
3. South-South	yes	no

第二,现行 FTA 模式多种多样,给经验不多的中国和 ASEAN 以选择。在通知了 GATT/WTO 的 474 个 RTAs 里,实际上并不是同一个模式,有辐轴模式"HUB AND SPOKE",也有大杂烩式"SMORGGASBORD OF FOOD

① 《中华人民共和国与东南亚国家联盟全面经济合作框架协议》(中文译文)第 12 条。商务部网站,http://gjs.mofcom.gov.cn/aarticle/Nocategory/200212/20021200056452.html,访问日期:2009 年 8 月 1 日。

② 杨丽艳:《东盟的法律和政策与现代国际法》,广西师范大学出版社 2000 年版,第 80 页。

③ David Evans, Peter HolmesETC. Evaluating Regional Trade Agreements: Deep and Shallow Integration. February 2006,访问日期:2011 年 5 月 12 日。

RELATED METAPHORS”，有传统型的，又有新形式型的（如不基于地理联系的簇星状的（CONSTELLATION），不基于过去一体化联系紧密基础而出于现实政治经济需要的）等，[①]或许 RTAs 应该定义为优惠贸易协定（preferential trade agreements，PTAs），理由是 FTAs，准确地说在贸易关系里是一些国家根据自己的贸易偏好而去缔结的，完全不是自由贸易，而是带有相当歧视的贸易。因为实际上这些协定并没有在缔约国之间创造出自由贸易。[②] 这些协议对全球经济起着建构或阻碍作用（building bloc or stumbling bloc），内容也五花八门，可以说是缔约国或成员方各取所需。

第三，双方的国情可能还不足以应付“深层一体化”。

2. 中国—东盟自由贸易区的“浅层一体化”模式的影响分析

第一，可能影响双方经济一体化的效果。中国和 ASEAN 的合作基本上是南南合作。而截至目前，事实证明，南南合作的效果并不是很好。因为根据 Ricardian and Heckscher-Ohlin（H-O）的比较优势理论（theories of comparative advantage），互相之间经济结构相似而没有比较优势，则效果受影响。

第二，可能会引发双方的思考：是否要进入到深层一体化？因为深层一体化可能会给双方带来更多的利益：如从发达国家向发展中国家的技术和知识转让，技术扩散可以提高生产力；从扩大的贸易中增加比较优势和“干中学”的效益，通过贸易自由化消除寻租活动；增加可以带来先进的技术和提高生产率的外国直接投资；通过跟多地介入世界市场增加竞争应对挑战。

第三，可能对于双方在国际地位和形象方面有影响：中国是一个贸易大国，也是一个不断在世界崛起的大国，应该在许多方面树立自己的形象，而深层一体化或许是一个可以表现的方面。而 ASEAN 则是一个区域国际组织，在树立形象和实际区域一体化程度加深方面也是有所需求的。

---

① *Bilateral and Regional Trade Agreements—Commentary and Analysis*, edited by Simon Lester and Bryan Mercurio. Cambridge：Cambridge University Press，2009，introduction，p. 5

② *Bilateral and Regional Trade Agreements—Commentary and Analysis*, edited by Simon Lester and Bryan Mercurio. Cambridge：Cambridge University Press，2009，introduction，p. 5

结 论

CAFTA是一个浅层一体化的模式,在双方经济发展和福利追求的过程中,应该向深层一体化发展,这对于双方是利大于弊的。

Study on Module-Selection in CAFTA

Yang Liyan*

Abstract

CAFTA has been set up . Its effects may be reviewed by the model perspective . CAFTA is the traditional FTA model, or "shallow model" : the limitation scope of regulation, and lower of the degree of regional integration . The reasons might be CAFTA 'membership nations whose national condition can't be deal with "deep integration". But "shallow integration" would have had adverse impact on the regional economic integration.

Keyword: China-ASEAN; FTA; Module-Selection

Content

---

* Professor of Law School of Guangxi Normal University, consultative member of the China-ASEAN Legal Research Lenter, PH. D.

中国—东盟自由贸易区

法律问题专论

CAFTA LEGAL ISSUES

中国—东盟自由贸易区争端解决机制：进一步完善的空间

Colin Yee Cheng ONG*

目　次

《中国—东盟全面经济合作框架协议》于2002年11月正式签署，2010年1月1日起生效。这个贸易协议非常重要，它影响着11个国家、世界1/4人口的生活。

到2015年，"高度敏感"商品的关税将被削减至50%以下。去年，中国与东盟的交易额达到1930亿美元。

2004年11月29日，《中国—东盟全面经济合作框架协议争端解决机制协议》在老挝首都万象签署。

《争端解决机制协议》与《东盟加强争端解决机制条约》在同一天签署。《框架协议》第11条第1款中提出在《框架协议》生效一年内为《框架协议》之

* Colin Yee Cheng ONG，博士，教授，文莱仲裁协会会长。

目的建立适当正式争端解决程序和机制。

依据《争端解决机制协议》(以下简称《协议》),有三种方式解决争端。《协议》第4条规定,争端当事方应尽最大努力通过磋商达成双方同意的解决办法,磋商不需要第三方介入;争端当事方也可以依据《协议》第5条的规定进行调解或调停,争端当事方在这些程序中的立场应当保密,这些程序不具有约束力;争端当事方也可以进入具有约束力的仲裁程序,很多情况下,如果当事方由于各种原因无法达成满意的解决方法,就可以依据《协议》第6条进入有约束力的仲裁程序。

本篇论文主要研究现有的《协议》规定是否充分,是否还有进一步完善、改进的空间。论文着重讲述仲裁,因为它是《协议》中最重要的争端解决程序。

一定程序规则的缺乏及现有的规则草案本身可能在将来的争端中引起实际问题。我们还想突出那些可以从2010年4月8日在越南首都河内签署的《东盟宪章框架内争端解决机制协议》中借鉴的观点。

一、现有《协议》仲裁程序规则及问题

在研究《协议》中哪些条款和规则可以进一步完善之前,先看一下《协议》中仲裁程序下现有的规则和程序。《协议》第9条第5款规定:"仲裁庭应遵守本协议附件1中的有关仲裁的规则和程序,除非仲裁庭在与争端各方磋商后另有决定。"

而附件1中对仲裁程序的规则和程序的说明只有一页A4纸。

诚然,简洁被普遍认为是好品质,但在法律问题上未必如此。争端当事方和他们的法律顾问能容易理解《协议》中任何仲裁所运用的规则和程序的确切参数,这是很重要的。

《协议》中宽泛的规则和程序对很多问题都没有具体的规定,比如仲裁庭应如何运作,应怎样处理一些简单问题,例如程序的时间规定、向仲裁庭提交的备忘录等文件的格式,怎样处理对仲裁员的质疑,怎样进行仲裁听审等。

如果仲裁庭的三位仲裁员对程序规则如何实施无法达成一致意见,就会产生混乱。

二、《协议》中仲裁庭主席人选确定规则及问题

有意思的是,《协议》第7条第3款规定,如果争端当事方无法就仲裁庭主

席人选达成一致，那么就应请求世界贸易组织的总干事来指定仲裁庭主席。当一争端当事方为非 WTO 成员时，由国际法院院长指定仲裁庭主席。

(一)《协议》与 WTO 争端解决机制的潜在冲突

起草《协议》时，起草人是否考虑到了不同的争端解决机制之间的潜在冲突。如果一个争端能同时采用世界贸易组织争端解决机制和《协议》来解决，那么有些法律问题是很难解决的。如果一争端当事方坚持使用世界贸易组织争端解决机制，而另一方想用《协议》解决，该怎么办呢？《协议》第 2 条第 5 款规定："在遵守第六款的前提下，本协定不妨碍缔约方依据其均是缔约方的其他条约，诉诸该条约项下争端解决程序的权利。"那么，争端当事方在争论究竟应该采用哪种争端解决机制的过程中会浪费时间。

在这种情况下，被请求指定仲裁庭主席的人该怎么办？更重要的是，如果一方向世界贸易组织争端解决机制申诉，世界贸易组织怎么办？

世贸组织的成员国有一定的义务，因此这两种机制下都会有很多国家申诉。建议中国—东盟自贸区国家首先修订现有的草案规定，鼓励各国在今后遇到同时涉及 WTO 和自贸区义务的争端时，首先使用自贸区争端解决机制，而不是立即求助于更为激烈的 WTO 争端解决机制。

(二)对《协议》中仲裁庭主席确定规则的技术审视

当《协议》规定世贸组织总干事指定仲裁庭主席时，给了他更多的责任，还有可能使他陷入一些冲突中。他必须在 WTO 争端解决机制下履行自己应尽的义务，还要在《协议》下为仲裁庭指定仲裁庭主席。对于《协议》的最终使用者来说，这不是理想的选择。

如果一争端当事方不是 WTO 成员，就请求国际法院院长指定仲裁庭主席同样也有问题。尽管国际法院院长毫无疑问可以履行这项职责，但国际法院并不是依照《协议》规定指定仲裁庭主席的最佳选择。他们更倾向于处理单纯的有关国际公法的案件，而不是涉及许多商法和商业内容的案件。

在这方面，永久仲裁庭的秘书长更适合为自贸区指定仲裁庭主席。更合适的方法是成立一个由独立的非政府法律和仲裁专家组成的轮值委员会，由这个组织的负责人指定仲裁庭主席。今天聚集在此的来自中国和东盟国家的咨询委员和法律专家们可以认真考虑一下这个建议。

三、仲裁员选定规则问题及改进

人们经常说,仲裁程序的好坏是由仲裁员决定的。自贸区争端解决机制的最终用户们需要指定合格的仲裁员。他们要有声望,对法律及涉及的争端领域有很深的了解,更重要的是要公正、忠实于事实和法律。很重要的一点是对仲裁员的选择要有具体、详细的标准,保证仲裁员们在裁决争端时能胜任并且没有偏见。

《协议》的第7条第6款规定了仲裁员的标准,具体表述如下:

"被指定为仲裁庭成员或者主席的人选,应在法律、国际贸易、《框架协议》涵盖的其它事项、或者国际贸易争端的解决方面具有专门的知识或经验,并且仅在客观、可靠、公正和独立的基础上严格任选。此外,主席不应为任何争端当事方的国民,且不得在任何争端当事方的境内具有经常居住地或者为其所雇佣。"

我们可以把它与《东盟宪章框架内争端解决机制协议》中对应的条款对比一下。《东盟宪章框架内争端解决机制协议》第11条第2款规定如下:

"所有的仲裁员必须:(1)在法律、《东盟宪章》涵盖的事项、与东盟相关的知识或者国际争端的解决方面具有专门的知识或经验;(2)在客观、可靠、公正的基础上严格任选;(3)独立于、不依附于、不听命于任何争端当事方;(4)没有参与处理过这个案件;(5)没有向争端当事方透露任何可能引起他们怀疑裁决公正的信息。"

第11条第3款规定:"仲裁庭主席不能为任何争端当事方的国民。"

《东盟宪章框架内争端解决机制协议》对于担任仲裁员人员的条件规定得更加严格,比《协议》要详细很多。如果修订《协议》的话,政策制定者们可以参考。

我们注意到,两个协议中都规定仲裁庭主席不能为任何争端当事方的国民。如果政策制定者们在修订《协议》时,在第7条第6款加上下面的标准会更好,即仲裁庭主席必须熟知中国法律或者处理过有关中国法律的问题,而且对于东盟任何一个国家的法律都有专门的知识或者经验。现有的表述可能会导致这样尴尬的局面,比如WTO总干事指定了一个非常有经验的仲裁员,但是他却对中国和东盟任何一国的基本法律一无所知。

仲裁庭主席了解争端当事方国家法律的基本原则是很重要的。除了客观、可靠、公正和独立的原则外,具有中国和东盟国家法律理论和实务方面的知识和经验也是很重要的。

四、《协议》对仲裁报告期限的规定及改进探讨

《协议》第 9 条第 8 款规定了散发最终报告的期限,规定如下:“仲裁庭应在其组成的 120 内向争端方散发最终报告。在紧急案件中,包括涉及易腐货物的案件,仲裁庭应力求在其组成的 60 天内将其报告散发各争端方。如仲裁庭认为不能在 120 天内散发最终报告,或在紧急案件中不能在 60 天内散发报告,则应书面通知争端方延迟的原因和散发报告的估计期限。自仲裁庭组成至报告散发争端方的期限无论如何不应超过 180 天。”

自贸区争端解决机制的仲裁比较特殊,它没有仲裁管理机构,因此在时间方面会导致一些问题,比如可能由于仲裁员效率低或者太忙而不能及时撰写最终报告或判决结果。

如果仲裁庭不能在 180 天内散发最终报告,就失去了裁决权,必须解散。如果这种情况发生,会对一直遵守程序期限但最终没有得到满意答复的争端当事方带来很多问题。

因此,政策制定者们可以考虑在第 9 条第 8 款加上这样一个规定,即如果一个仲裁员(包括仲裁庭主席)不能及时履行职责,另外一个或两个仲裁员可以撰写判决结果。

五、《协议》关于第三方定义的规定及问题

《协议》第 10 条关于第三方的定义应该更严谨一些。第 10 条规定:“任何对仲裁庭审议的争端有实质利益并且已将其利益书面通知争端当事方和其它缔约方的缔约方,应享有向仲裁庭提交书面陈述的机会。这些书面陈述也应提交争端各当事方,并应反映在仲裁庭报告中。”

第 10 条中“实质利益”的定义会引起争论。对这个定义应该有客观而不是主观的解释。如果现有行为的结果会对第三方产生影响,可以认为涉及第三方的实质利益。重要的是,想要进入仲裁的第三方必须不仅能证明它的合法利益受到损害,而且仲裁庭的任何判决会对其合法利益造成不容易挽回的损失。

结　论

以上总结的几个问题代表了《协议》中需要进一步改进和修订的方面。中国—东盟自贸区 11 个国家的领导人会尽力解决争端解决机制和程序规则方面的问题,但这是很漫长、很复杂的任务,需要几年的时间才能完成。与《协议》同一天签署的《东盟加强争端解决机制条约》的完善和修订经过六年的时间才得以完成。

就论坛来说,咨询委员和来自中国和东盟的法律专家们如果能认真考虑怎样使《协议》中现有的规则和程序更加完善,将是非常有意义的。如果这样,就能对中国—东盟自由贸易区争端解决机制中核心的、重要的法律问题有更加深刻的理解和思考。

Dispute Settlement Mechanism for CAFTA: Any Room for Future Refinement?

Pro. & Dr. Colin Yee Cheng ONG *

Abstract

The China-ASEAN Free Trade Agreement (CAFTA) which was officially announced and signed in November 2002 and came into force on the 1st January 2010. CAFTA is an important trade agreement as it now affects the lives of people in 11 countries who represent a quarter of the world's population.

By 2015, duties must be cut to no more than 50 percent on "highly sensitive" items. China's trade with ASEAN amounted to US $ 193 billion last year.

The Agreement on Dispute Settlement Mechanism of the Framework Agreement on Comprehensive Economic Co-Operation Between the Association of Southeast Asian Nations and the People's Republic of China ("CAFTA DSM") was signed by the Leaders in Vientiane on the 29th November 2004. The CAFTA DSM was signed on the same day as when the ASEAN leaders signed the ASEAN Protocol on Enhanced Dispute Settlement Mechanism.

This paper looks at whether the current DSM is adequate as it currently stands or whether there is any room for further improvement and refinement. The author will attempt to both point out areas which may require additional attention and will also examine whether there are any useful ideas that can be adapted from the 2010 Protocol to the ASEAN Charter on Dispute Settlement Mechanisms that was signed in Hanoi, Vietnam on the 8th April 2010.

---

* Pro. & Dr. Colin Yee Cheng ONG, President of the Brunei Arbitration Society.

KeyWords: CAFTA DSM; the Third Party; Arbitrator Selection; Arbitration Report; Arbitration Procedure

Content

《中国—东盟投资协议》述评*

魏艳茹**

内容摘要

《中国—东盟投资协议》在中国—东盟自由贸易区范围内创建了统一的国际投资保护法制，在保护外国投资者私益的同时试图兼顾东道国国家主权，此为其成就。但该协议也存在重大不足，如所约束的国家行为范围过于狭窄、缺乏审慎的措施条款、根本安全例外条款未受到必要的制度性约束等。目前的当务之急是有针对性地完善该协议。

关键词：《中国—东盟投资协议》；调整范围；审慎措施；根本安全例外

目　次

---

* 基金项目：国家社科基金青年项目“双边投资协议核心条款研究”(10CFX082)；广西哲学社会科学“十一五”规划项目“中国—东盟国家投资法律环境比较研究”(08CFX001)；广西大学“211工程”建设项目“中国—东盟经贸法律制度研究”(09211FX09)。

** 魏艳茹，广西大学法学院教授，法学博士，中国—东盟法律研究中心研究员，专研国际投资法。

2009 年 8 月 15 日，中国与东盟 10 国在泰国曼谷正式签署了《中国—东盟投资协议》，该协议随后于 2010 年 1 月 15 日开始在中国以及文莱、柬埔寨、印尼、马来西亚、菲律宾等东盟成员国之间正式生效。[①] 随着其他东盟成员国的陆续批准，其空间适用范围将进一步扩大。与中国和东盟国家之间所签订的《货物贸易协议》、《服务贸易协议》以及《争端解决机制协议》相比，《中国—东盟投资协议》的迷人之处在于，它为外国投资者创设了国际法上的出诉权，即外国投资者有权将其与东道国之间的纠纷提交至国际仲裁庭，诉称东道国的某些行为违反了该协议，并要求东道国给予赔偿。考虑到衡量东道国行为是否违反国际法的标准是国际法而非国内法，符合国内法的东道国行为完全可能构成违反国际法，故人们有理由期待，《中国—东盟投资协议》的达成和生效将在很大程度上抵消中国—东盟自由贸易区范围内 11 国国内法的不确定性以及由此衍生的法律风险，最终大大促进该自由贸易区范围内的跨国直接投资。[②] 遗憾的是，由于存在诸多重大缔约缺失，该协议的效果恐难达到预期。目前法学界仅有寥寥数篇文章涉及《中国—东盟投资协议》，且内容均为简单介绍性质，[③]就笔者的接触范围而言，尚未发现对该协议本身的缔约缺失问题予以专题探讨的著述。鉴于迄今国内学界对该协议仍缺乏必要的研究，本文拟就其成就、缺漏与完善进行述评。

一、《中国—东盟投资协议》的成就

根据《中国—东盟投资协议》第 2 条，该协议的目标在于，促进东盟与中国

---

① 该协议第 27 条规定，“本协议自签订之日起 6 个月生效”，“缔约方承诺完成使本协议生效的国内程序”。根据东盟秘书处的数据，上述 6 个国家及批准日期分别为：中国（2009 年 12 月 12 日）、文莱（2009 年 12 月 21 日）、柬埔寨（2010 年 9 月 15 日）、印尼（2010 年 10 月 11 日）、马来西亚（2009 年 8 月 28 日）、菲律宾（2009 年 12 月 29 日）。

② 商务部国际司商务参赞就签署《投资协议》答记者问，http://news.xinhuanet.com/fortune/2009－08/15/content.htm，访问日期：2009 年 8 月 15 日。

③ 目前法学界仅有寥寥数篇文章涉及《中国—东盟投资协议》，且内容均为简单介绍性质，如曾文革、王怡：《中国—东盟〈投资协议〉实施探究》，载《经济问题探索》2010 年第 4 期；李光辉：《中国—东盟自由贸易区〈投资协议〉》，载《中国对外贸易》2010 年第 1 期；武燕琼：《中国—东盟自由贸易区〈投资协议〉的法律评析》，载《思想战线》2009 年第 S2 期，等等。就笔者的接触范围而言，尚未发现对该协议本身的缔约缺失问题进行专题探讨的著述。

之间投资流动，建立自由、便利、透明和具有竞争性的投资体制。该协议共 27 条，主要规定了投资待遇、征收与损失补偿、转移和利润汇回、代位求偿、缔约方间争端解决、缔约方和投资者间争端解决、一般例外、安全例外等内容。在笔者看来，该协议的成就主要体现在以下几点：

第一，在中国—东盟自由贸易区范围内创建了统一的国际投资保护法制。

自 20 世纪 80 年代开始，中国与东盟国家便开始通过缔结国际投资协议的方式加强彼此之间的投资保护。截至 2001 年，中国与东盟 10 国间均分别缔结了双边投资协议。① 需要特别指出的是，由于在上述双边投资协议中只有中国—文莱双边投资协议迄未生效，而文莱又一向不在意通过双边投资协议的方式改善本国投资的法律环境，②该双边投资协议的生效时间难以预期，故除特别说明外，本文以下将不研究与该双边投资协议相关的问题。由于缔约时不同伙伴国家的理念差异及我国在双边投资协议核心条款问题上的态度变迁，上述双边投资协议中的投资保护水平参差不齐。鉴于投资者与东道国之间的争端解决条款是有关投资保护水平高低的关键性条款之一，我们不妨以该条款为例，分析上述双边投资协议的投资保护水平差异大到何种程度。

考察这些双边投资协议可以发现，其有关投资仲裁（investment arbitration，专指投资者与东道国之间因投资争端而引起的国际仲裁）的规定非常芜杂：

有的双边投资协议不但允许投资者就东道国违反该协议义务的所有争端提起投资仲裁，甚至还允许投资者就东道国违反国内法意义上的合同义务的所有争端提起投资仲裁，如 2001 年的《中国—缅甸投资协议》。这意味着投资者可以随时通过投资仲裁的方式迫使东道国履行国际投资协议义务（或合同义务），投资协议（甚或合同）中的每一个条款对投资者都有直接的意义。

有的双边投资协议则仅允许投资者就征收、国有化的补偿款额争端提起投资仲裁，如 1992 年的《中国—越南投资协议》、1988 年的《中国—马来西亚投资协议》。这意味着就该协议其他条款而言，在东道国违反相关国际义务的情况下，投资者只能请求母国出面，按照国家间争端的模式来酌情处理。由于

---

① 这 10 个双边投资协议的缔结年份分别是：泰国（1985 年）、新加坡（1985 年）、马来西亚（1988 年）、菲律宾（1992 年）、越南（1992 年）、老挝（1993 年）、印尼（1994 年）、柬埔寨（1996 年）、文莱（2000 年）、缅甸（2001 年）。

② 目前文莱所缔结的 BIT 仅有 8 个，其缔约伙伴分别是：德国、阿曼、韩国、中国、乌克兰、巴林、印度、科威特。

投资者与其母国间利益取向的差异,母国完全可能出于政治修好等其他方面的考虑而不肯替投资者讨还一个公道。

有的双边投资协议甚至完全不允许投资者对东道国提起任何投资仲裁,如1985年的《中国—泰国投资协议》。

我们知道,进行跨国投资的企业往往都进行复杂的股权安排,在多国境内成立各种子公司、母公司等,上述国际投资保护水平上的参差不齐将令在中国—东盟自由贸易区范围内投资的企业如入国际法的迷宫,难以安全、便捷地进行商业筹划,这显然阻碍了整个区域内的国际直接投资的流动。令人欣慰的是,新签订的《中国—东盟投资协议》恰好弥补了上述不足,统一了国际投资保护标准。

第二,在保护外国投资者私益的同时试图兼顾东道国国家主权。

尽管外资能给东道国带来资金、技术、管理经验等方面的益处,但也可能对东道国的国民经济、国家安全造成不利影响,尤其对经济结构欠佳、抗风险能力弱的资本输入国而言,情况更是如此,故资本输入国莫不保留外资管制权以维护国家主权。[①]

然而,现今世界各国所签订的国际投资协议,虽措施、内容不尽相同,但皆或来源于美国式模板[②]或来源于欧洲式模板[③]。这两大模板的核心条款均系发达国家拟定,且此种包含投资仲裁的国际投资协议长期以来主要在发达国家与发展中国家之间以及发展中国家间签订,发达国家彼此之间并不签订这种协议,故投资仲裁的"被申请人"(通常为东道国)角色传统上都是由发展中国家扮演,发达国家则几乎固定地扮演着申请人(通常为外国投资者)的母国这一角色。结果便是,发达国家并不关注东道国主权之维护,而将注意力全部放在千方百计保护外国投资者私有财产权方面。这就形成了国际投资协议片面保护外国投资者私人权益,不维护东道国主权的局面。我国与东盟国家所签订的上述双边投资协议都存在这种问题,即并未设立维护东道国主权的必要条款。

从国际投资仲裁实践看,在国际投资协议缺乏必要的保障东道国主权条

---

① Ha-Joon Chang, Foreign Investment Regulation in Historical Perspective, *The European Journal of Development Research*, Vol. 16, No. 3, Autumn 2004, pp. 687～715.

② 美国双边投资协议范本即为这种模板的典范。

③ 德国双边投资协议范本即为这种模板的典范。

款的情况下，投资者可能仅因东道国保护公众健康、[1]保障金融安全、[2]保护环境、[3]贯彻执行条约等行为而提起投资仲裁，[4]声称东道国的这些措施损害了其投资，违反了国际投资协议中的征收条款、公平公正待遇条款等，而崇尚“私有财产神圣不可侵犯”理念的投资仲裁庭则倾向于僵化地理解“有约必守”，支持投资者的主张，认定东道国确系违反了上述条约义务，从而有必要予以赔偿。[5]

由于《北美自由贸易协议》首次在发达国家之间引入投资仲裁机制，而美、加两国的海外投资者又具有非常强的诉讼意识，因此，美、加等一向倡导投资仲裁的发达国家不得不亲自体会作为被申请人（东道国）的苦衷，这一经历使得美、加等国开始有意识地在投资协议中增加旨在保护东道国主权的新条款，如税收措施例外条款、一般例外条款、安全例外条款等，以确保东道国有权在不受羁绊的情况下保障此类主权利益。

因此，《中国—东盟投资协议》仿效最新美式双边投资协议范本的上述做法，在协议中明文增设了税收措施条款和一般例外、根本安全例外等条款，这着实有利于在保护外国投资者私益与维护东道国主权之间求取平衡，其意义值得肯定。

二、《中国—东盟投资协议》的缺漏

瑕瑜互见的是，《中国—东盟投资协议》也存在诸多重大缺漏，以至于严重影响了该协议效用之发挥。限于篇幅，本文仅拟探讨如下三个问题：

---

① See Methanex Corp. v. The United States of America (NAFTA Chapter 11 arbitration).

② See Fireman's Fund Insurance Company v. The United Mexican States, ICSID Case No. ARB(AF)/02/1.

③ See Metalclad Corporation v. The United Mexican States, ICSID Case No. ARB (AF)/97/1.

④ See Pope & Talbot Inc. v. The Government of Canada (NAFTA Chapter 11 arbitration).

⑤ Shalakany, Amr A. Arbitration and the Third World: A Plea for Reassessing Bias Under the Specter of Neoliberalism. *Harvard International Law Journal*, 2000, 41: 419～424.

(一)所约束的国家行为范围过于狭窄

《中国—东盟投资协议》第3条规定了其适用范围问题:“本协议适用于一缔约方对下列相关情形采取或保留的措施:(1)另一缔约方的投资者;(2)另一缔约方投资者在其领土内的投资。”由此可见,并非东道国的所有针对外国投资者或其投资的行为均受该协议约束,能够受该协议约束的仅是构成“措施”的行为。那么,何谓“措施”呢?

根据该协议第1条第7款,所谓“措施”是指一缔约方所采取的,影响投资者和/或投资的,任何普遍适用的法律、法规、规则、程序、行政决定或行政行为……也就是说,这一规定将“措施”局限于“普遍适用”(of general application)的“法律、法规、规则、程序、行政决定或行政行为”。尽管该协议并未就“普遍适用”一词进行专门的界定,但作为常用的法律术语,在“普遍适用的措施、行为”之类的语境下,“普遍适用”指措施、行为的抽象性,申言之,这类措施、行为针对的是不特定的对象,这一解读在国际法领域并无明显分歧。比如,2010年《欧盟—韩国自由贸易协议》第12章(透明度)第12.1条明确规定:“普遍适用的措施指的是任何普遍的或抽象的行为、程序、解释或其他要求,包括不具有约束力的措施。它不包括适用于特定的人的裁断。”2006年《新加坡—巴拿马自由贸易协议》第14章(透明度)第14.6条亦规定:“普遍适用的行政裁断指的是适用于其调整范围内的所有的人或事并确立了行为准则的行政裁断或解释,但不包括:(a)在个案中,经由行政程序作出的,适用于缔约另一方的特定的人、货物或服务的判决或裁断;或(b)针对特别的行为或做法而作出的裁断。”有鉴于此,《中国—东盟投资协议》第3条的上述规定就排除了东道国国家机关的具体行政行为和司法行为,因为后两类行为不具有普遍适用性。

《中国—东盟投资协议》的这种规定是否妥当呢?为此,我们有必要研究投资仲裁实例,以查明在实践中困扰外国投资者的国家行为是否主要为具有普遍适用性的行为。

鉴于世界银行集团之内的“解决投资争端国际中心”(以下简称ICSID)系专门性的投资仲裁机构,它所处理的投资仲裁案件占当今世界同类案件的绝大多数,我们不妨以ICSID仲裁案件为剖析的样本。需要说明的是,由于仲裁的非公开性所致,我们所研究的对象并不周延,仅限于其裁决文书已被公开披露出来的那部分ICSID仲裁实例。根据笔者收集的资料,从2010年1月1日至2010年6月24日,ICSID共对15个投资仲裁案件发布了包括管辖权决定、中期裁决、最终裁决在内的各类仲裁文书。通过这些仲裁文书我们发现:

(1)当事双方争议的主要国家行为具有普遍适用性的案件共有3个,占所有样本的20%,均与东道国颁布和实施新立法有关;[①](2)当事双方争议的主要国家行为不具有普遍适用性的案件共11个,占所有样本的73%,分别涉及东道国关闭企业、[②]违反特许协议、[③]法院审判不公、[④]拒绝发放采矿许可证、[⑤]扣押船舶[⑥]、国有化、[⑦]拒不清偿主权债务、[⑧]不履行和解协议和不分配无线电频率、[⑨]税务检查及相关刑事调查[⑩]等行为;(3)根据目前公开披露的信息,尚无法判断当事双方争议的主要国家行为是否具有普遍适用性的案件共1个,约

---

① Mobil v. Bolivarian Republic of Venezuela, ICSID Case No. ARB/07/27 (Netherlands/Venezuela BIT); Burlington Resources Inc. and others v. Republic of Ecuador and Empresa Estatal Petróleos del Ecuador (PetroEcuador), ICSID Case No. ARB/08/5 (US/Ecuador BIT); Corn Products International, Inc. v. United Mexican States, ICSID Case No. ARB (AF)/04/1 (NAFTA).

② Alasdair Ross Anderson and others v. Republic of Costa Rica, ICSID Case No. ARB(AF)/07/3 (Canada/Costa Rica BIT); Victor Pey Casado and President Allende Foundation v. Republic of Chile, ICSID Case No. ARB/98/2 (Spain/Chile BIT).

③ Railroad Development Corporation v. Republic of Guatemala, ICSID Case No. ARB/07/23 (US CAFTA/DR FTA); Quiborax S. A., Non Metallic Minerals S. A. and Allan Fosk Kaplún v. Plurinational State of Bolivia, ICSID Case No. ARB/06/2 (Bolivia/Chile BIT); Rumeli Telekom A. S. and Telsim Mobil Telekomunikasyon Hizmetleri A. S. v. Kazakhstan, ICSID Case No. ARB/05/16 (Turkey/Kazakhstan BIT).

④ ATA Construction, Industrial and Trading Company v. The Hashemite Kingdom of Jordan, ICSID Case No. ARB/08/2 (Turkey/Jordan BIT).

⑤ Pac Rim Cayman LLC v. Republic of El Salvador, ICSID Case No. ARB/09/12 (CAFTA).

⑥ Inmaris Perestroika Sailing Maritime Services GMBH and Others v. Ukraine, ICSID Case No. ARB/08/8 (Germany/Ukraine BIT).

⑦ CEMEX Caracas Investments B. V. and CEMEX Caracas Ⅱ Investments B. V. v. Bolivarian Republic of Venezuela, ICSID Case No. ARB/08/15 (Netherlands/Venezuela BIT).

⑧ Giovanna a Beccara and others v. The Argentine Republic, ICSID Case No. ARB/07/5 (Argentina/Italy BIT).

⑨ Joseph Charles Lemire v. Ukraine, ICSID Case No. ARB/06/18 (US/Ukraine BIT).

⑩ The Rompetrol Group N. V. v. Romania, ICSID Case No. ARB/06/3 (Netherlands/Romania BIT).

占所有样本的7%。[1]

上述数据显然说明,在国际投资仲裁实践中,导致外国投资者提起投资仲裁的主要不是具有普遍适用性的行为(也即立法或者抽象行政行为),而是不具有普遍适用性的行为(主要包括具体行政行为或司法行为)。因此,《中国—东盟投资协议》所约束的国家行为范围确实过窄。

(二)缺乏审慎措施条款

审慎措施条款是2004年美式双边投资协议范本所创设的一种新条款,其目的是为了保护东道国的金融监管主权,其内容则主要涉及国际投资协议不妨碍东道国出于审慎原因而采取或保持与金融服务有关的措施,也即东道国出于审慎原因采取的影响外国投资者及其投资的措施不受国际投资协议约束。

在笔者看来,审慎措施条款的产生乃是基于如下两方面的迫切需要:

第一,服务贸易自由化进程导致金融业领域外资大量增多,东道国对金融业的正当监管权与其所承担的国际投资保护义务之间的冲突加剧。

20世纪90年代以来,随着WTO《服务贸易总协定》以及诸多以该协议为蓝本的区域性、双边性服务贸易协议的达成和生效,全球金融服务贸易自由化进程大大加快。由于直接在东道国设立旨在提供服务的商业机构能够降低跨境贸易的成本,并可利用东道国在要素价格方面的竞争优势,故在跨境提供、消费者移动、商业存在、自然人流动等四种服务贸易的提供方式中,商业存在方式颇受金融服务提供者的青睐。可是,跨国服务提供者在他国设立商业机构的经济活动不但属于国际服务贸易,亦属于国际直接投资。虽然顾及金融服务贸易的特殊重要性以及发展中国家的特殊情况,上述服务贸易协议在促进金融服务贸易自由化之余为主权国家预留了一定的管制空间,但考虑到国际服务贸易协议从未为私人创设国际法上的出诉权,而多数国际投资协议则恰恰允许外国投资者就东道国违反该协议的行为提起国际仲裁,故如无保护东道国金融监管权的必要制度设计,则难以在保护金融业外资私益与维护东道国金融主权之间保持适当的平衡。

第二,经济一体化条件下金融体系的脆弱性和金融危机的传染效应增强,东道国的货币政策制定权与其所承担的国际投资保护义务之间的冲突加剧。

---

① Alpha Projektholding GmbH v. Ukraine, ICSID Case No. ARB/07/16 (Austria/Ukraine).

“在一体化条件下，国际资本投机性、趋利性和大规模快速流动等特点，使国际金融市场充满风险和不稳定性，一国金融体系的脆弱性加剧，金融危机爆发的概率加大。”①一旦金融危机在经济一体化范围内的某个国家或地区爆发，它往往能够通过贸易联系与竞争性贬值、政策调整、随机总需求流动性冲击等非偶发性途径，以及投资者或金融市场其他参与者行为（特别是非理性行为）等偶发性途径，像传染病一样迅速从最早爆发危机的国家或地区蔓延到其他国家和地区，②此即外部因素引发金融危机，亦称金融危机的传染效应。为应对金融危机，国家通常需要对自己的货币政策等主要的宏观经济调控工具进行适度调整，而这往往会影响到各行各业的外国投资者及其投资。倘若允许受此影响的外国投资者根据国际投资协议提起投资仲裁索赔，则东道国的货币政策制定权必将受到严重侵蚀。

所以，晚近一些年来，包括美国、加拿大、日本、挪威以及我国在内的一些国家开始在国际投资协议中订入审慎措施条款。相形之下，《中国—东盟投资协议》中却没有规定该条款，这确为严重缺漏。

（三）根本安全例外条款缺乏必要的制度性约束

根本安全例外条款首次出现于2004年美式双边投资协议范本，随后被许多国家在缔结投资协议时采纳，其目的在于确保东道国在保障国家根本安全利益的时候，不受国际投资协议的掣肘。

《中国—东盟投资协议》中规定根本安全例外的是其第17条：“本协议的任何规定不得解释为：(1)要求任何一方提供其认为如披露会违背其根本安全利益的任何信息。(2)阻止任何一方采取其认为对保护根本安全利益所必需的任何行动，包括但不限于：①与裂变和聚变物质或衍生这些物质的物质有关的行动；②与武器、弹药和作战物资的贸易有关的行动，及与直接或间接供应军事机关的其他货物和物资的贸易有关的行动；③为保护关键的公共基础设施免受使其丧失或降低功能的故意袭击而采取的行动；④战时或国内、国际关系中其他紧急情况下采取的行动。(3)阻止一方为履行其在《联合国宪章》项下的维护国际和平与安全的义务而采取的任何行动。”

为最大限度地维护东道国的根本安全利益，该协议通过“其认为”（which

① 游家兴：《经济一体化进程会放大金融危机传染效应吗——以中国为样本》，载《国际金融研究》2010年第1期。

② 梅新育：《国际金融危机传染机制的新特点》，载《中国金融》2007年第18期。

it cosiders)一语赋予了东道国在采取根本安全例外措施时的自行判断权。鉴于该协议并未明文规定东道国自行判断的范围和限度,故其在实践中的具体运作方式还有赖于国际投资仲裁庭的裁断。尽管目前尚无投资者依据《中国—东盟投资协议》提起投资仲裁,受该协议约束的东道国因此也尚无启用根本安全例外条款进行抗辩的实例,但考虑到其他同样包含了根本安全例外条款的国际投资协议项下业已发生过相关案件,故我们仍可通过实证研究的方式了解仲裁庭在实践中如何理解此类条款中的自行判断权。

根据目前已披露出来的裁决书,迄今多数仲裁庭认为,如果一项根本安全例外条款没有赋予东道国自行判断权,如没有使用"其认为"等措辞,则仲裁庭有权对下述两方面问题进行审查:对国家基本安全利益的严重威胁是否存在、东道国所采取的措施是否控制在保护国家基本安全利益的必要限度内;倘若此类条款通过"其认为"等措辞赋予了东道国自行判断权,则对上述两方面问题的唯一判断者就是东道国本身,仲裁庭并无实质审查权。① 当然,鉴于《维也纳条约法公约》第26条规定,缔约国应善意履行条约义务,故仲裁庭此时应有权审查东道国采取措施时的主观心理状态,也即是否善意。② 不过,对东道国主观心理状态的揣测通常难以获得确切的证据支持,有关善意原则的国际法案例又非常鲜见,故不可高估善意原则对东道国自行判断权的约束潜力。当然,也有个别仲裁庭认为,自行判断性质的基本安全例外条款并非意味着东道国有权杜撰并不存在的国家基本安全之威胁,故仲裁庭此时应有权审查对国家基本安全的严重威胁是否存在,以确定东道国是否有权启动该条款。③ 此外,联合国贸易和发展会议的一份出版物也持此观点。④

综上,对于自行判断性质的基本安全例外条款,投资仲裁庭的看法并不一

① CMS Gas Transmission Co. v. Republic ofArgentina, ICSID Case No. ARB/01/8, Award of May 12, 2005, 44 ILM 1205 (2005), paras. 366~376; Enron Corporation and Ponderosa Assets, L. P. v. Argentine Republic, ICSID Case No. ARB/01/3 (United States/Argentina BIT), Award of 22 May 2007, paras. 331~339; Sempra Energy International v. The Argentine Republic, ICSID Case No. ARB/02/16 (US/Argentina BIT), Award of 28 September 2007, paras. 373~374.

② See supra.

③ Continental Casualty Company v. Argentine Republic, ICSID Case No. ARB/03/9), Award of September 5, 2008, para. 182.

④ UNCTAD, The Protection Of National Security In IIAs, UNCTAD Series on International Investment Policies for Development, 2009, p. 93.

致:多数仲裁庭认为,东道国有权自行确定对国家基本安全的严重威胁是否存在及其所采取的对策措施是否必要,而此时仲裁庭除可考察东道国的主观心理状态是否为善意外,别无任何实质审查权。鉴于上述主流看法实际上给拥有自行判断权的东道国预留了滥用权利的极大空间,而《中国—东盟投资协议》中的根本安全例外条款恰属于自行判断性质,故如无适当的制度设计防止东道国滥用权利,则投资者的权利保护势必成为空谈。

三、《中国—东盟投资协议》的完善对策

据我国商务部统计,截至2009年8月,我国已开展了14个自由贸易区谈判,涉及31个国家和地区。其中,除中国—东盟自由贸易区外,中国—新西兰自由贸易区、中国—巴基斯坦自由贸易区、中国—秘鲁自由贸易区也涵盖了投资的内容。此外,在我国与澳大利亚、智利、挪威等国开展的自由贸易区谈判中,投资均为主要内容①。在我国目前正在建设的诸多自由贸易区中,中国—东盟自由贸易区具有非常重要的标志性意义:它不但是我国对外商谈的第一个自由贸易区,同时也是东盟作为一个整体对外商谈的第一个自由贸易区,故《中国—东盟投资协议》的完善不仅关系到该自由贸易区范围内国际投资法制的合理构建,还关系到我国今后在参与创建其他自由贸易区国际投资法制时的谈判立场确定,意义非常重大。

笔者认为,应如是完善该协议:

(一)扩大受约束的国家行为之范围

如上所述,目前世界各国所签订的国际投资协议主要以下述两种范本为模板:美国式双边投资协议范本、欧洲式双边投资协议范本。考虑到尽管美国式双边投资协议晚近日益风行,但至今世界上仍有许多国家继续签订欧洲式双边投资协议,故在探索如何扩大《中国—东盟投资协议》项下受约束的国家行为之类型时,有必要同时考察这两种典型范本的做法。

笔者认为,在扩大受约束的国家行为之范围问题上,《中国—东盟投资协议》有两种可选择的方案:

第一,采用美式双边投资协议的做法,对该协议所约束的"措施"之含义进

① 商务部官员就中国—东盟自贸区《投资协议》答问,http://www.chinanews.com.cn/cj/cj-gncj/news/2009/08-15/1819891.shtml,访问日期:2009年8月15日。

行明确界定:在内涵界定方面删除“普遍适用的”这一限制词,在外延界定方面使用弹性词汇将具体行政行为和司法行为均涵盖进来。可资参考的便是美国(2004 年)、加拿大(2004 年)双边投资协议范本第 1 条的规定:“‘措施’包括任何法律、规章、程序、要求或做法。”上述界定一举囊括了东道国立法、行政、司法机关所从事的所有行为,从而使得东道国不但需要对国家机关所为的具有普遍适用性的行为负责,也需要对国家机关所为的不具有普遍适用性的行为负责。从各国缔约实践来看,不但美国对外缔约时采用这种宽泛的界定方法,而且一些东盟国家也已在缔约实践中接受了这种做法,如 2007 年《泰国—日本自由贸易区协议》第 8 章(投资)第 91 条规定:“‘措施’一词指的是缔约方以法律、规章、规则、程序、决定、行政行为或其他形式所采取的任何措施。”

第二,采用欧洲式双边投资协议的做法,对该协议所约束的“措施”之含义不做任何界定。可资参考的便是德国(2008 年)、法国(2006 年)、印度(2003 年)双边投资协议范本的规定。考虑到根据国际公法的国家责任原理,执行政府职能的立法、行政、司法机关的所有行为都可以归因于国家,都可以被视作国家的行为,故若《中国—东盟投资协议》不对“措施”概念进行任何界定,缔约国同样有义务确保其立法、行政、司法机关的所有具有、不具有普遍适用性的行为符合该协议的规定。从各国缔约实践来看,不但早期的双边投资协议均采用这种不界定“措施”的简洁式缔约技巧,而且德国、法国等采用传统欧洲式范本的国家一直在采用这种缔约技巧,此外,迄今一些东盟国家在缔约实践中也保持这种做法,如 2002 年《泰国—德国促进和保护投资协议》即是如此。

当然,从整体内容和结构来看,《中国—东盟投资协议》确系以美式双边投资协议范本为模板,但这并不意味着《中国—东盟投资协议》必须采纳第一种方案。实际上,上述两种方案的效果是完全一样的。也正因为这个原因,主要借鉴美式范本的 2007 年挪威双边投资协议范本便没有对“措施”进行任何界定。

(二)增设审慎措施条款

不同的双边投资协议,其有关审慎措施条款的内容设定有所不同。具体来说,可以区分为两类:其一是实体内容型,也即仅规定了可以援引审慎措施例外的实体条件,如 2007 年挪威双边投资协议范本便是如此;其二是实体兼程序内容型,也即不仅规定了可以援引审慎措施例外的实体条件,而且还规定了涉及审慎措施例外的争端解决程序,如美国和加拿大的双边投资协议范本便是如此。笔者认为,《中国—东盟投资协议》在增设审慎措施条款时,其内容应采纳实体兼程序内容型：

第一，实体内容部分的设定。这部分内容是审慎措施条款的公认核心组成部分，其以《服务贸易总协定》的《金融服务附件》第2(a)条为蓝本，强调东道国有义务为了维护整个金融系统以及单个金融机构的安全、稳健、统一或金融责任而进行干预，且此种干预不应被视为违反相关投资协议义务。其惯常表达模式为："本条约的任何其他规定不得阻止缔约一方出于审慎原因而采取或保持与金融服务有关的措施，包括为保护投资者、存款人、保单持有人或金融服务提供者对其负有信托责任的人而采取的措施，或为保证金融体系完整和稳定而采取的措施。如此类措施不符合本协议的规定，则不得用作逃避该方在本协议项下的承诺或义务的手段。"上述规定可资《中国—东盟投资协议》借鉴。需要注意的是，上述规定同时还强调了东道国"不得逃避相关投资协议承诺或义务"。申言之，一国有权采取审慎措施且不对外国投资者承担赔偿责任，但倘若因此发生争端，投资仲裁庭仍有权对这种具有审慎措施性质的国家行为进行实质性审查，以确定东道国是否借此逃避了相关投资协议义务，以防东道国滥用审慎监管权。

第二，程序内容部分的设定。如上所述，为防止东道国滥用审慎措施权，国际投资仲裁庭有权就东道国是否属于"以采取审慎措施之名、行逃避国际投资协议义务之实"进行审查。然而，由于国际投资仲裁员通常具有片面强调"私有财产神圣不可侵犯"的倾向，不大考虑东道国的国家主权，将东道国的金融监管行为完全交由仲裁庭来裁断并不合适。所以，《中国—东盟投资协议》有必要借鉴2004年美国、加拿大的双边投资协议范本的最新做法，在审慎措施条款中增加必要的程序性内容，以适当约束仲裁庭。具体为：(1)投资仲裁庭有义务应东道国的要求提请双方提交报告。也就是说，倘若投资者提起投资仲裁，而东道国援引审慎措施条款进行抗辩，那么，在东道国提出要求的情况下，投资仲裁庭应请求该东道国及投资者母国出具书面报告，以澄清在该案中东道国能否以及在何种程度上提出审慎措施抗辩。仲裁庭在收到报告之前不得继续审理。(2)双方的报告对投资仲裁庭有约束力。也就是说，缔约双方在收到仲裁庭的上述请求后，应通过下述途径准备报告：双方之间的争端解决程序、双方金融监管机构之间的磋商由双方指定的仲裁专家组处理。缔约双方应将报告转交给投资仲裁庭，该报告对投资仲裁庭具有约束力。(3)在缔约双方逾期未提交报告的情况下，投资仲裁庭可继续审理。也就是说，若仲裁庭发出要求后若干天内，缔约双方没有作出报告，仲裁庭也没有收到报告，则仲裁庭可自行继续审理、自行裁断。

(三)对根本安全例外条款予以必要的制度性约束

在对根本安全例外条款进行制度性约束方面,目前主要存在两种做法:实体性约束、程序性约束。笔者认为,《中国—东盟投资协议》应采用程序性约束的方法。

首先,实体性约束方案不尽合理。所谓实体性约束,也即对东道国援引根本安全例外条款一事附加实体性要求。如2003年匈牙利—印度双边投资协议第12条规定:"本协议不妨碍缔约国在正常、合理、非歧视的基础上依照自己的法律,为了保护自己的根本安全利益或……而采取行动。"在这种方案中,不但东道国有义务"正常、合理、非歧视"地"适用自己的法律"采取保护根本安全例外的措施,而且投资仲裁庭也有权对东道国是否依法、是否正常、合理、非歧视进行实体审查。考虑到这种方案对东道国的自由裁量权约束太大,不利于东道国在诸如国防安全利益受到严重威胁等紧急情况下权宜行事,笔者认为不宜采纳。

其次,程序性约束方案可资借鉴。所谓程序性约束,也即对东道国援引根本安全例外条款一事附加程序性要求。目前国际投资协议中的根本安全例外条款均系以WTO《服务贸易总协定》第14条为蓝本,而《服务贸易总协定》第14条已在其第2款中对根本安全例外条款设定了必要的程序性要求,其内容主要为:根据根本安全例外条款采取措施的缔约方应在最大程度上通知服务贸易理事会如下事项——所采取的措施、这些措施的终止情况。倘《中国—东盟投资协议》采用类似的程序性约束方案,一方面,东道国酌情采取适当措施保护本国根本安全利益的权利未受到实质性侵蚀,东道国的主权利益得以保全,另一方面,上述程序性通知义务也迫使东道国必须将影响受益人的措施及时通知相关方面,从而无法在违反相关协议后以"保护根本安全利益"为借口逃避责任,外国投资者的利益亦得以适当保全,实为两全方案。

在程序性约束方案的具体设计上,笔者认为,可以借鉴2003年《日本—越南双边投资协议》第15条,具体规定如下:如果缔约方依据根本安全例外条款采取与本协议战乱损失赔偿条款以外的其他条款义务不符的任何措施,则该缔约方应当在该措施生效前或生效后的尽可能早的时间内通知另一缔约方,通知内容应包括如下几方面:(1)受影响的部门和分部门或事项;(2)该措施所涉的义务或者协议条款;(3)该措施的法律渊源;(4)对该措施的简要描述;(5)采取该措施的目的。

The China-ASEAN Investment Agreement: Achievements, Shortcomings and Improvements

Wei Yanru*

Abstract

The China-ASEAN Investment Agreement not only creates a uniform international investment protection system in China-ASEAN Free Trade Area, but also tries to balance the private rights of foreign investors and the sovereignty of host countries, which is its achievement. At the same time, severe problems exist in the Agreement, e. g. , regulating too narrow scope of state conducts, lacking a prudential clause, and lacking necessary systemic restrictions in the essential security clause, etc. It is very urgent for us to improve the Agreement.

Keywords: the China-ASEAN Investment Agreement; scope of application; prudential measures; essential security exception.

Content

* Professor of the Law School of Guangxi University, researcher of the China-ASEAN Legal Research Center, mainly engaging in the international investment law.

中国、东盟国家

国内法专论

DOMESTIC LAWS OF CHINA AND ASEAN COUNTRIES

Adjustment of National Laws of Vietnam in Conjunction with the Implementation of ASEAN—China Free Trade Area

Nguyen Xuan Anh*

Content

- Vietnam's national laws under the demand of the implementation of ACFTA.
- Implementation of ACFTA—how to gain win-win results?

Vietnam, a full member of ASEAN, participated as one Signing Party in the Framework Agreement on Comprehensive Economic Co-Operation between ASEAN and the People's Republic of China in 2002, leading to the establishment of ASEAN - China Free Trade Area (ACFTA) and other specific Agreements on Trade in Goods (2005), on Trade in Services (2006), and on Investment (2009). It is one of the very important milestones in the process of international economic integration of Vietnam. In practice, while Vietnam has been taking active steps in the adjustment of national laws for the implementation of ACFTA, much remains to be done to take full advantage of ACFTA.

* Nguyen Xuan Anh, vice-director of the Viefnam-China-ASEAN Legal Information and consultancy.

Ⅰ. Vietnam's national laws under the demand of the implementation of ACFTA

In the process of integration, Vietnam has goodwill of maintaining to fully and actively implement international trade commitments signed and pledged by itself. On such basis, under all agreements in the framework of ACFTA, especially the Agreement on Trade in Goods (TIG), Vietnam has quickly promulgated and executed domestic laws and documents to implement these agreements.

For its content, these documents can be listed as followed:

(1) A group of documents with the content of tax adjustments for the-implementation of tariff reduction.

In fact, it is the group of import lists and tariff provided by Vietnam in order to make them legally adjusted (by annual scale) in the framework of ACFTA. Up to now, the implementation of annual tariff reduction in line with this group of documents has been quite smooth with no negative feedbacks or complaints.

> Box 1 - Legal documents of adjusting tariff in line with the implementation of ACFTA
>
> -Decree No. 99/2004/ND-CP dated February 25, 2004 of Vietnam's Government promulgating Vietnam's 2004—2008 list of goods and their import tax rates for implementation of the early harvest program of the Framework Agreement on ASEAN—China Comprehensive Economic Cooperation.
>
> —Circular No. 16/2004/TT-BTC dated March 10, 2004 of the Ministry of Finance guiding the implementation of the Government's Decree No. 99/2004/ND-CP dated February 25, 2004 which promulgates Vietnam's list of goods and their import tax rates for implementation of the early harvest program under the Framework Agreement on ASEAN-China Comprehensive Economic Cooperation.
>
> —Decision No. 35/2006/QD-BTC dated June 12, 2006 of the Ministry of Finance promulgating Vietnam's 2006 list of goods items and their particularly preferential import tax rates for implementation of the ASEAN-China Agreement on Trade in Goods.

—Circular No. 52/2006/TT-BTC dated June 12, 2006 of the Ministry of Finance guiding the application of Vietnam's particularly preferential import tax rates for the implementation of the ASEAN-China Agreement on Trade in Goods.

—Decision No. 26/2007/QD-BTC dated April 16, 2007 of the Ministry of Finance promulgating Vietnam's particularly preferential import table of rates for the implementation of the ASEAN-China Free Trade Area.

—Decision No. 20/2008/QD-BTC dated May 05, 2008 of the Ministry of Finance promulgating Vietnam's special preferential import duty schedule for implementation of the ASEAN-China Free Trade Area.

(2) A group of documents on origin of goods applied for im-export administration under the framework of ACFTA.

The main content of these documents is to "domesticize" the articles and terms on the origin of goods under the Agreement on Trade in Goods within the framework of ACFTA. The specific and detailed provisions on conditions and procedures to determine the origin of goods that can enjoy preferential tariff under ACFTA have paved the way for the practical implementation of the most important agreements in the framework of ACFTA.

Box 2 - Legal documents on the origin of goods for the implementation of ACFTA

—Decision No. 1727/2003/QD-BTM dated December 12, 2003 of the Ministry of Trade with regulations on the issuance of Vietnam's certificate of origin form E for preferential tariff treatment of goods under the framework agreement on comprehensive economic cooperation among the Governments of the People's Republic of China and the member countries of the association of the Southeast Asian nations.

— Legal dispatch No. 4992/TCHQ-GSQL of the General Department of Customs on the time of the acceptance of Vietnam's certificate of Origin-Form E with the backin Chinese.

(3) Legal documents providing for the implementation of commitments under the framework of ACFTA on specific cases are arisen in practice.

The practice of implementation of ACFTA provisions has arisen quite a few difficulties for specific cases. In order to solve the problems in a timely manner and for the smoother implementation of ACFTA, relevant authorities of Vietnam often seek the correspondence from the tantamount organs of China for the timely solutions in favor of the involved businesses. These are only the uncommonly - applied legal documents but making not small contribution to the implementation of ACFTA.

Box 3 - Typical legal documents instructing the implementation of ACFTA in specific cases. — Legal dispatch No. 16562/BTC-HTQT of the Ministry of Finance regulating special preferential tariff for the goods originated from ACFTA. — Legal dispatch No. 6823/TCHQ-GSQL of the General Department of Customs about the enjoyment of preferential tariff under the Agreement on Trade in Goods within ACFTA. — Legal dispatch No. 6821/TCHQ-GSQL of the General Department of Customs regulating preferential tariff on exports within ACFTA.

(4) Vietnam's general legal documents for the implementation of international trade commitments/agreements.

In fact, Vietnam's negotiation on ACFTA was carried out simultaneously with the other agreements as ASEAN Plus, WTO…, the implementation of ACFTA has also been performed concurrently with the other trade commitments.

Along with the adjustment of national laws and legal regulations toward the performance of ACFTA, Vietnam also issued other legal documents for the implementation of other/all commercial commitments/agreements. All such legal documents made quite large contribution to the synchronous and systematic implementation of Vietnam's commitments/agreements on trade specifically and fruitfully.

The preliminary consideration of these legal documents showed that:

①ACFTA is mainly subjected to Vietnamese laws over the matters of tariff and tax in relation with China; other relating matters of institution or conditions or transparency… have also been performed along the process of Vietnam's implementation of other trade commitments/agreements (especially under the framework of WTO), therefore meeting the demands by ACFTA.

②Vietnam's domestic legal system has fundamentally adjusted in an appropriate and timely manner for the realization of commitments under the framework of ACFTA. Such adjustment was made under both "hard" commitments on national laws as well as legal regulations and "flexible" pledge over legal instructions on specific cases.

The process of implementation of ACFTA in Vietnam has, in practice, shown few big difficulties. Vietnam's partners among ASEAN nations and China as well raised no huge complaints referring the performance of Vietnamese Government's commitments within the framework of ACFTA.

Ⅱ. Implementation of ACFTA—how to gain win-win results?

In the aspect of legality, Vietnam can be said to have taken firm and active steps in the performance of all commitments/agreements within the framework of ACFTA.

However, from economic perspective, Vietnamese economy in general and enterprises in particular seem to face not small challenges and difficulties (with less corresponding interests and benefits respectively).

In overall, the most transparent benefits from ACFTA that Vietnam have been looking forward to is from the Agreement on Trade in Goods (because Vietnamese are still quite weak and less competitive in exportation, services and investment so that they will be hardly achieving fruitful results from the Agreements on Trade in Services and Investment within ACFTA), but the fact showed that at the very most hopeful domain, Vietnam might not be satisfactory.

A series of researches by both foreign and local organizations have indicated that out of 6 FTA signed by Vietnam with 15 partners, ACFTA represented the only one that Vietnam gains very few considerable economic outcomes up till now.

Typically, since the official implementation of ACFTA, Vietnam has been subjected to negative impacts on both importation and exportation at certain periods while Vietnam has not fully complies with tariff reduction (under the Agreement on Trade in Goods, by 2015, the roadmap of tariff reduction will have ended).

From the export aspect, Vietnamese market share in China has been continuously narrowed since 2004 (the point of application of early harvest program), except the 2009 inconsiderable expansion. From the import triangle, after 2004, Chinese imports have been strongly pumped into Vietnamese market in correspondence with the sudden and non-stop enlargement of Chinese market share in Vietnam. In overall, Vietnam has been subjected to huge trade deficit against China. Vietnam's import gap from China has doubled within 3 years from 2004 to 2007, though reduced a little in 2008 - 2009, basically being at a large scale at present.

For the export structure, ACFTA has not really exerted positive impacts in the improvement of Vietnam's export structure, especially when Chinese imports are more and more diversified (including the textile and garments of 17%, steel of 18%, 23% for materials used for domestic manufacturing…) while Vietnamese exports to China are mainly from agricultural products of 39% and raw materials of 33%.

Such figures has risen deep concerns among a large number of experts because an FTA is only sustainable if it brings interests and benefits for both sides in both short term and long term. An FTA with large disadvantages or handicaps will inspire great pressure on enterprises and laborers, causing huge difficulties for the government to master the macro-economy and create the social consensus for the issuance of relating economic and integration policies as well as other policies in the future.

From that point of view, it is necessary to overcome the on-going difficulties and challenges in trade relations between ASEAN countries and China in general, between Vietnam and China in particular, via appropriate solutions, thus turning ACFTA into a practical legal tool for the sharing nations to enjoy win-win results and satisfying the expectations of leaders and peoples of all related nations.

In short, Vietnam has been trying all the best for the full implementation of ACFTA and in fact Vietnam has been doing very well. However, from the perspective of interest and benefit, there should be more general solutions from all nations, including China for the real win-win ACFTA as an economic solution. On such basis, all concerning parties can foster the voluntariness and cooperation in the process of implementation of ACFTA, thus bringing genuine prosperity and happiness for people around the region.

中国—东盟自由贸易区成立后越南法律的调整

阮春英*

内容摘要

中国与东盟间经贸关系的全面建立对于越南参与国际经济一体化具有非常重要的意义。目前,越南积极采取相应的措施对国内法进行调整以更好地实施ACFTA。本文首先从法律角度考察越南国内法与实施ACFTA间的契合性,但同时从经济角度指出,应采取相应的措施实现越南与其他国家间的双赢局面,从而促进各国自觉、自愿地遵守并实施ACFTA。

关键词: ACFTA的实施;国内法;经济一体化;双赢局面

目　次

* 阮春英,越南—中国—东盟法律信息咨询中心副主任。

Development of Business Laws in Myanmar

Win Myint*

Abstract

In the past decades, the global trading system has become much more liberalized and the establishment of regional trading agreements and free trade agreements , or RTAs and FTAs have become increasingly integrated. Myanmar has also been implementing economic and legal development relating the regional dimension and direction. Myanmar has cooperated with other Asian countries such as Japan, Korea and China and implemented open regionalism under the framework of ASEAN. In the process of free and fair trade and trade liberalization, Myanmar has been taking part as an active participant in the various regional and international forum. Myanmar entered into China-ASEAN Free Trade Agreement (CAFTA) which was officially announced and signed in November 2002, ASEAN and China envision the liberalization of their bilateral trade in stages: by 2010 for the ASEAN 6 and China; and 2015 for Cambodia, Laos, Myanmar and Vietnam.

The objective of this paper is to present Myanmar business laws and experiences of making legal reforms in several sectors which Myanmar has changed her centralized economic system to market-oriented economic system in 1988 before Myanmar entered into CAFTA. Moreover, According to Article 8 (h) of CAFTA agreement, the facilitation and promotion of effective and adequate protection of trade-related aspects of intellectual property

* Win Myint, deputy director general from the Office of the Prosecutor General of Myanmar.

rights are so important between parties. Therefore, I will present the current situation of Myanmar business laws and laws relating Intellectual Property Rights.

Key Words: Business Law; Intellectual Property Law; Centralized Economic System; Market-Oriented System

Content

- Introduction
- Legal system of Myanmar
- Export Policy
- Import Policy
- Myanmar and FTAs
- Legal Development in Domestic Business Area
- The Current situation of Myanmar Intellectual Property Laws
- Conclusion

Introduction

International Trade is carried on by all nations to varying degrees. No country is so self sufficient that it can put up barriers and ignore the rest of world and a free interchange of products and services. ① In the changing of global legal and institutional Framework respecting economic relations of the nation states from the multimodal regulations made among them at different areas and levels. This effects the inter-dependence among developed and developing countries, least developing countries to grant such changes on the

① Mark S. W. Hoyle, *The Law of International Trade*, The laureate Press London 1981 , 1st edition ,p. 1.

other hand. There have been surges of Free Trade of Area networks and cluster around the world. Myanmar also make progress on this way to ensure that Myanmar can exist in the competitive market. Myanmar is now playing an important role in the strategic economic development of China and the countries in ASEAN to attain their rapid economic growth.

Legal system of Myanmar

The legal system of Union of Myanmar is based on the Common Law Legal system to the Common Law legal family. It uses the principles of Common Law legal system and adopted them into the statute laws that are promulgated by the legislature. As mentioned above many of the principles of Myanmar legal system and in particular the commercial, economics and corporate laws are based upon the Common Law legal system and thus belonging to the common law legal family.

Trade Regime of Myanmar[①]

Since Myanmar has changed it's economic course from a centralized economy system into a market-oriented system, a series of structural reforms had been introduced and new legal policy instruments given the private sector including foreign investors and businessmen, the right to do business and to make investment in the country were enacted. The Government of the Union of Myanmar has recognized, in the context of the market-oriented economic system, the private sector as a prime-mover of the market mechanism and pays great attention for its development. All-out efforts are being made to encourage the active participation of private sectors in foreign trade and giving full support in every angle.

For the above reasons, trade liberalization measures were introduced as follows:

(1) To be in line with the changing economic system, the private individualsor enterprises are allowed to carry out the export import business which was previously monopolised by the state.

(2) Border Trade was regularised in order to develop and strengthen the

① Directorate of Trade, advance forward through commerce.

bilateral trade relations with the neighbouring countries. Department of Border Trade was established and its 11 branch offices providing one-stop service for border trade matters in collaboration with various departments concerned.

(3)Export and Import procedures were realigned.

(4) Lowered the technical barriers to trade and simplified export/ import procedures geared towards trade facilitation and promotion.

(5) Incentives are being given to exporters by allowing 100 % retention of export earnings for importation of goods.

(6) Trade notifications are being issued by specifying necessary rules in conformity to the changing internal and external business environment.

(7) The role of Chambers of Commerce and Industry had reactivated and reorganized the Union of Myanmar Federation of Chambers of Commerceand Industry-UMFCCI for the promotion of trade and industry of the private sector.

To be in line with the market-oriented economy, the foreign trade policy of Myanmar is also a very independent one. We can trade with any country in the world except some countries that are trade embargoed by the United Nations Resolutions or a few countries and territories which we have cut off diplomatic relations.

Myanmar believes in trade liberalization and also wants free and fair trade in the world. Myanmar was a founder member of the old organization, GATT and a member of the new organization, WTO. Hence, our foreign trade policies are generally governed by the rule-based multilateral trading system.

Export Policy

Myanmar's export policy is to export all exportable surplus and diversify foreign markets by using of natural and human resources. Increasing and diversifying exports and improving the quality of products are among the main objectives of the export promotion policy.

We give top priority for the development of agriculture as the base and all-round development of the economy as well. A number of new items in the manufacturing and processing sectors have been introduced in the past few years. Main export items include agricultural products, forest products, fishery products, metals & minerals, precious stones and industrial products.

The registered exporter/importer has the right to do trading business. The registered exporters/importers are allowed to enjoy 100 percent export retention money for the import of goods. There exists no export quota nor ceiling for any exportable product or any individual or organization.

Import Policy

Regarding the import policy, import is allowed against the export earnings with a view to promote export and to overcome the balance of trade deficit problems. The private businessmen are encouraged to import capital goods, industrial machineries including raw materials and other essential items while the consumer choices can be fulfilled equally at the same time.

Licence should be applied for any export or import. The authority to issue export/import licences and permits is dedicated to Directorate of Trade and Department of Border Trade under the Ministry of Commerce. Directorate of Trade is authorised to issue export/import licences and permits for conventional export/import by overseas. The Department of Border Trade is authorised to issue export/import licences for overland trade with the neighbouring countries.

The validity of export/import licence/permit issued by the Directorate of Trade is three months from the date of issue, and it cannot be extendable. Export licence fee is not payable on export of any commodity including agricultural crops. All the imports are subject to pay the licence fees, customs duty and commercial tax.

Customs duty together with the commercial tax are collected at the point of entry and the time of clearance of imported goods. Raw materials and other essential imports are taxed at very low rates, while the highest rate is applied to luxury items.

Commercial tax is levied according to the Schedules appended to the Commercial Tax law 1991, and the rates vary depending on the types of goods and services. For the items not exempted from commercial tax, the rates of tax on imported goods are 5%, 10%, 20%, 25% according to the respective schedule of goods. Another schedule represents specific types of foods such as cigarette, liquor, etc. carrying rates above 25%.

Assessment of Import Duty is based on the assessable value, which is the sum of CIF value and the landing charge (0.5 % of the CIF value) for the goods imported. The commercial tax together with the custom duty are collected at the point of entry and the time of clearance of imported goods.

There are three state banks namely Myanmar Foreign Trade Bank-MFTB, Myanmar Investment and Commercial Bank-MICB and Myanmar Economic Bank-MEB, conducting foreign trade transactions of the Union of Myanmar. MEB opens branch offices at the border checkpoints for the commercial transactions of overland trade with the neighboring countries.

Myanmar and FTAs

Myanmar has implemented the economic and legal development according to the regional dimension and direction. In addition, Myanmar has also entered into bilateral FTA with its trading partners. Therefore, the development has been made at bilateral level and regional level. Myanmar has cooperated with other ASEAN countries and has been implementing open regionalism under the framework of ASEAN. Moreover, Myanmar is active in negotiation many FTAs with its economic/trading partner at regional① and bilateral level. Furthermore, Myanmar has signed a Framework Agreements with BIMSTEC② countries so as to establish an FTA by 2015/2017. Apart from the establishment of ASEAN Free Trade Area, Myanmar is now working closely with other ASEAN members, at a regional level, to establish a

---

① Myanmar is a member of ASEAN and in this regional organizations, there are many economic integration programs launching for attaining the objectives of liberalization, for example of the ASEAN Investment area , the Framework Agreement on Trade in Services.

② BIMSTEC or the Bay of Bengal Initiative for Multi-Sectoral Technical and Economic Cooperation consists of Bangladesh, Bhutan, India, Myanmar, Nepal, Sri Lanka, and Thailand.

free trade area with China. Myanmar entered into China-ASEAN Free Trade Agreement (CAFTA) which was officially announced and signed in November 2002, ASEAN and China envision the liberalization of their bilateral trade in stages: by 2010 for the ASEAN-6 and China; and 2015 for Cambodia, Laos, Myanmar and Vietnam. Preparing the economy for the introduction of CAFTA is one of the major steps awaiting the Myanmar government.

Legal Development in Domestic Business Area

Being on this traditional aspect of contemporary legal history, Cooperate laws and Commercial laws also belong to the same fundamentals or modalities of principles of Myanmar Legal system. Today, corporate laws, commercial laws and economic laws are pillars of our market economic system. Historically , these laws which have the principles of common law are kept intact during the past twenty-five years before 1988, when our country adopted the market economic system , a new legal injection has given to these laws and they came into life once again . Commencing from State Law and Order Restoration Council and later the State Peace and Development Council not only put life onto those laws but promulgated new laws for investment, introduced privatization and developed the market economic system that there will be a promotion of foreign investment ,citizens taking active part in the economy, the developing of the market economy and the achieving of better quality of life for our people.① Among those changes of laws and developments, I will mainly focus on the Union of Myanmar Foreign Investment Law and State-owned Economic Enterprises Law in order to understand how those laws are salient for Myanmar and its trading partner.

Myanmar's long experience with foreign investment extends back to its early trading relations with China. By 1941, one quarter of Myanmar's capital stock was owned by foreign investors - Britain, China and India being the dominant countries of origin. Following the end of the Second World War and upon Myanmar's achieving independence from Britain in 1948, for-

---

① H. E. Dr. Tun Shin, Business Law of Myanmar, *Law Journal*, Vol. 2, No. 1, p. 105.

eign companies returned and were permitted to operate through to the early 1960s, receiving official encouragement by way of the Myanmar government's 1955 Investment Policy Statement and the passing of the 1959 Union of Myanmar Investment Act.

In the late 1988, Myanmar changed its centrally-planned economic system that had been practiced for more than two and a half decades to a market oriented system. One of the first instruments of its promised economic reforms was the 1988 Foreign Investment Law (FIL). It provided a number of attractive incentives for foreign investors.

The basic principles set out in the FIL show that the governmentencourageswas desperate for foreign capital-hard currency either by way of direct investment or export earnings, and high technology. Section 4 of the FIL states that foreign investment shall be made in accordance with the following basic principles:

(a)promotion and expansion of exports;

(b)exploitation of natural resources which require heavy investment;

(c)acquisition of high technology;

(d)supporting and assisting production and services involving large capital;

(e)opening up of employment opportunities;

(f)development of works which would save energy consumption; and

(g)Regional development.

The FIL also established the Myanmar Investment Commission (MIC), with various duties and powers, to scrutinize and approve foreign investment. The attractive incentives offered by the FIL begin in Section 21, where the MIC may grant a series of tax relieves and exemptions, including the following:

①an income tax exemption for three consecutive years in the case of enterprises producing goods and services;

②an income tax exemption on profits if reinvested within one year;

③a right to accelerate depreciation on machinery, equipment, building, and other capital;

④a 50 percent tax relief on the profits earned from exported goods;

⑤the deduction of income taxes paid for foreigners from assessable income, and their taxes to be calculated at the same rate as citizens;

⑥the deduction of research and development expenses;

⑦the right to carry losses for three consecutive years; and

⑧the full exemption of customs duty and internal taxes on parts, equipment and raw materials for three years.

The State-owned Economic Enterprises Law was enacted in March 1989. Section 3 gives the Government to perform certain activities through this law. Section 3 empowers only State-owned Economic Enterprises to undertake the twelve activities① such as the extraction and sale of teak, some gems, petroleum and natural gas, electricity generation, mining, dockyard services and air and rail transport. But in both mining and oil/gas exploration and development, the foreign party was required to sign a production or profit-sharing contract with the relevant government entity. The exemption is made through in Section 4. Under section 4, the private business man or institutions may do business even the State-owned Economic Enterprises Law as the Joint Ventures with government institutions or under the permit. To do so, this section also serves as vehicle for privatization②.

Foreign investors are permitted to lease land and immovable property at reasonable rates from the government. Duration of the lease is generally for an initial period of 30 years and extendible from three to five-year terms. Myanmar still has the comparative advantage in wages compare to other developing countries. Existence of fairly trained and literate labour force attracts labour intensive and export-oriented industries.

Myanmar's accession to full membership status in ASEAN in July 1997 would be viewed as an attractive proposition for most prospective foreign investors. Concerning "Myanmar's Commitment in ASEAN for Foreign Direct Investment (FDI) Promotion", Myanmar has decided to follow the resolu-

---

① H. E. Dr. Tun Shin, Business Law of Myanmar, *Law Journal*, Vol. 2, No. 1, p. 106.

② H. E. Dr. Tun Shin, Business Law of Myanmar, *Law Journal*, Vol. 2, No. 1, p. 106.

tion adopted at the Fifth ASEAN Summit held on 15th December 1995 in Bangkok where the Framework Agreement on ASEAN Investment Area (AIA) was drafted in the light of the creation of an ASEAN Economic Region. This agreement is to implement the realization of an ASEAN Investment Area in 2010 and promotion free flow of investment by 2010. It had already been signed at the 30th ASEAN Economic Ministries (AEM) Meeting in Manila on 7th October 1998.

Three broad-based programmes which will govern the realization of ASEAN Investment Area (AIA) are Cooperation and Facilitation Programme; Promotion and Awareness Programme and Liberalization Programme. All these programmes are expressed as the inputs of the Hanoi Plan of Action (HPA). Key measures of HPA with regard to the implementation of the Framework Agreement on ASEAN Investment Area (AIA) shall have to be undertaken through individual and collective manner within schedules and timetable. Myanmar is putting all out efforts to realize these provisions called for in the framework agreement.

The Current situation of Myanmar Intellectual Property Laws

Relevant laws as well as official rulings recognizing and enforcing the principle of Intellectual Property rights in Myanmar of British Colonial rule periods looks very impressive and had timely developed to a substantial extent. However, as time passed, those laws were not kept modified in accordance with the dynamism of the global economic trends, to say especially because of political formalities of the past requires consideration to be compatible with the times. Most of such old laws need updating. ①

Relevant Laws related to Intellectual protection in Myanmar are the Code of Civil Procedure (1808), the Penal Code (1860), the Specific Relief Act (1877), the Sea Customs Act (1878), the Myanmar Merchandise Marks Act, (1889), the Code of Criminal Procedure (1898), the Registration Act (1908), the Myanmar Copyright Act (1914), the Land Customs Act

---

① U Than Maung, Protection of Trademark rights in Myanmar, *Law Journal*, Vol. 3, No. 1, 1st edition, p. 155.

(1924), the Myanmar Patents and Designs (Emergency Provisions) Act (1946), the Science and Technology Development Law (1994), the Computer Science Development Law (2002), the Television and Video Law (1996), Motion Picture Law (1996), National Drug Law(2006), Traditional Drug Law (2006) and Electronic Transaction Law (2004).

In current situation, Myanmar being a founding member of WTO has an obligation to implement the provision of TRIPS Agreement. The new Intellectual Property Laws including Copyright Law, Trademarks Law, Patents Law and Industrial Designs Law are under process of drafting by the Ministries concerned. The draft new laws are based upon the WIPO model law and in line with the TRIPS Agreement and Conventions and Treaties administered by WIPO. In Myanmar future those laws of the provisions will also be contained in accordance with the International Minimum Standard.

Conclusion

CAFTA is a fair and equitable legal and institutional framework for implementing such economic agreements. The building of ASEAN Community and China-ASEAN Free Trade Area will enter into a new stage. Therefore, Myanmar like other new members of ASEAN will face a newer and greater challenges and development opportunity. In order to strengthen and harmonize its legal and institutional frameworks such as challenging and changing global economy that affects Myanmar, some areas of laws concerning the implementation of FTA need to be in line with the current situation.

In order to overcome these challenges, Myanmar is now drafting new laws relating to Intellectual Protection Rights (IPRs) and Myanmar offer technical know-how and investments to raise up the economy. Moreover, we need effective and valid protection of IPRs for encouragement in promoting investment and economic development in CAFTA. The future works for Intellectual Property protection in Myanmar are to establish necessary infrastructure, to train official and staffs, to close cooperation with WIPO and ASEAN members and China. Furthermore, Myanmar needs comprehensive and effective IP protection to promote foreign investment and technology transfer as well as for boosting industrial development. It is important to set up an appropriate legal IPRs system and also need to upgrade system practices. In conclusion, Business Laws still remain today or it was as the back-bone of the Business world of Myanmar. Law will advance together with the economy of the country to keep abreast with Myanmar's ASEAN neighbour. ①

REFERENCES

1. Mark S. W. Hoyle, "The Law of International Trade", The laureate Press London 1981, 1st edition.

2. Directorate of Trade, "Advance forward through commerce".

3. H. E. Dr. Tun Shin "Business Laws of Myanmar" Office of the Attorney's Law Journal Vol 2 (1), 1st edition.

4. H. E. Dr. TunShin "Business Laws of Myanmar Revised" Office of the Attorney's Law Journal Vol 8 (1), 1st edition.

5. U Than Maung, "Protection of Trademark rights in Myanmar" Office of the Attorney's Law Journal Vol 3 (1) ,1st edition.

6. www. wto. org.

7. www. asean. org.

---

① H. E. Dr. Tun Shin, Business Laws of Myanmar Revisted, *Law Journal*, Vol. 8, No. 1, 1st edition.

缅甸商法的发展

温·敏特*

内容摘要

在过去的几十年,全球贸易体系趋于更加自由化,区域贸易协议和自由贸易协议的建立,或称为 RTAs 和 FTAs 已日益一体化。缅甸同样进行了与区域层面和方向相关经济和法律发展。缅甸与其他亚洲国家如日本、韩国和中国进行合作并在东盟框架下实行开放的地区主义。在自由和公平贸易以及贸易自由化的进程中,缅甸积极参与各种区域和国际论坛并成为其中一员。缅甸加入了于 2002 年 11 月正式宣布并签署的中国—东盟自由贸易区(CAFTA),东盟和中国分阶段预设他们的双边贸易自由化:至 2010 年东盟六国和中国实现贸易自由化;2015 年和柬埔寨、老挝、缅甸和越南。

本论文旨在介绍缅甸商法和在缅甸在加入 CAFTA 之前,于 1988 年由计划经济体制转变为市场经济体制后在几个方面进行法律改革的经验。此外,根据 CAFTA 协议第八章,各缔约方对和贸易相关的知识产权的便利和有效的推广和适当保护是如此的重要。因此,我将介绍缅甸商法当前的形势和与法律相关的知识产权。

关键词: 商法;知识产权法;计划经济体系;市场导向体系

目　次

* 温·敏特,缅甸总检察长办公室副主任。

中国—东盟自由贸易区下中国公司法的发展

赵万一 *

内容摘要

中国—东盟自由贸易区的建立,将进一步促进中国和东盟之间的经济合作。立足已建立的较完备的外资法律制度,中国应进一步构筑吸引外资的良好公司法律制度,改善公司生存环境,加强对外商投资者的保护力度,强化平等、互惠互利原则,和平解决经贸争端。

关键词:发展;中国—东盟自贸区;公司法

目 次

* 赵万一,西南政法大学民商法学院院长、教授,中国—东盟法律研究中心咨询委员。

一、中国—东盟自由贸易区的发展现状

自2002年《中国一东盟全面经济合作框架协议》签署后，双方加快自由贸易区进程。2004年11月，中国和东盟签署《中国—东盟全面经济合作框架协议货物贸易协议》和《中国—东盟争端解决机制协议》两个文件，所有的东盟成员国承认中国的市场经济地位。2010年1月1日起中国—东盟自贸区正式建成。

在中国与东盟国家双向投资中，过去一直以东盟对华投资居多，然而随着中国一东盟自由贸易区的建设和建成，这一趋势已得到逐渐改变。东盟国家向中国大量投资的主要原因是中国市场巨大，对于东盟企业家具有很大的吸引力。而自由贸易区的建设促使投资壁垒不断消除，贸易投资更加便利化，使中国企业向东盟投资兴趣盎然，投资额增长迅猛。

越来越多的中国企业把东盟国家作为主要投资目的地。中国商务部已经批准成立的10个境外经贸合作区，其中三个设在东盟国家，分别在印尼、越南和柬埔寨，这表明东南亚成为中国企业"走出去"战略的重点地区。中国—东盟自贸区建成后，加大了消除投资壁垒的力度，客观上为中国企业走向东南亚创造了条件，将巩固东盟作为中国对外投资的首选地位。如果东盟经济一体化形成，对中国企业而言，只要进入东盟任何一个国家就等于进入了10个国家的市场，而且东盟已与日本、韩国、澳大利亚等国建立了自贸区，中国企业可借此拓展国际市场。

中国—东盟自由贸易区是一个国家和一个区域性经济组织的合作。东盟这个区域组织内部的状态不但直接影响着该自由贸易区的成败，而且也影响到与中国的经济合作前景。由于东盟本身具有严重的经济结构雷同性的内生的脆弱性，因此这在很大程度上阻碍了自由贸易区的建设。但中国—东盟之间的贸易与投资与双边的经济发展水平并不相适应，因此仍有较大的发展潜力。为了扩大中国和东盟之间的经济合作，有必要在涉外法律和国内法上消除阻碍双方发展的各种法律障碍，从而为双方的经济合作与贸易往来创造良好的法律环境。

二、中国现行外资法律制度评析

在改革开放之后，为了充分利用外国的资金和技术以促进中国的经济发

展,我国颁布了大量的涉外方面的法律法规,构筑了较为完整的涉外法律制度体系和外商投资保护法律体系。同时在国内法方面也在吸收和借鉴外国先进经验的基础上,建立起了较为完备的市场主体和市场行为法律制度。

(一)市场主体制度已基本成型,但内外资主体制度上的差异还有待消除。公司是接纳外资的主要组织形式和载体。公司规范的制度设计对吸引外资具有决定性影响。从总的方面说中国已经构筑了较为全面和较为先进的主体制度,特别是2005年修改后的中国公司法为吸引外资提供了有力的法律保障。(1)中国公司法修改的目的在于为中外投资者提供良好的法律环境和制度选择机会。利用制度优势促进社会经济的发展。(2)公司法所确立的一些理念和原则(如效益优先原则和公司自治理念),有利于保障外国投资者实现投资目的。(3)公司法修改中对外国先进公司制度的借鉴和创新,为东盟国家的公司立法提供了丰富的立法经验和制度借鉴样板。(4)公司法修改中对国际惯例的尊重使外国投资者在中国的投资行为更具有可预期性。但我们不能不看到的一点是在公司法的适用上还存在内资企业和外资企业的制度差异,内外资企业统一立法的目标还没有实现。

(二)涉外投资法律、政策的系统性和稳定性有待加强。中国现行有关立法长期以来一直采用分部门、多渠道、多层次、单向立法的方式,缺乏中央和地方、地方和地方之间法规的统一性。中央的有关规定原则性太强,各地多层次、多方面制定的优惠政策造成了引资的地区差别,导致歧视性待遇。中央各部门的有关立法没有协调一致,出现法律冲突。地方政府的有关立法存在越权和滥用权力的现象,即"土政策"的规定超过了法律的规定,在给予外商优惠方面竞相攀比。而且,地方政府招商引资方面的规定多采用红头文件方式,政策性强,缺乏法律的稳定性,使外商缺乏安全感。

(三)外资法律、政策透明度逐步提高,但执法仍须加强。法律、政策的公开化是实现法治的标志之一,也是世贸组织追求的透明度的目的。近几年来,中国政府大力推行依法行政和政务公开,使外资法律、政策在更大范畴和更高程度上实现公开化,透明度逐步得到提高。但仍存在一些非公开的内部文件、行政指示、内部通知和大量的司法解释,造成有关法律法规未能正确、公正实施,影响到法律的执行效率。

(四)外商投资的范围等方面的限制还没有完全消除。中国将外商投资项目分为鼓励、允许、限制和禁止四类,其中涉及国家安全和社会公共利益的领域对外商投资加以禁止或严格限制,此外对外商投资服务业也有一定限制。有关法规还规定,外商所需原材料和设备同等条件下应优先在中国购买,虽然没有明文规定外汇平衡的要求,但仍要求自行解决外汇收支平衡。另外在审批手续和服务收费方面,对外资企业仍存在歧视现象。

三、构筑吸引外资的良好公司法律制度

适应中国—东盟自由贸易区建成后经济发展的需要,有必要从以下方面加以完善。

(一)改善公司的生存环境,强化对外商投资者的吸引力。从总体上看,东盟与中国发展水平很接近,产业结构和外贸结构相似,在国际分工体系中处于同一层次,因而,在出口、吸引外资等一系列问题上既存在合作的契机,同时也存在竞争的可能性。中国应根据本国利益和实际需要,进一步明确规定鼓励、允许、限制和禁止外资的领域和项目,以引导外商投资方向和规范外商投资行为,对创新工业,扩充产能自动化和提升服务业水准的行业进行奖励。同时进一步改善投资环境,进一步加强对外招商活动的规范化、法律化建设。

(二)进一步加强对外商投资者的保护力度。目前中国已通过外资企业法和与相关国家签订双边投资协定等方式,规定不对外国投资者在中国投资设立的企业采取征收、国有化或其效果相当于征收、国有化的其他措施,即使为法律所准许的目的,采取征收、国有化措施,也必须建立在非歧视性基础上,并进行合理补偿。同时通过相关规定和承诺,保证在中国设立的企业可自由转让其资本及各种利润。但对其中的社会公共利益保留条款目前还缺乏明确的法律界定,从而使投资者的权利预期受到一定影响,因此有必要通过相关法律对此加以明确。

(三)通过合理的制度设计,降低外商的投资风险。为提高招商引资成效,对确定为重大高新科技的工业项目,为减轻外方对投资风险的担心,可以由中国企业与外国投资者一起出资,共担风险,共负盈亏,以此增加外商对高科技项目的信心。也可考虑设立专门的金融担保公司,对国家扶持的外商创新投资项目提供专项担保。同时应扩大外商可以出资的范围,明确允许外商可以以多种方式如货币、实物、知识产权、债权、探矿权以及法律允许的其他财产权利等出资,均可用来出资。

(四)确立内外投资者之间的国民待遇。中国与东盟大多数国家都出于大量吸引外资和对本国企业和市场保护的双重目的,对外商投资既有市场准入及审批程序上的较多限制即进入本国前的“低国民待遇”,又有进入本

国后的税收优惠等“超国民待遇”,即存在不同形式的“非国民待遇”。而按照《中国和东盟全面经济合作框架协议》,中国—东盟自由贸易区的主要内容之一就是扩大投资领域的合作。1992年启动的东盟自由贸易区(AFTA),也把取消对外商投资的壁垒,创建东盟投资区,实行投资自由化作为其主要内容。因此同属发展中国家的中国与东盟各国应在实现国民待遇上作进一步的努力。

(五)创新企业组织形式。按照学界通说,组织法为强行性规范,而行为法则大多为任意性规范。我国现行的公司组织形式还比较简单,与复杂多变的市场经济发展要求存在不适应。有必要通过修改法律或制定单行法的方式,有条件允许外商投资企业在组织形式上进行创新和探索。可借鉴新加坡的企业组织形式,充实中国的企业组织形式。新加坡的企业组织形式分为商行与公司两类。商行又分独资与合伙两种。个人与公司都可以设立商行,非新加坡公民或法人可以设立商行。商行不是法律个体,在其名下不能注册成立另一商行。个人与公司均可设立公司。公司分为私营有限公司、非私营公司、特免私营公司、以担保为限的有限公司和无限公司五种。其中私营有限公司、非私营公司属于以股份为限的有限公司。按照新加坡法律的规定,私营有限公司的资本必须私募;非私营公司在向(公司商行注册局)呈交发股计划书后可发行股票或债券向大众筹募资金,所发行的股票或债券可以自由转让。在取得新加坡证券交易所批准后,其股票可上市挂牌交易。特免私营公司的股东完全自然人组成,公司不须向呈报账目,条件是其中一名董事、公司秘书或审计师须签发一份证明书以确定公司有能力负担其债务,公司经审核的账目已在股东大会上由股东查阅过。以担保为限的有限公司通常是慈善团体或非营利机构,公司成员分别以个人身份担保公司结束时将负责公司的债务。无限公司中公司成员对公司债务负无限清偿责任。上述五种公司的设立者均不限于新加坡公民或法人。新加坡还允许外国公司按公司法规定呈交有关文件与办理有关手续后,在新加坡设立子公司(辅助的)和合资公司(合资)。相对来说中国的公司组织形式还比较单一,投资者可供选择的比较少。因此有必要通过创新企业组织形式的方式扩大对外资的吸引力。

(六)充分发挥司法的导引功能。中国目前仍存在投资环境不够稳定的问题,部分现行法律、法规的执行力度不够,随意性较大,有法不依的现象时有发生。因此有必要通过公正的执法原则和严明的司法制度、多样化解决争端机制和完善的损害补偿机制维护外来投资者的合法利益。同时提高法律制度的效率与可靠性,降低投资风险。特别是要充分发挥仲裁、调解等非讼机制在解决公司纠纷中的作用。

(七)进一步强化对外交往中的国际惯例原则。根据《中国—东盟全面经济合作框架协议争端解决机制协议》,争端各方可以通过谈判、调解或和解、仲裁等方式来解决,尤其鼓励争端方通过谈判解决争端,并不鼓励争端各方采取报复措施。这与世界贸易组织《争端解决谅解》有诸多相同之处。此外,中国与东盟各国在其他诸多方面也强调参照国家惯例原则。比如,在环境保护,税收抵免或税收减让,资金、利润的自由流动等方面均遵守国际惯例原则。

(八)进一步强化平等、互惠互利原则。中国与东盟各国的政治、经济、文化、宗教、民族、种族及法律制度等国情不同,对经济一体化和投资贸易自由化的接受和认可程度也不同。因此在外商投资法领域更应当充分体现平等、互惠互利的原则,更加强调将平等、互惠互利作为立法的基本考量要素。

Development of China's Company Law under the CAFTA

Zhao Wanyi*

Abstract

The establishment of CAFTA would further the economic cooperation between China and the ASEAN countries. Based on its initially shaped foreign investments legal system, China should continue constructing a better company legal system to attract foreign investments by improving living environment for companies, enhancing protection level for foreign investors, promoting fair and reciprocal principles, and settling disputes peacefully.

Keyword: Development; China; Company Law; CAFTA

Content

* Dean and professor of Civil and Commericial School of Southwest University of Political Science and Law, Consultative member of China-ASEAN Legal Research Center.

越南投资法律制度的演变及完善

黎氏利[越南]　阮如政[越南]*　米　良** 译

内容摘要

越南自1975年获得全国统一，完成了民主革命的任务，将国名改为越南社会主义共和国后，至1986年越共"六大"之前的11年间，越南实行的是计划经济体制，国家不承认各经济主体独立的法律地位，因此也不需要投资立法，在发展对外经济关系的态度上基本上是否定的；1986年召开的越共"六大"改变了计划经济的模式，转而实行"有国家管理的计划经济"模式，此后，越南走上了一条"革新开放"的道路，越南开始承认市场主体独立的法律地位，并允许外国投资以解决越南经济建设中的资金不足、技术落后、管理落后的问题。25年来，越南先后出台了《公司法》、《企业法》、《保险经营法》、《鼓励国内投资法》、《民法典》、《合作社法》及数部《外国投资法》，从开始的允许外国投资到后来的大量吸引外国投资，经历了逐步开放、逐步与世界通行的外国投资制度接轨，到加入WTO，越南的投资法律制度发生了巨大变化。

关键词：越南；投资法；演变；完善

目　次

---

* 黎氏利，越南河内法律大学副教授；阮如政，越南河内法律大学副教授。

** 米良，云南大学法学院教授，博士，云南大学东盟法研究中心主任。研究方向：东盟法。

一、越南投资法的演变

纵观当代越南投资法律制度的发展,可以将其分为三个主要阶段:第一阶段(1975—1986)是投资立法的起步阶段,这一阶段越南在指导思想上从长期闭关锁国带来经济落后的现实中认识到必须实行对外开放,这是一个战略性的改变;第二阶段(1986—2005)是越南投资立法的产生阶段,这一阶段越南从国会的层面制定了系统、专门的投资法;第三阶段(2005 至今)是越南投资法体系的完善阶段,这一阶段越南加入了世贸组织,市场经济的法律体系基本形成,越南完善了投资法律体系并制定了《知识产权法》、《企业法》等配套法律,全方位对外开放、对内搞活的格局形成。

(一)越南投资立法的起步阶段

1975 年,越南实现了南北统一。长期的战争使得越南百孔千疮,经济也走到了崩溃的边缘,人民生活贫困,百废待兴。统一后的政府资金匮乏、技术落后,但国家的统一使得越南南北方两个地区共同拥有了统一的政策,便于发展国家经济。重建国家和发展经济需要巨大的投资,在此背景下,越南制定了许多积极的政策旨在争取国外有利的国际条件、资金和技术的援助以便发展国家的经济。

1977 年 4 月 18 日,部长会议(现在改为中央政府)颁布了《外国投资条例》(称为 1977 年《外国投资条例》)。这是越南当代第一部规范外国投资的法律文本。规定了外资在越南投资的投资领域、投资形式、投资期限、外资适用税率、外汇管理和会计、统计制度、投资手续、清算和投资争端解决等问题。由于在这一阶段,私营经济未被承认合法,所以没有引导投资的各种法律文本。因此,在这一阶段,外国在越南投资仅在法律上确认,由于缺少具体的、操作性强的具体制度,加之战后的越南投资环境极差,因此,这一阶段到越南投资的企业极少。

这一阶段,越南由于实行计划经济体制,国内投资立法是一个空白。

(二)越南投资立法的发展阶段

1. 外国投资立法的变化

这一阶段以 1986 年越共“六大”的召开为标志,它被视为越南“革新”事业的开端。1987 年 12 月 19 日,八届国会 2 次会议通过了《外国投资法》。与

1977 年颁布的《外国投资条例》相比，它在内容和形式方面都有了较大的进步，同时，它为外国在越南的投资活动奠定了具有价值的法理基础。为了施行 1987 年颁布的《外国投资法》，越南中央政府颁布了第 139 号决议和二十七部与外国投资相关的不同的法律文本。然而，1987 年颁布的《外国投资法》的许多规定仍然存在许多缺陷。如：允许外国投资的形式只有三种，一是通过经营合作合同投资，二是通过成立联营企业形式投资，三是通过成立外资 100%全资企业形式投资，BOT、EPC 等形式则未被允许；另外，外国独资企业和合伙式合作经营不得享受减免税待遇，同时，优惠措施也仅限于减免所得税，外国投资者也不享有国民待遇和最惠国待遇。

为了继续完善外国在越南投资法律规范体系，1990 年 6 月 30 日，越南八届国会 7 次会议通过了《1987 年外国投资法部分条款修改、补充法》(简称为 1990 年修改的《外国投资法》)。《1990 年修改的外国投资法》颁布以后，在越南的外资投资活动步入了一个新的发展阶段，标志着越南进一步开放和融入国际经济体系。然而，新的《1990 年修改的外国投资法》只是解决了 1987 年颁布的《外国投资法》一些较大的局限，但在投资活动实践中出现了许多问题，阻碍了许多外资在越南的投资活动。在此背景下，对 1990 年颁布的《外国投资法》进行修改、补充的呼声又高了起来，理由主要是，由于各国都在进行鼓励投资，所以吸引外资日益呈现激烈的竞争，为了吸引外资进入越南，改善投资环境的问题成为首要问题。1992 年 2 月 23 日，国会通过了《1987 年外国在越南投资法部分条款修改、补充法》(简称为《1992 年修改的外国投资法》)。在《1992 年修改的外国投资法》得以通过后，一批与外国投资相关的各种法律文本相继颁布。直至 1996 年《外国在越南投资法》颁布之前，越南颁布了大约 110 部与外国投资活动相关的法律文本，为外国在越南的投资活动营造了相对完整、配套的法律环境。

越共“八大”要求将“融入更高的社会经济程度发展经济—社会”指导思想体制化。1996 年 11 月 12 日，国会颁布了新的《外国投资法》。1996 年《外国投资法》颁布以后，政府 1997 年 12 月 18 日颁布的政府 1997 年第 12 号决议颁布了《外国在越南投资法》实施细则和 15 部与外国在越南投资相关的其他法律文本。

在这一阶段，国内投资立法也得到加强，1990 年颁布了《公司法》，接着，《私营企业法》、《鼓励国内投资法》、《信用组织法》等与投资相关的重要法律也相继颁布。1994 年 6 月 22 日，国会还通过了《鼓励国内投资法》。

自 1997 年以后，特别是亚洲金融危机以后，越南乃至地区和世界的形势发生了许多的变化。虽然外国投资领域依然继续在越南的经济发展中做出积极的贡献,但是,在其后几年中,外国到越南投资的速度连续衰退,面对这种实际情况,为了扼制衰退,同时满足全面革新经济事业、主动融入新时期国际的需求,2000 年 6 月 9 日,越南国会通过了《外国在越南投资部分条款修改、补充法》。该法补充了两条新条款,对 1996 年颁布的《外国投资法》的 20 条进行了修改、补充。2000 年《外国投资法》(修改)主要集中于下列部分问题:

(1)扩大外资参股企业的自主权;

(2)在税收和财政领域中提高了投资者优惠程度;

(3)简化了行政审批程序。

2000 年的《外国投资法》(修改)制定了许多新的规定,旨在为投资者排除障碍、困难,降低风险。此后,政府颁布了政府第 14 号决议(共 14 章、125 条附两条附录),履行了越南的各项国际承诺,同时为日益吸引、吸收和有效使用外资直接投资营造了法律环境。截止 2004 年年底,越南有效使用外资投资项目达到 5300 个以上、登记注册资金总额达到 470 亿美元以上,实现投资达到 310 亿美元。2004 年,外国投资领域占社会投资资金总额的 17%,创造了占越南全国 14.5%的国内生产总值,占全国工业行业生产总值近 37%和出口金额近 54.5%。

2. 国内投资立法的变化

这一时期,越南各种私营经济成分也得到迅猛发展,使得这一阶段的国内投资立法日益完善。在这一阶段中,与投资相关的各种重要法律文本相继出台,它们是 1999 年颁布的《企业法》、《保险经营法》。1999 年的《企业法》取代了原来的《公司法》。根据这些法律,越南的自然人、企业可以在法律没有禁止的所有各个领域中自由经营、投资。《鼓励国内投资法》的诞生和施行同样为吸引国内投资做出了重要的贡献,截止 2005 年,已有 15 万多个民营企业成立,为国内私营领域投资比重跃升至 2004 年投资发展总额的 26.7%贡献了力量,提供了上百万个新的就业岗位。

2003 年的《合作社法》取代了 1996 年颁布的《合作社法》,该法以许多崭新的内容创立了各种新型的合作社模式,主要有农村土地承包给农民家庭户、推行农村庄园经济,这些创新模式使农业、农村呈现了一片崭新的面貌,大量投资被吸引到这一领域,为推动农业现代化贡献了力量。

这一时期越南还颁布和施行《国有企业法》及与之相关配套的政府行政法规和部门规章。该法继续肯定了国有企业在各行各业和国民经济支柱领域发展过程中的重要作用。从 2001—2005 年,国家投资的资金 526 万亿盾,占全社会投资总额的53.3%,包括:国家财政预算资金占22.8%;国家信用资金占13.3%;国有企业投资资金占17.7%。以上数据可以看出,国有经济依然占据国民经济的主导地位。

(三)越南现行投资法的特点

上述外国投资法律体系、国内投资法律体系的实施,对越南经济发展起到了巨大的促进作用。仅从1999年至2004年的5年间,募集的投资资金总额达到986万亿盾。然而,直至2005年以前,越南仍然存在两个独立的区分国内投资法和外国投资法的法律体系,越南政府意识到正是这一点削弱了越南投资环境的吸引度,并了解到在使用法律调整投资活动的实践中,许多国家不区分国内投资和外国投资。“随着越南革新开放的深入,出于大力推进国家的工业化、现代化、主动融入国际事业的需求必须制定一部不区分国内投资法和外国投资法的统一的《投资法》,旨在为经济—社会的发展加强动员一切资源。”在这样的背景下,2005年的《投资法》正式诞生。

2005年11月29日,越南第十一届国会第8次会议通过了《投资法》。该法共十章、89条,对在越南进行的国内投资和外国投资所涉及的相关制度作了统一的、详细的规制。之后,2005年颁布的《企业法》、《贸易法》、《证券法》、《知识产权法》和其他相关法律相继颁布,标志着越南在“市场经济体制化和开放融入国际经济路线”的立法初步建立和相对完善。

1.2005年《投资法》的特点。

(1)将“社会主义定向市场体制发展多种成分经济”的路线、方针、政策法律化,旨在继续保持、扩大和发展自主经营权,最大限度地动员为经济—社会发展投资的资源。

(2)继续革新国家对于经济中投资活动的职能,将鼓励、引导、扶持投资者视为主要职能,将投资者视为国家行政机关的服务对象。国家尊重投资者的自主经营权、自主投资权,采用注册登记制度取代许可证制,取消与自主投资原则背道而驰、给企业造成麻烦的“申请—下拨”规定,使各种调解与投资相关争端的活动司法化。

(3)保证投资活动中的透明性,各种与投资相关的经济信息公开化。

(4)该法的内容与越南签订或加入的双边和多边条约的内容特别是关于国民待遇、最惠国待遇等各项原则相符,为建立平等、透明、稳定和具有较高竞争性的投资经营环境创造了条件。

2005年《投资法》与2005年《企业法》共同为各种经济成分的各个企业和

投资者创造了一个总的投资法律平台和条件。然而,值得注意的是,外国投资者和企业仍然必须执行一些特殊规定,特别是在市场准入乃至在程序方面必须符合一些特殊规定,有的领域、行业、职业和地区,国内的企业和投资者可以从事,但外国的企业和投资者不能从事、限制从事。

2005年颁布的《投资法》的亮点是向WTO成员国、东盟成员国开放了投资市场,同时取消了与贸易相关的各种投资壁垒,具体是不强制投资者必须履行各种要求,如:优先采购国内商品、劳务或者从国内特定生产或者提供劳务的地点采购商品、服务;商品出口或者劳务输出达到某一种特定的比例;限制出口商品数量、价格、种类和劳务输出或者国内生产、供应;进口商品须保持与出口商品的数量和价格相应的数量和价格或者必须自行从出口源平衡外币以满足进口的需求;在商品生产中达到特定的内地化比例;在国内或者国外某一个具体的地点提供商品、劳务等。

2.2005年投资法增加的新内容。

为了履行越南在签订或参加的国际条约中的各项承诺,2005年颁布的《投资法》增加了下列主要内容:

(1)自由投资权得以扩大,投资者可以投资经济的所有领域,被禁止和限制的领域除外。对于外国投资者限制投资领域要保障与国际承诺相符。各部、各行业、各地、总公司无权颁布各种禁止和限制投资的条款。

(2)补充、扩大各种直接和间接的投资形式(合并和回购企业(M&A)、经营合作合同(BCC)、合资、购买股份)。

(3)扩大外国投资者的企业类型(外国投资者不仅准许成立有限责任公司而且可以依照《企业法》成立一切类型的公司)。

(4)法律制定鼓励优惠投资的各种规则统一适用于外国投资者和国内投资者。

(5)废除“一个外国企业、一个项目”的规定;简化对于外国投资者准入市场、成立企业的手续。

(6)关于调解争端,《投资法》规定,外国投资者有权向外国仲裁组织提出调解各种争端的申请。外国投资者同样有权向越南国家机关提出在越南仲裁机关或者法院调解争端的申请,国家主管部门代表与外国投资者之间订立合同中或者越南作为成员国的国际条约中达成协议的情形除外。

(7)对于投资的行政(审批)手续,法律进行了显著的改革;对国家管理和地方投资进行了大力的分级。国家对投资的管理主要依据各种技术基础设施结构规划、使用土地规划、建设规划、矿产和各种资源规划。

除了上述各项内容外，对于依照建设—经营—移交(BOT)合同、建设—移交—经营(BTO)合同、建设—移交(BT)合同形式投资、到国外投资、投资和使用国家资金的各种活动，法律同样制定了总体原则性规定并由政府颁布。

总而言之，2005年颁布的《投资法》调整所有在越南的各种投资活动和从越南到国外的投资活动，包括所有的直接投资和间接投资活动；从国家和个人的资金投资；国内投资者和国外投资者。其满足了所有投资者的愿望，同时满足了越南融入国际经济需求的投资。

二、越南投资法的完善

2005年《投资法》诞生尽管有了许多进步的地方，但是，法律本身和各种施行说明文本仍然存在许多的困惑、不足。因此，还需要制定解决的办法旨在完善总体投资法律和各种直接投资形式的法律、特别是外国直接进入越南投资的法律。只有这样才能保证国内投资者和国外投资者之间的平等。保证各种法律文本与法律以下各种文本乃至其它各种专门法律文本之间的统一。保证投资法与各种国际条约之间的和谐。要做到这些，需要采取下列各项措施：

1. 加强国家机构的工作能力。按照将鼓励、引导、扶持企业视为是主要职能、将投资者和企业视为国家机关服务对象的方向加强与施行《投资法》相关的国家机构的能力。在自身职责和权限范围内展开施行《投资法》的过程中，与指导、引导和适用2005年《投资法》工作相关的国家和地方各部委、各部门应该明确重心，掌握自身辖区的强项、弱点、迫切的问题以便集中解决，为投资活动创造有利的前提条件。同时，必须把投资者的正当利益放在首位以便鼓励他们。这是决定法律效果的非常重要的问题。

2. 大力改革行政审批手续。国家各个主管部门必须大力革新和改善行政审批手续以便在为投资者办理经营登记注册中按照“一道门”、“一个公章”的体制有所突破，规定一套标准的档案材料以便投资者可以向各个职能机关提供一切必需的信息，为每一个登记注册成立的企业发放一个通用的编码(经营登记注册编码同时是税务编码)。应用必需的信息技术以便为投资者在了解与经营登记注册程序、手续相关的信息和快捷办理经营登记注册、节省费用和时间创造便利的条件。同时，国家各个主管部门同样需要及时受理、处理了结发放许可证、投资证明书过程中的各种疑难问题。加强与各部、相关部门之间管理外国投资的配合体制。目前，所有不同的各部委、各部门正在积极执行政府关于以两项主要内容为特征的行政手续简单化的政策：核查各种行政手续和提出裁减不需要、多余的行政手续("30 提案")。对于投资活动,必须要加强相关各部委、各部门之间管理投资的配合体制以便保证最大限度地发挥管理活动的效果,同时及时解决企业的各种问题。对于地方,省级人民委员会按照与投资者解决档案材料头绪、时间透明、清楚的方向颁布关于辖区管理投资的各种文本,旨在为投资活动创造便利的条件。

3. 法律透明化,保证为投资者提供完整、及时的信息。法律透明化是一种要求也是融入国际经济的一种原则。在投资活动中,透明化为营造平等、竞争、公平的投资环境,创造提高投资效果的条件贡献力量,为降低来自投资环境的风险贡献力量。一个具有吸引透明投资政策体系的国家什么时间都有明确、公开保障投资者财产所有权的条款。因此,透明化将为投资者增加资金和财产安全性贡献力量。透明化同样与要求各种政策和法律体系必须清楚、一贯、容易预测紧密相连。为了满足这种要求必须采取下列解决措施:

(1)各种投资手续透明化,在投资者与管理机关之间使用双向通信如互联网……坚决废除各种不必要的中间环节、各种多余、重叠的手续。必须在内部建立一种随时监督、检查、独立、客观的体制,在为投资者办理行政手续中克服封闭、缺乏公开、容易产生消极的状况。

(2)提高行政机构能力,建立一个真正强大、确保专业性的行政机构便于为投资者服务。为了公权机构活动有效果需要从"申请—下拨"体制向服务体制的"颁发"思维转变。建设一支专业、具有专门技能和与国际接轨能力的公务员干部队伍。

只有这样,透明化才能为减少由政策带来的风险因素下降到投资者可以接受的最低限度贡献力量。同时,一方面需要制定措施以提高投资者对与总体投资活动相关的政策、法律公开、透明的共同认识。另一方面,需要大力开展参考、学习世界上一些国家在建设和完善投资法方面的经验。在当今时代,各种经济基础不断地相互影响,在经济方面,各国都在一个共同的游戏场中运动,所以,不可能有具有个别性的特殊法律或者依照一个国家特殊习惯的法律体系。

4. 检查、修改投资法和相关规定之间重叠的规定。国家各个主管部门需要及时检查在投资活动方面现行法律和各项规定以便修改、补充、废除、重新颁布与 2005 年《投资法》规定相符的各项法律规定,以便具有处置方向,旨在营造真正通畅和具有吸引力的投资环境。目前,存在下列一些可以看得到的困惑:

(1)《投资法》和《企业法》还存在许多不相符的地方，根据政府2007年第139号决议(第9条)，外国投资者投资不超过49%(股份)则办理经营登记注册手续以便成立企业，对于国内投资项目相应适用投资登记注册。凭借这项规定，外国投资者与越南投资者成立有外国投资资金不超过49%(股份)的企业，然后，按照经营登记注册证明书调整程序(手续)实施转让部分或者全部越南方的股本。因此，《投资法》(第46条、第47条、第48条、第49条)关于登记注册、审查发放投资证明书的各项规定不能适用于对该投资项目的审查。

(2)此前投资优惠分类目录分散在很多相互不同的文本中，给投资者在投资适用、选择中造成了困难。政府2006年第108号决议诞生，进行了统一、具体的规定，满足了投资者的需求。然而，政府2008年第124号决议对《企业所得税法》颁布的一份各个经济—社会条件困难地区的特殊分类目录进行了详细规定，以便在其它优惠类型仍然依据政府2006年第108号决议的分类目录统一适用时适用优惠税率。这一条造成了不同步，在履行过程中带来了许多困惑。

(3)按照现行《投资法》确定直接投资、间接投资的方法正好看出与企业管理中不相符的条款。据《投资法》规定，投资者不直接参与投资活动管理的是间接投资。但是，一旦投资者已经合资、购买股份，则即使他们在企业中没有占据管理位置，在该企业的活动过程中他们依然具有一定的影响。或者在外国投资者开始合资时未参与，但是，随后参与管理则如何处理和确定直接投资、间接投资？因此，当前对关于投资的各项规定和相关法律的各项规定进行核查、同步化是非常必要的。

5.在越南参与的各种国际协议总体性之下完善投资法。在目前全球化的背景下，越南参与的各种关于投资的国际条约是营造吸引、促进投资者和外国投资者投资活动环境的重要工具。过去许多年，越南与世界各国缔结了将近50个鼓励和保护投资的投资协定，特别是加入世界贸易组织时关于开放市场的承诺。

履行上述各种协议要求国家法律、各种双方协议、各种多方协议必须要同步，特别是保证国家待遇和最惠国待遇各项原则。为了履行这一条，要求各个主管部门必须履行提供关于越南已经签订的各种双方和多方协议的名册和内容信息便于投资者可以抓住各种机会、实现投资，促进经济—社会的发展。

On the Evolution and Improvement of Vietnam's Investment Legal System

Lee Lai & Ruanru Zheng*

Abstract

Vietnamese national unity since 1975, and completed the task of democratic revolution, changed its name to the Socialist Republic of Vietnam after the 1986 Communist Party of Vietnam, "six"before 11 years, Vietnam implemented a planned economy system, countries do not recognize The legal status of an independent economic entities, the legislation does not need to invest in the development of foreign economic relations is basically a negative attitude; CPV held in 1986, "six"changed the planned economy model, switching to "A national management of the planned economy "model, then, Vietnam embarked on a" reform and opening up "of the road, the Vietnamese began to recognize the independence of the legal status of the main market and allow foreign investment in Vietnam to address the lack of economic construction in the capital, backward technology, Backward management issues. 25 years, Vietnam has issued a "Company Law", "Enterprise Law", "Insurance Business Act", "to encourage domestic investment law", "Civil Code", "Cooperative Law "and several of "foreign investment", from the beginning Allowed a large number of foreign investment to attract foreign investment later, through the gradual opening up, step by step with the world's foreign investment regime prevailing standards, to join WTO, Vietnam's investment in the legal system has changed dramatically.

Keywords: Vietnam; Investment Law; Evolution; Improvement

---

* Lee Lai, assistant professor of Hanoi University of Law; Ruanru Zheng, assistant professor of Hanoi University of Law.

Content

中国—东盟自由贸易区的司法及实务合作

JUDICIAL AND PRACTICAL COOPERATION IN CAFTA

中国—东盟自由贸易区争端解决机制框架下的司法协助问题

王 瀚*

内容摘要

《中国—东盟国家全面经济合作框架协议争端解决机制协议》的出台奠定了中国和东盟全面的经济贸易合作中争端解决机制的法律基础。协议规定争端解决的基本问题，但尚留有很多问题待进一步明确，而争端解决机制框架下各国的司法协助是其中的关键问题之一。基于仲裁在争端解决中所起到的作用，在选择为仲裁裁决提供司法协助的路径时，应当遵循一定原则，并与一般外国仲裁裁决作出必要的区分。

关键词：争端解决机制；仲裁；司法协助

目 次

* 王瀚，西北政法大学副校长，教授，法学博士，中国—东盟法律研究中心咨询委员。

一、关于争端解决机制的简评

2010 年 1 月 1 日,中国—东盟自由贸易区这一全球第三大自由贸易区全面建成,中国和东盟国家开始步入“零关税”时代。建成后的自由贸易区,东盟和中国的贸易占到世界贸易的 13%,成为一个涵盖 11 个国家、19 亿人口、GDP 达 6 万亿美元的巨大经济体,是目前世界人口最多的自由贸易区,也是发展中国家间最大的自由贸易区。

自由贸易区的建立,对中国与东盟都有着积极的意义:一方面有利于巩固和加强中国与东盟之间的友好合作关系,有利于中国与发展中国家、周边国家的团结合作,也有利于东盟在国际事务上提高地位、发挥作用;另一方面,有利于进一步促进中国和东盟各自的经济发展,扩大双方贸易和投资规模,促进区域内各国之间的货物流通、资金流通和信息流通,促进区域市场的发展,创造更多的财富,提高本地区的整体竞争能力,为区域内各国人民谋求福利。与此同时,中国—东盟自由贸易区的建立,有利于推动东盟经济一体化,对世界经济增长也有积极作用。尽管中国—东盟自由贸易区的进程充满风雨,但是我们有足够的理由对自由贸易区的前景充满信心。今后一段时间内,自由贸易区以及双边经贸关系将呈现贸易额度增长、贸易结构进一步合理化、双方的相互直接投资逐步扩大、经济合作领域日益拓宽等趋势。

在欢庆欣喜的同时,我们也应当看到,中国—东盟自由贸易区是一个由发展中国家组成的自由贸易区,是以一个大国和另一个自由贸易区为基础而形成的一个全新的自由贸易区,是一个发展存在着巨大差距的自由贸易区,是一个有着复杂历史条件、依然存在主权争议的敏感地区。因此这些国家之间进行贸易投资活动,将不可避免地遇到市场不规范、政府政策多变、相关国家国内法律制度不健全等问题,进行长期的、全面的经济合作难免会出现争议。历史的经验告诉我们,贸易争端发生的背景基本上是因为各国文化传统、思想意识、政治制度、经济架构、社会发展程度等因素的不同而导致各国经贸政策的差别。因此,合作中产生争端是正常的,但必须要建立健全的争端解决机制来解决争端。欧洲著名 WTO 专家彼得斯曼也说过:“所有文明社会有个共同特征,都需要有一套适用与解释规则的、和平解决争端的规范和程序。这是国际、国内法律制度的共同经验。”[①]争端解决机制是多边贸易体制的支柱之一，是多边贸易体制保持稳定性的前提之一，也是贸易往来能够按照公平、公正的原则正常进行的基本要求。

因此，《中国—东盟国家全面经济合作框架协议争端解决机制协议》的出台喻示着自由贸易区的发展迈出了坚实的一步。争端解决机制对中国和东盟全面的经济贸易合作奠定了法律基础，起到重要的维护和促进作用，是整个自由贸易区的“安全卫士”。

二、目前争端解决机制框架下司法协助的重点对象——仲裁

客观地说，现行的争端解决机制更大的作用在于给我们指明了一条解决纠纷的途径，其本身的构建远未到完善的一步。虽然《中国—东盟争端解决机制协议》对争议适用范围、磋商程序、调解或调停、仲裁庭的设立、仲裁庭的职能、仲裁庭的组成和程序、仲裁的执行等问题作了规定。但不难看出，这些内容明显缺乏可操作性。目前，虽然中国与东盟间发生贸易争端可以依照该《争端解决机制协议》寻求解决，但结果孰难预料。这其中有很多问题尚待进一步明确，其中很关键的一个环节就是争端解决机制框架下各国的司法协助亟待明确化。虽然争端解决机制就司法协助未作任何规定，但我们不能就此否认该问题亟待解决的迫切性。毕竟，若争议的解决由各国提供司法保障，则争端解决机制的运作将达到能够妥善、彻底解决问题的完美状态。我们应当清醒地认识到，由于中国和东盟各国文化传统、思想意识、政治制度、法律体系等方面均存在差异，故而争端解决机制框架下的司法协助问题不能一蹴而就，需要有计划、有步骤地开展和实施。就目前而言，可以先将重点放在对仲裁的司法协助上。原因如下：

第一，相较于其他几种制度，仲裁获得司法协助的可能性更大，操作性更强。在国际民商事纠纷解决领域，仲裁制度优于诉讼已是公认的事实。仲裁的民间性使其在域外申请承认和执行时不会触及外国司法主权的底限，而《纽约公约》更是从制度层面对裁决的效力提供了坚实的保障。另外，若对《争端解决机制协议》的内容稍加分析，即可看出条文关于仲裁的规定最为体系化、制度化。加之仲裁所具有的一裁终局性、时限短等特点，使得使争端解决机制

① Ermst-Ulrich Petersmann: The Dispute Settlement System of the World Trade Organization System Since 1948, *Common Market Law Review*, 1994, p. 1157.

的效率得到保障。因此,相对于其他争端解决方式而言,仲裁制度在CAFTA争端解决机制中居于至关重要的核心地位。

第二,争端解决机制框架下的仲裁需要司法协助。《争端解决机制协议》第8条第4款规定:“仲裁庭裁决为终局,对争端当事方有约束力。”争端解决机制的最终目的是解决争议,而争议解决的核心取决于执行。关于“执行”,《争端解决机制协议》主要从两个方面予以保障:首先,《争端解决机制协议》希望争端当事方能够执行仲裁庭的建议和裁决;其次,在仲裁庭的建议和裁决未在合理期限内执行时,争端当事方可以以补偿和中止减让或利益作为可获得的临时措施,《争端解决机制协议》第13条对补偿、减让、利益从范围、时限等方面做出了具体的规定。这一规定虽然给予了仲裁裁决得到执行的一定的保障,但效果相对有限。若能从司法角度得到相关国内法院的支持,则争端解决机制的权威性将得到极大的维护。

三、对仲裁裁决提供司法协助的路径

首先,作为一个多法域国家,中国在“一国两制三法系四法域”的复杂情况下就如何解决区际法律冲突及区际司法协助问题已积累了不少经验。虽然不能将国内的方式照搬到中国与东盟之间,但我国已有的做法还是能够给我们提供一些思路。在司法协助这一问题上,中国与东盟若想通过政府间的谈判走条约化道路并不现实。但是,可以尝试由各国的法院系统出面来就涉及仲裁的司法协助问题进行协商。在成功后还可以向争端解决机制框架下的其他方式扩展。

其次,根据中国—东盟自由贸易区自身的特点,我们在探讨争端解决机制框架下的司法协助问题时,必须要明确的就是应当遵循的基本原则。这些原则至少应当包括:

1.平等互利原则。平等互利原则是我国在处理国际商事交往中一贯遵循的原则之一,中国—东盟自由贸易区本身的目标也是促进各方之间的经济发展,从而达到“双赢”。平等互利原则是中国与东盟建立自由贸易区时必须遵循的原则,这一原则同样也要在司法协助领域得到遵循。司法协助本质上是一种互助行为,只有通过协商,在互利互惠基础上才能促使协助顺利有效进行。具体来说,平等互利原则可以表述为:(1)各国法律的地位平等,各自司法机关在合作中的活动权限和特定要求方面,经平等协商,相互给予同样的优惠和便利;(2)在司法互助内容方面,应当在同等范围的程序上互相开展;(3)在司法互助程序中，应确保各国的法律制度和司法机关处于平等地位；(4)各国公民应地位平等、不受歧视。

2.效率原则。建立民商事司法协助机制的直接目的之一就是为了实现民商事司法便利、民商事司法经济，更好地保护当事人合法利益的实现。中国—东盟自由贸易区建立后，各国之间的民商事活动十分频繁，互涉案件必将逐步增多，为促进各国友好交往与经济繁荣，各国间应当尽量简化民商事司法程序，提高效率。

最后，在对争端解决机制下仲裁裁决定位时也需要注意，要将其和一般的外国仲裁裁决加以区分。一般的外国仲裁裁决是指在被请求承认和执行仲裁裁决的国家之外的另一个国家领土内作出的裁决，或被请求承认和执行仲裁裁决的国家不认为该裁决是其内国裁决的裁决。而中国—东盟自由贸易区争端解决机制下仲裁裁决则具有其特殊性，不能按照以往的标准来进行界定。中国和东盟各国的仲裁裁决无论是否在其国领土内作成，也无论该裁决是否属于契约或非契约性商事法律关系争议，应均在成员国内得到承认和执行，当然中国和东盟各国对其成员国仲裁裁决的承认和执行还可以采取更为宽松的规定。

The Issue of Legal Assistance under the Framework of CAFTA Dispute Settlement Mechanism

Wang Han*

Abstract

Agreement on Dispute Settlement Mechanism of the Framework Agreement on Comprehensive Economic Co-operation between the People's Republic of China and the Association of Southeast Asian Nations has provided a legal foundation of dispute settlement mechanism for the comprehensive economic co-operation between China and ASEAN. Though the agreement has formulated the basic problems in dispute settlement, some issues including the legal assistance under the framework of DSM are needed to further defined. With the consideration of the role of arbitration in dispute settlement and the path determination for the legal assistance to arbitration, it is necessary to abide by some principles and to distinguish the awards rendered by other foreign arbitration organizations and the awards from DSM .

Keywords: Dispute Settlement Mechanism; Arbitration; Legal Assistance

Content

- A Brief Review of the Dispute Settlement Mechanism
- The Existing Important Legal Assistance means under the Framework of DSM—Arbitration
- The Route to Provide Legal Assistance for the Arbitration Decision

---

* Vice president and professor of Northwest University of Politics and Law, consultative member of China-ASEAN Legal Research Center.

CAFTA下外国法查明制度之CAFTA化

张春良*

内容摘要

CAFTA的有效运行离不开纠纷排解机制的支撑,其统一私法纠纷排解机制并未建立。此种结构性缺失致使传统国际民商事争议解决机制成为替补路径,而法律选择及其必然涉及的外国法查明因此成为其中不可或缺的核心环节。它对于CAFTA功能的正常发挥、区域法律的协调、互信合作的司法态度以及东亚和平崛起的司法平台之建构具有举足轻重的意义。由于CAFTA下多元语言、多元文化、多元法系的并存和历史合作基础的匮乏,以传统国别自力救济方式查明彼此法律的做法业已不合时宜,必须因应经济的CAFTA化而伴生一场外国法查明的CAFTA化之辅佐运动方为标本兼治之进路。CAFTA下既有法律合作为CAFTA化的查明方式的重构奠定了现实基础,中国—东盟法律研究中心的新设有望成为激活这个一体化查明方案的画龙点睛之笔。

关键词:CAFTA;争议解决机制;法律合作;外国法查明;CAFTA化

目　次

* 张春良,法学博士,西南政法大学副教授,中国—东盟法律研究中心研究员,硕士研究生导师,武汉大学博士后,研究方向:国际私法。

- CAFTA 下外国法查明之障碍
- CAFTA 下现行外国法查明之评析
- 外国法查明之 CAFTA 化
- 余论:刺猬的依偎

引言:落拍的 CAFTA 的"牙齿"

中国—东盟自由贸易区(China-Association of Southeast Asian Nations Free Trade Area,以下简称 CAFTA)是中国—东盟在政治、经济、社会和文化等领域全面展开合作过程中的一个重要举措和成就,其政治和法理根据可追溯至 2002 年 11 月双方所签署的旨在建立 CAFTA 的《中国与东盟全面经济合作框架协议》(Framework Agreement on Comprehensive Economic Cooperation)。根据该协议的安排,CAFTA 之建成运行将分为两个阶段:第一阶段是在文莱、印度尼西亚、马来西亚、菲律宾、新加坡、泰国六国和中国之间于 2010 年首先实现区域自由贸易;第二阶段在第一阶段所建成的自由贸易区基础之上进一步将自由贸易的区域范围扩展至其余四国,即柬埔寨、老挝、缅甸和越南,最终将于 2015 年实现中国与东盟之间的完全的自由贸易区域化。

要真正实现 CAFTA 可持续的有效运作,必须立足于健全的纠纷排解机制。相比于 CAFTA 高效合作进程,作为其反向的制度安排即纠纷排解机制之建设却显得落寞且落拍。双方就争端解决所达成的制度安排屈指可数,在中国与东盟签署的一系列文件中,以争端解决为主题的文件只有一个,即双方于 2004 年 11 月 29 日在万象签署的《关于中国与东盟全面经济合作框架协议之争端解决机制的协定》,该协定已经于 2005 年 7 月开始实施。从该协定的特征来看,它是一种公法争端解决机制,针对的是中国与东盟两大主体之间的公法性争端。[①] 根据该协定的引言部分之声明,它是 2002 年《全面经济合作框架协议》第 11 条的延续。根据该条之规定,各缔约方应在该协议生效后 1 年内为该协议的实施建立适当的正式的争端解决程序与机制。而 2002 年的

① 马永梅:《中国—东盟自由贸易区争端解决机制的法律剖析》,载《广西民族大学学报》(哲学社会科学版)2008 年第 1 期。

框架协议是国家间的公法性协议，由此延伸出的争端解决专题安排也就是公法性争端解决机制，此种定位将私法性争端排除在外。

考虑到自由贸易区的绝大多数商业交易是私人间行为，而在中国与东盟之间的私法性争端解决机制却尚付阙如，这就出现了一个巨大的纠纷排解统一制度安排之缺失。反过来也就挑明了，CAFTA 下国际私法性争端之解决只能诉诸传统的国际民商事纠纷解决模式，[①]其主要方式有二：一是国际民事诉讼；二是国际商事仲裁。本文不探讨统一的 CAFTA 民商事争议解决机制的创设，其现实可行性尚需进一步观察，而是就现行 CAFTA 背景下民商事争议解决机制所必然涉及的外国法查明问题做一专题研究，以期改变各国各自为政的外国法查明方式，建构 CAFTA 化的外国法查明统一制度。

一、CAFTA 下外国法查明之意义

除非存在可供援引的统一实体规范，否则在任何国际民商事争议的处理之中不可避免地会涉及外国法的适用问题。[②] 在 CAFTA 背景下，外国法查明尤其具有值得特别探讨的意义。

（一）促进 CAFTA 功能的正常发挥

凡有利益之存在必然伴生着争讼之可能，CAFTA 是一个巨大的利益场，因此奢求在其中能够实现国家之间、公民之间的永久和平是不切实际的假想。争讼的发生既然不可避免，CAFTA 功能的正常发挥也就离不开对纠纷解决机制的倚赖，外国法查明是各种纠纷解决机制不可或缺的重要环节，谨慎且合理地查明外国法将会促进 CAFTA 下争议的正常解决，从而促进 CAFTA 功能的正常发挥。有学者说得真切："冲突法特定理念能否实现，不仅仅取决于冲突规范在理论上的精巧设计；在一国冲突规范确定由外国法来调整当事人之间的权利义务关系时，更依赖于司法实践中能否及在多大范围和程度上查

① 程信和、张永忠：《论中国—东盟自由贸易区法律模式的构建》，载《环球法律评论》2005 年第 6 期。

② 张春良：《冲突法的笛卡尔式沉思——第一沉思：冲突法的本体论》，肖厚国主编：《民法哲学研究》（第二辑），法律出版社 2010 年版。

明外国法内容并予应用之。"[①]由此足见外国法查明承载着冲突法的"光荣与梦想"之重任。外国法查明上的不当做法将会根本毁灭冲突法之理念,影响案件的公平处理,这首先会引发当事人之间的抵触,进而可能影响国家之间的政治经济关系,[②]为 CAFTA 功能的有效发挥带来消极影响。

(二)建构互信合作的司法姿态

外国法查明常被人视为是排除外国法适用的"逃避机巧",[③]即为了不适用外国法而去查明外国法。在这样的观念定位下,查明外国法之目的不在于去真诚地查找并理解外国法,相反,其目的乃在于经过形式查明之后"发现"无法查明,从而规避掉通过谨慎勤勉的查明本应查实且应予适用的外国法。对外国法的此种恶意态度显然将会引发国家之间的"法律冷战",在对等与反报过程之中破坏彼此互信合作的司法态度之建构。但事实上,外国法查明并不只是一种玩弄外国法情感的魔术,它是解决涉外私法争议的必须环节,[④]它既可以被滥用成为排除外国法得以适用的卑劣行径,同时也能够被正直诚信地运用以合理解决案件争议,成为对他国公民、法律及国家展示开放坦诚态度的窗口。由此看来,外国法查明对于国家间在司法方面,同时也就间接地在政治经济层面的合作具有辩证效果:用之得当,能够提升彼此互信与合作程度;用之不当,则会毁坏彼此的合作基础。CAFTA 的功效虽然表现在商业或经济层面,但司法方面的互信与合作是其内在维度。CAFTA 作为区域化的经济合作成就尤其对成员方之间的司法互信与合作提出了更高的要求,更紧密的、一体化的经济联盟需要与之匹配的法律合作予以支持,外国法查明作为国家间法律合作的一个方面便因此具有了特别的意义。

---

① 徐鹏:《外国法查明:规则借鉴中的思考——以德国外国法查明制度为参照》,载《环球法律评论》2007 年第 2 期。

② 隆茨曾经指出:跨国私人间的任何商事交易都可能被还原成为国家与国家之间的公法关系,在每一个商业主体背后都站立着一个主权国家。(参见隆茨:《国际私法》,吴云琪等译,法律出版社 1986 年版。)

③ Albert A. Ehrenzweig, David W. Louisell, Geoffrey C. Hazard. *Jurisdiction in a nutshell: State and Federal*. West Pub. Co., 1980.

④ 有观点指出:"外国法的查明是正确适用外国法的前提,直接影响案件的审理和判决的结果"。(参见郭玉军:《近年中国有关外国法查明与适用的理论与实践》,载《武大国际法评论》2007 年第 2 期。)

(三)实现国别法律的区域协调

冲突法的调整理念对法官的智识提出了极限要求，由于可能适用外国法，而按照法官知法的司法认知预设，[①]法官就应当在逻辑上被预定为对万民之法无所不知的法律领域的全知的“上帝”。但这种预设显然不符合现实，外国法查明制度之功能便在于辅助法官延伸自己的认知范围。法官都可能怀有“致命的自负”[②]，但在不定的外国法之适用问题上能够最好地教会他们明白谦逊的美德。外国法查明并不只是简单的技术活，查明外国法同时也是理解外国法、对话他者的事情。这种理解和对话就是一种比较，有比较才有鉴别，有鉴别才有自我批判；有自我批判才有借鉴，有借鉴就能促进国别法律的协调。[③] 因此，在CAFTA更密切的政治经济关联之下，各成员国法律之间的交流与对话在司法领域主要是通过外国法查明来直接实现的，在查明外国法的过程之中才能真正了解外国法的精神与立意。作为法律存在的各种可能样态，CAFTA下各成员国立法将会在比较、交流、适用之中进行多边自我调整，从而在宏观上呈现出法律趋同的走势。就此而言，外国法查明的积极意义便在于实现CAFTA下国别法律的区域协调。

(四)奠定东亚崛起的司法平台

CAFTA是中国和ASEAN相互需要的结果，CAFTA的成功将同时实现ASEAN和中国的和平崛起。中国和ASEAN的和平崛起必须立足于区域地缘政治经济的稳定，CAFTA首先是区域地缘经济结构，同时也因为政治与经济的关联性而作为区域地缘政治结构，它的稳定、发展与繁荣是双边和平崛起的必需条件。CAFTA的稳定、发展与繁荣最终是通过方方面面的国别多层次接触、交流与合作得以实现的，涉外司法方面的合作便是其中重要一维。有观点立足于我国角度富有远见地指出：“要把从我国国家利益和国家战略的高度来考虑，作为处理涉东盟民商事关系法律适用的最大价值取向”，“在处理我国涉东盟民商事法律纠纷(案件)时，我们应高度注意避免以狭隘的民族利

---

① Symeon C. Symeonides, Wendy Collins Perdue, Arthur T. von Mehren. *Conflict of Laws: American, Comparative, International: Cases and Materials* (2nd edition). Thomson West, 2003: 108.

② [美]波斯纳：《法官是如何思考的》，苏力译，北京大学出版社2009年版。

③ 张春良：《冲突法的历史逻辑》，法律出版社2010年版。

己主义或狭隘的国家主义的做法……否则便会破坏中国与东盟民商事交往关系在平等互利的基础上和谐稳定地向前发展，进而影响中国—东盟自由贸易区的建立。”[①]外国法查明并不是奠定和平崛起司法平台的唯一因素，更不是决定因素，但毫无疑问，外国法查明所折射出来的对他国法律的态度彰显着该国的处世立场和处事方略，[②]它通过影响 CAFTA 功能的发挥来间接地影响东亚崛起。因此，外国法查明尽管不是唯一的、决定性的因素，但它必然将是影响东亚崛起的重要因素。只有建构出多边接受的外国法查明方式才能清除影响 CAFTA 高效运行的司法方面的消极负面因素，以此方式奠定东亚崛起的司法平台。

二、CAFTA 下外国法查明之障碍

与一般外国法查明相比，CAFTA 下查明外国法受困于一些特别因素的限制。这些障碍因素包括多元的语言、多元的法系、多元的文化和历史合作基础的缺乏。

(一)语言障碍

语言是人际、族际与国际交流与合作的首要影响因素。CAFTA 下各成员国所使用的语种存在幅度极大的差异，除菲律宾、柬埔寨、新加坡三个东盟成员国允许使用英语作为官方语言之一外，其他成员国均有自己独特的官方语言。即便是使用英语作为官方语言的国家，中国法院的法官在查明其法律时也倍感吃力，这也是为什么说法院地法得到更多地适用的一个客观原因，沃尔夫早就说过：除了对本国法律的偏爱之外，适用本国法实在地有很多客观益处[③]。因此，在 CAFTA 下几乎各国立法均有自己独特的语言表达，这就在客观方面提高了查明法律的额外难度。

---

① 邓崇专：《东盟自由贸易区的特点及我国涉东盟民商事关系法律的价值取向》，载《河北法学》2007 年第 1 期。

② 与外国法查明并列的公共秩序保留问题就为国外学者所特别强调指出，不当的公序保留将会是在特定时期引发国家对抗乃至战争的着火点。(参见[英]马丁・沃尔夫：《国际私法》(上卷)，李浩培等译，北京大学出版社 2009 年版。)外国法查明的不当适用尽管不会产生如此严重的后果，但引发国家之间的司法“冷战”从而为国家间政治关系渗入冷调因素却是现实的。

③ [英]马丁・沃尔夫：《国际私法》(上卷)，李浩培等译，北京大学出版社 2009 年版。

(二)法系障碍

法律具有双重语言:一是用以表述法律的语言系统;二是法律自身的语言系统。对于表述法律的语言系统即为通常所谓之语言学,这种语言障碍尚可以通过强化语言培训得到克服,但是对于法律自身的语言系统则难以短期之内得以“速成”。法律自身的语言系统是由整个法律体制所建构的,它涉及对整个法律体制的结构、立意、精神的整体把握,如果没有对整个体制的法意之了解是无法真正理解、解释和适用外国法的。但要对一国之法律体制整体予以把握,显然并非朝夕可成之事。更何况,当一国法官业已习惯了自身法律体制的思维逻辑时,它再要进入他国法律体制进行理解、解释和适用就可能按照其固有的思维惯性而对他国法律体制进行“侵略性”查明。[①] 当这两国的法律体制隶属于同一法系时尚可维持大体合理性,但当它们隶属于不同法系、立足于不同法律历史基础时,此种查明就难免陷入一种“印象主义”。[②] CAFTA下各成员国的法系归属就具有较大差距,有观点认为东盟成员国作为亚洲国家,带有明显的亚洲法的痕迹。[③] 但事实上,CAFTA下各成员国均有被他国入侵、侵占或殖民的经历,这使它们或多或少受到英美法系、伊斯兰法系、大陆法系的影响:“历史上,东盟不少国家曾经是英国、美国、荷兰、西班牙、葡萄牙等国的殖民地,因此在殖民地时期被移植的法律还深深根植在这些国家中,如菲律宾在被西班牙统治的三个多世纪中移植了西班牙法,后在美国的殖民统治之下又移植了美国法。因此,世界两大主要法系英美法系和大陆法系的传统给这些国家的法律和法律制度发展印上了深深的历史烙印。”[④]

另一方面,CAFTA成员国在完全拥有主权之后也仍然为着本国法律的现代化而主动地借鉴、移植和学习大陆法系和英美法系的精髓,这就再次导致它们法文化的融合和法系归属的困难。不独如此,CAFTA下11国尽管在借鉴欧盟先进法律文化,但同时也更加自觉和能动地利用本土的法制资源,走具有本国特色、符合本国国情的法律发展道路。如此一来,东盟各国“积极从西方国家引进法律,还以经济发展为目的制定了大量的符合各国国情的开发法,加之各国固有的反映各自特定历史背景和文化的传统法,可以说,东盟自由贸

---

① Juenger, F. *Choice of Law and Multistate Justice* (Special edition). NY, 2005.

② Juenger, F. *Choice of Law and Multistate Justice* (Special edition). NY, 2005.

③ 杨丽艳:《区域经济一体化法律制度研究》,法律出版社2004年版,第394页。

④ 申华林主编:《东盟国家法律概论》,广西民族出版社2004年版,第2页。

易区的法律是世界各主要法律文化和其传统的交融”[①]。基于上述原因,导致它们的法律文化即便具有融合性特征,也具有不同的融合风格。这些因素极大地限制了东盟成员国与中国彼此之间对对方法律的查明,在语言、法系的消极限制之外,还多了各国地方法文化的掣肘。

(三)文化障碍

从更彻底的角度来看,CAFTA下各国文化的差异在根底处为查明、理解和解释彼此之间的法律带来了制约。外国法的查明本身还包括理解和解释外国法,然后才谈得上适用的问题。要理解和解释外国法既要掌握外国语言和外国法的意义,同时还要知晓外国法的生成根据,而不能离开外国法所赖以依托的文化母体而机械理解。[②] 不同的文化滋生不同的法律立场,不同的法律立场进一步才具体化为特定的法律规则。因此,在冲突法的视野之中才会存在在一国被认为耻辱卑劣者却在他国被饰以“紫金色的荣光”之背反现象。[③] 剥取了外国法所立足的文化语境也就剥夺了外国法的解释力和说明力,同时也就阉割了外国法之生命力。失去了生命力的外国法将连带丧失掉其正当性和合理性。因此,要本真地查明外国法就不得不尊重其文化背景,而对文化背景的尊重则再次为外国法之查明提出了更高的要求。CAFTA下11国均具有幅差极大的文化背景,除少数国家之间具有文明的同构性之外,绝大多数国家走上了不同的文化发展轨道。

应当看到,东盟十国与中国之间在文化背景方面具有一些共享的成分,诸如佛教的影响便成为一种精神纽带,在一定程度上限制了文化离心的力量,而且某些国家如越南等还受汉文化影响颇深。特别是考虑到中华文明在悠久历史过程中,在其最光辉灿烂的时刻,对东南亚周边国家的辐射和示范作用,CAFTA并不完全缺乏文明方面的合作基础。但此种文明合作的同质性结构伴随着中华文明于清末开始衰败以来便开始丧失向心凝聚力,加上西方列强对东南亚国家的入侵与殖民,更加速了东南亚各国文化多样性的形成。发展至今,不同的文化底蕴成为外国法查明过程之中的“先见”,此种先见的消极性

---

① 邓崇专:《东盟自由贸易区的特点及我国涉东盟民商事关系法律的价值取向》,载《河北法学》2007年第1期。

② Frances Olsen, Alexander Lorz and Dieter Stein edited. *Translation Issues in Language and Law*. Basingstoke Palgrave Macmillan, 2009.

③ [德]尼采:《查拉图斯特拉如是说》,孙周兴译,上海人民出版社2009年版。

在于它成为了制约外国法本真查明的前提性偏见。在它的干扰和"染色"下，被查明的外国法往往并不是真正的外国法，而是多多少少受到法院地国文化所"调整"过的外国印象。这就如同用油画的技法来绘山水，或者用山水画的技法来绘油画，二者不是相互成全，相反，它们只是相互"伤害"、相互"扭曲"。

(四)历史障碍

CAFTA 下各国查明对方法律的障碍还在于彼此之间较少有过查明法律方面的司法协助之合作经验。如果能够得到被查明国的协助，外国法之查明无疑会起到事半功倍之效果。但 CAFTA 下各国之间迄今鲜有此方面的安排，历史合作基础严重匮乏。以中国为例，虽然最高人民法院关于《民法通则》的司法解释之中规定了五种查明外国法的方式，其中一种便是通过"与中国签订有司法协助协定的缔约对方的中央机关提供"，但遗憾的是，经查阅我国与 CAFTA 下其他成员国之间的司法协助协定，即可发现它具有巨大的缺失。对此可先浏览下表：

表 1　中国—X 之间的司法协助协定一览表[①]：

国别	司法协助条约
中国—文莱	无
中国—菲律宾	2000 年 10 月《中华人民共和国和菲律宾共和国关于刑事司法协助的条约》 2001 年 10 月《中华人民共和国和菲律宾共和国引渡条约》
中国—柬埔寨	1999 年 2 月《中华人民共和国和柬埔寨王国引渡条约》
中国—老挝	1999 年 1 月《中华人民共和国和老挝人民民主共和国关于民事和刑事司法协助的条约》
中国—马来西亚	无
中国—缅甸	无

① 本部分经过整理，其原始资料来源于中国法院网，http://www.chinacourt.org/，访问日期：2011 年 1 月 11 日。

续表

国别	司法协助条约
中国—泰国	无
中国—新加坡	无
中国—印度尼西亚	2009 年 7 月《中华人民共和国和印度尼西亚共和国引渡条约》 2000 年 7 月《中华人民共和国和印度尼西亚共和国关于刑事司法协助的条约》
中国—越南	1998 年 10 月《中华人民共和国和越南社会主义共和国关于民事和刑事司法协助的条约》
CAFTA	无

首先,从整个 CAFTA 的制度安排来看,它并没有一个统一的关于外国法查明的多边司法协助安排;其次,就双边司法协助的缔结来看,要完全展开 CAFTA 下 11 个成员国两两之间的司法协助安排之检索,工作量极大,为此,本文仅以中国为不变量,通过考察其分别与 CAFTA 及其他成员国之间的双边司法协助安排,以之作为一个样本来揭示 CAFTA 下双边司法协助安排之梗概。

从上表整理的结果可以看出,“中国—X”的双边司法协助安排可总体上划分为三类:一是没有任何司法协助;二是仅有刑事司法协助;三是含有民商事司法协助。中国与文莱、马来西亚、缅甸、泰国、新加坡等东盟五国之间就属于第一种类型,彼此之间无任何司法协助。中国与印度尼西亚、菲律宾、柬埔寨仅有刑事司法协助。中国与越南、老挝之间不仅有刑事司法协助,而且还有民事司法协助。由于本文所探讨的外国法查明仅限于民商事领域,因此就中国与 CAFTA 下其他成员国之间的双边司法协助而言,只有越南和老挝存在协助查明的法律依据,其他八国与中国之间的外国法查明便无法采取此种便捷的查明方式。如果中国样本具有典型性的话,那就意味着,大多数 CAFTA 成员国之间的外国法查明只能通过原始的当事人查明、法官查明的方式进行。但当事人查明易生争端,法官查明却又因为上述种种原因的存在而使法官常常拘泥于“仅仅通过国外规则文字的‘地方性阅读’”[①]来望文生义，弃外国法本身而就外国法之镜像，颇多误解发生。可见，正是由于首先在 CAFTA 层面缺乏多边的司法协助安排，其次则在 CAFTA 下各成员国之间缺乏普遍的两两双边司法协助安排，从而为 CAFTA 下外国法查明形成了本可克服的消极障碍。

三、CAFTA 下现行外国法查明之评析

(一)CAFTA 下外国法查明的现行方式

从法律逻辑的角度看，CAFTA 下查明外国法的途径应当是：首先，如果 CAFTA 各成员国具有统一的规则，则适用该统一规则。需要指出的是，此种统一规则包括两大方面，一是 CAFTA 各成员国专门达成的统一安排；二是 CAFTA 下 11 国共同缔结或参加了其他的全球性或地区性的有关查明外国法的条约或协定。其次，在没有此类统一安排的情况下，则看 CAFTA 各成员国是否局部地形成多边统一安排或者双边统一安排。再次，在缺乏局部多边或双边统一安排的情况下，只能由各国按照本国国内立法的方式查明外国法。最后，在无法查明外国法时，通常由法院地法予以替补救济。

根据 CAFTA 现行相关条约或协议，它并不存在统一的制度安排，因此，CAFTA 下各成员国在查明彼此的法律时就只能按照双边协定及国内立法规定的方式予以执行，在无法查明或者无法充分查明时，则适用受理案件的法院所在地法。

(二)立足中国视角的国别考察

中国法院在审理涉东盟成员国的民商事案件时必将遭遇外国法查明的问题。由于统一查明制度的缺乏，中国法院在查明东盟成员国的立法时就不得不诉诸双边约定和国内立法。不同国家彼此之间就查明对方法律存在着参差不齐的双边安排，就中国角度来看，由于中国只与越南和老挝两国分别达成了两两互助的民事司法协助协定，因此，中国法院在需要查明越南法律或者老挝法律时，可寻求司法协助的途径请求越南或老挝的相关机关(一般是该国国内

---

① 徐鹏：《外国法查明：规则借鉴中的思考——以德国外国法查明制度为参照》，载《环球法律评论》2007 年第 2 期。

的最高司法机关或司法行政机关)予以提供。

在案件准据法涉及越南或老挝之外的其他东盟成员国的法律时,由于中国与它们不存在统一的、双边的民事司法协助协定,因此,其查明方式就只能由受理案件的中国法院按照本国国内立法予以执行。但中国有关立法即《民法通则》第八章并没有对查明外国法之方式作出规定,而在最高人民法院对《民法通则》的司法解释之中有所体现。根据《最高人民法院关于贯彻执行〈民法通则〉若干问题的意见》第193条之规定,查明外国法的途径包括五种类型:(1)由当事人提供;(2)由与我国订立司法协助协定的缔约对方的中央机关提供;(3)由我国驻该国使领馆提供;(4)由该国驻我国使馆提供;(5)由中外法律专家提供。除此之外,在涉外民商事合同的法律适用方面,最高人民法院新增加了法官的查明责任,要求人民法院对根据最密切联系原则确定的作为合同准据法的外国法依照职权予以查明。[①]《涉外民事关系法律适用法》第10条将之总结为法官查明和当事人查明两种方式,

尽管查明方式看起来足够丰富,外国法之查明似乎也就不存在多大问题,但就对中国法院涉外审判的实证统计数据显示,中国法官通常采取简单化的查明方式:首先由当事人提供;在当事人无法提供或者彼此互有分歧时,可由中外法律专家提供协助;在通过此种方式无法查明外国法时,则认定外国法无法查明,从而以中国法取而代之。这种简化的外国法查明方式首先在查明质量上值得商榷,其次则在查明态度上值得反思。前已述及,外国法查明之方式与态度反映了一国的涉外司法态度,司法权作为国家主权的一个重要方面,其涉外司法态度也就直接彰显了该国的涉外主权态度。以这样简化得略显草率的查明方式适用于CAFTA下成员国之间彼此法律的查明,必将对CAFTA功效之发挥产生重大的负面冲击。

(三)现行方式之评析

在CAFTA场景下从中国查明ASEAN成员国法律的司法实践可看出,驻外使领馆、法官、法律专家在查明方面的功效并未得到充分发挥,现实做法简单地退化为主要由当事人查明,查明外国法的重要责任由此落到了彼此对抗的当事人之肩上。此种现实有效的查明模式表现出这样几个消极方面:

---

① 见最高人民法院2007年6月11日法释[2007]14号,即《最高人民法院关于审理涉外民事或商事合同纠纷案件法律适用若干问题的规定》第9条。

1.查明效率低下

"法官知法"虽为"天理",但该命题只在国内法体制下有效;在超出一国法律之外而对于他国法律,法官与一般公民相同,通常也只是程度略有不同的"法盲"而已。被查明的外国法在CAFTA情境下往往生长于不同的法律文化,隶属于不同的法系类别,体现了不同的法律观念;不仅如此,法律自身也是一个有机体,它还存在发展生长的动态变化。因此,当习惯了按照成文法方式来理解和查明法律的中国法官或者当事人需要去查明CAFTA下另外一个隶属于英美判例法系的国家如马来西亚的法律时,他面对浩如烟海、零散且不断发展变化着的司法判例时,可以想象其查明效率会有多高。毫无疑问,每一个国家的司法机关对本国法律是最熟悉、最权威的查明主体,但按照现行CAFTA下的查明体制来看,由于并不存在统一的多边查明协助安排,而且在双边的查明协助也屈指可数的情况下,此种本可利用的权威查明方式便被束之高阁、无法发挥现实功效了。

在查明主体方面,中国虽然罗列了当事人、法官、驻外使领馆和法律专家四大查明主体,但驻外使领馆因另有重任在身,理论和实践上都极少接受查明协助之请求。法官查明虽然符合法律预设,但由法官查明也存在着上述查明效率低下之情形。从《泰国国际私法》第8条来看,它甚至提出了更高的查明标准,即不仅要求法官要查明外国法,而且必须能够做到"充分认定",否则不得适用外国法。至于法律专家之查明,其最大的局限性在于它往往体现了较大的主观性,使学术观点通过此种方式成为法院司法的间接渊源,而这是不符合中国否认学者学说可以作为法律渊源的现行立法体制的。

2.外国法被"漫画化"

脱离法律生长的语境而对该法律进行查明,其效果无异于"镜花水月"。特别是由于CAFTA下各国均有自己独特的语言系统,不同的语言系统之间虽然可以进行大体对译,但是由于语言基本元素的不同,始终存在着无法对译的方面。在那些最能体现各国语言独特性而无法对译的场域之中,法律无疑是其中一个主要方面。因此,除非是由生于斯且长于斯的人士对自身的法律进行查明并予以阐释,除外之人进行查明和解释就不可避免地会导致该外国法的变样走形。我们也不乏这样的现实体验,即对于外国法中的某些制度或者规定,乃至本国历史上的某些制度或者规定,往往无法理解其存在的意义和价值,但一旦还原其生成基础和语境便能够合理地理解那些初看起来不合理的规定。而这种生成基础和语境就是赋予特定法律以精神、立意的文化母体。所以,按照中国现行的查明外国法的方式,不管是由当事人查明,还是由法官查明,都可能是一种外部的形式化的查明,流于对法律规则而不是内在法意的掌握,这就可能导致外国法被机械地扭曲、剪切,然后被合成为既不是内国法、也不是外国法的混合法。如此被适用的法律就既不是适用法院地法,也不是适用外国法,外国法查明也就失去了意义。

除了由于“釜底抽薪”而形式化地误解外国法之外,一种更根深蒂固的误解根源发生在内国法官或当事人的先天认识结构之中。按照古典认识论的立论,主体总是按照特定的范畴来构造世界,也按照相同的范畴去认识事物的。按照康德的见解,这些范畴是先验的,因此为认识如何可能这一究底之问提供了担保。但按照当代存在主义现象学的理解,存在始终有一个生存论境遇,不同的生存论境遇将会有不同的范畴,范畴的先验性因此被生存论化了。这就表明,不同的法律体系总是存活于不同的生活共同体之中,而查明外国法的行为实质上就是两大不同的生活共同体之间的对话与交往,但不同的生活共同体有不同的范畴,当按照某一共同体的范畴去解读另一共同体的法律时便可能发生一种“创造性误解”。对此,法国国际私法学者巴蒂福尔和拉加德就指出:按照内国法的范畴去理解外国法,无异于将外国法律的“衣料”放入内国法律的“抽屉”之中,内国法官和当事人因此置精美的“衣料”于不顾,却执著于且满足于外国法的“漫画”。[①] 这是在CAFTA下各成员国查明彼此法律时的共同命运。

3.外国法被规避

外国法查明尽管重要,但它存在两大致命缺陷:一是历经千辛万苦查明的却是外国法的印象,而非本真的外国法;二是即便假定查明的确切无疑的是该外国法本身,但为获得这一结果却付出了不成比例的、畸高的时间、费用和人力成本,得不偿失。或许正是出于此种正反两方面的考虑,法官通常都倾向于在案件审理过程中适用本国法而非外国法。为达到这一目标,为查明外国法之目的而设计的外国法查明制度便可能被司法能动地规避,这便是在简单查明之后即以无法查明为由,遂适用法院地法替代之。CAFTA的11个参与国几乎都对外国法无法查明的救济方式作出了不约而同的做法,这便是适用法院地法。理由不一:或者直接推定该外国法与法院地法相同;或者将法院地法列为最后的兜底规则。理论上虽然将法院地法的适用视为是外国法无法查明时的救济,而不是目的;但实践中法官却往往采取“结果导向”的做法,即为适

---

① [法]巴蒂福尔、拉加德:《国际私法总论》,陈洪武等译,中国对外翻译出版公司1989年版。

用法院地法而未穷尽外国法查明之手段，或者在查明外国法时未尽到勤勉谨慎之查明责任，然后便将外国法进行“短路”，直接越过之而适用法院地法。

这是一种不成文的司法能动规避，另外在CAFTA的一些成员国的国际私法立法之中甚至还存在着一些制度化的规避措施，比较突出和奇特的便是反致制度的确立问题。反致作为国际私法上一个独特的现象，它在很大程度上便是为法院地法之适用而开辟的“反射”途径。其作用方式类同于能回飞的飞盘，向外抛投之后能够重新返回到出发点，其实现原理简述如下：法官根据本国冲突规范指向外国法，但该外国法中的冲突规范却反向指回了本国法，法官因此不是适用外国法而是适用本国法裁决案件。在反致情形下根本就不发生外国法的查明问题，因此也就不会存在查明外国法的上述“烦恼”。中国立法是否排除了反致，存在着一定的争议，但主流观点是认为立法应当排除反致，除非在婚姻家庭领域之中基于对等做法采取反致措施。[①]《泰国国际私法》和《越南社会主义共和国民法典》都完整地保留了反致制度。正是基于反致这样一些措施具有排除外国法适用的功能，美国现实主义学者艾伦茨威格将它们视为是一套“迷人的智力操练”，法院地法因此应当被当作为冲突法的首要原则。[②] 此种做法将外国法的适用一笔勾销，自然地，当外国法被排除之后也就不再存在查明外国法的困扰了，这是最彻底的“排忧解难”之方式。但这种做法一方面使当事人对法律适用的预期落空，[③]另一方面则可能引起国家之间的法律适用对抗，并最终将此种对抗积累并传递到判决的彼此承认和执行环节，导致判决无法获得域外认可，涉外民商事关系之调整因此陷于滞涩。最后，此种消极效应反向传递到涉外经贸交往过程之中，必将冲击CAFTA之有效和有序运行。

4.有伤冲突法之理念

从CAFTA现行体制安排可以看出，除了少量地存在着双边司法协助协定而可以便捷高效且本身地查明外国法之外，更常见的做法乃是由一国法官或当事人对另一CAFTA成员国之立法进行“离岸想象”。以这样想象的产物作为案件的准据法，显然是有违冲突法之基本理念的。冲突法的基本理念其实很朴素，这便是通过预先的选择规则对关涉两个及其以上的法域的案件确

---

① 赵生祥等：《国际私法学》，法律出版社2005年版。

② 转引自邓正来：《美国现代国际私法流派》，中国政法大学出版社2006年版。

③ Symeon C. Symeonides. *Private International Law at the end of the 20th century: progress or regress?*. Kluwer law international, 2000.

定法律,然后据之裁决案件。因此,从冲突法基本理念出发,当法律选择规则指向外国法时,该外国法便应当是唯一适格的适用于案件的法律。近千年来国际私法史上的大师们都对这种适用的"适格"问题进行了研究,德国萨维尼被誉为国际私法近代之父,他就将这种被选择出来的法律视为是"本座法",是特定法律关系的"家"。[①] 很显然,通过如此选择出来的外国法如果在外国法查明环节被有意或无意地扭曲、漫画、规避或短路,那么这就不仅伤了国际私法史上大师们的"心意",[②]同时也就是损害了冲突法之基本理念,连带着根本否定了冲突法存在之必要。

职是之故,不论是为了合理地调整案件,维护当事人的合法权益,捍卫冲突法的指令,还是为了优化涉外民商事新秩序,促进 CAFTA 功能的有效发挥,或者为了东亚及中国之崛起等等宏观使命,重构 CAFTA 下外国法查明之方式业已成为 CAFTA 成员国的共同使命和责任。至于如何重构 CAFTA 下外国法查明之具体方案,问题本身已经提示了解决问题的思路。这个思路的总体观念便是实现外国法查明之 CAFTA 化,因为 CAFTA 化的区域政治经济关系需要 CAFTA 化的外国法查明。

四、外国法查明之 CAFTA 化

(一)查明机制 CAFTA 化的现实基础

CAFTA 是通过政治合作而实现的经济领域的一体化安排,此种安排将会自然扩展及法律领域的一体化安排。争端解决机制作为法律领域的终端救济环节也将受到一体化发展的影响,而一体化的争端解决机制正好就是解决经济一体化过程中所产生的一切纠纷之最佳方案。国际公法层面的统一争端解决机制已经生效运作,国际私法方面的统一争端解决机制尚未建立。在这样的格局之下,外国法查明等机制不得不诉诸双边协定,但更主要地依赖于与一般的查明外国法并无二致的国别自力救济之方式。现有解决方式易陷入各

---

① [德]萨维尼:《法律冲突与法律规则的时间和地域范围》,李双元等译,法律出版社 1999 年版。

② 如萨维尼的国际私法追求便是四个大同:同一个世界,同一个案件,同一个法律,同一个梦想。参见张春良:《论萨维尼冲突法思想的情调——萨维尼"本座说"的抱负、梦幻及其宿命》,载肖厚国主编:《民法哲学研究》(第一辑),法律出版社 2009 年版。

自为政、矛盾冲突之现象，因此可在现有解纷体制之下逐点地实现国际私法争端解决机制的渐进式协调。由于各种私法争端解决机制都必须解决法律适用的问题，因此，外国法之查明便是其中最紧迫、最具有战略意义、同时也具有统一协调的最现实操作基础的环节。

1. CAFTA 法律合作现行结构

围绕 CAFTA 的建设，中国与东盟已经形成了具有一定规模、虚实结合、富有成效的法律合作基础。法律合作的轮廓结构初具雏形成型，[①]CAFTA 下法律合作主要通过实体机构和主题论坛两种方式进行。其中，实体机构包括中国—东盟法律培训基地和中国—东盟法律研究中心；主题论坛则包括中国—东盟 FTA 法律事务论坛和中国—东盟法律合作与发展高层论坛。实体机构推动下的法律合作是 CAFTA 法律合作的实体性方面，主题论坛则是 CAFTA 法律合作的非实体性方面，前者为常设性法律合作机制，且有专门的硬件、人力资源等支持，后者则为周期性法律合作机制，以会议形式进行，并不具有专门且固定的常设性硬件、人力资源等支持。此种配合机制可谓虚实结合，确保了 CAFTA 下常设性与临时性法律合作、灵活性与稳定性法律合作、综合性与专题性法律合作。CAFTA 下法律合作机制为争端解决机制的建设提供了丰富和有效的智识支持，统一的公法争端解决机制业已建成，剩下的历史使命只是如何进一步完善和改进，而统一的私法争端解决机制尚未建立，目前务实的做法是渐进式地推进统一私法争端解决机制之建设，依赖 CAFTA 下法律合作机制提供的成就，逐步实现司法协助（包括外国法查明）、解纷方案的统一。

2. CAFTA 法律合作现有成就

第一，中国—东盟法律培训基地已经于 2007 年开始连续举行了 3 届东盟学员培训班和 2 届中国学员培训班，对彼此的宏观法律体制和某些部门法律

---

① 需要指出的是，还有一些提供商业性服务的法律服务中心，典型的如中国—东盟联合服务中心，该中心依托中国—东盟博览会得以建立，并在 CAFTA 法律事务论坛组委会主导下运行。该联合服务中心的功能重心落脚在中国与东盟的法律服务方面，同时兼及投资、金融和评价等内容。该中心汇集全球智识精英，组建顾问团与专家库，并按照不同类别组成专家组以提供直接的、具有针对性的服务，弥补投资双方对项目投资国及投资国法律、政策方面的信息缺乏，有效解决 CAFTA 内涉及国际贸易和地区投资的法律服务。（进一步的详细信息可查阅：http://www.dmfl2004.com/lhfw/html/? 321.html，访问日期：2010 年 12 月 12 日。）因其为商业性服务机构，故未纳入中国与东盟的法律合作结构之中，它与其他商业性法律服务机构一样，充其量只能算广义的法律合作。

知识进行了较为系统的培训。但从培训课程的开设看,具有单边性和双边非对称性:即在课程设置及内容讲解上主要是对中国法律的介绍和讲解,更多的东盟成员国的法律体制尚未得到全面覆盖,东盟成员国之中主要是新加坡、马来西亚、泰国和越南等国家的法律得到了相对详细的介绍,主讲人员也更应该突出和强调本国背景,最好是由所涉法律所属国专业人士主持讲解;即便是中国法律体制的介绍也尚未完全覆盖。这将在后续的培训课程之中得到进一步的完善和优化。

第二,中国—东盟 FTA 法律事务论坛已经连续召开了 6 届会议,会议紧扣 CAFTA 建设对其中紧迫的法律问题如争端解决机制、司法协助、国别投资、多边合作项目、合作发展、共同应对危机等议题进行了深入、系统、务实和有效的探讨与交流,这些会议交流为 CAFTA 正式成立后的功能发挥及其改善具有重要的支持意义,也为 CAFTA 今后可能遭遇的难题进行了排解方案的预先论证。

第三,中国—东盟法律合作与发展高层论坛包括本次议程在内已经连续举办了 4 届高级别的会议,从 4 届会议的主题来看,都是围绕 CAFTA 中的"法律合作"予以展开的。至今,高层论坛业已对东盟与中国的法律制度进行了系列的比较研究,分别因应会议举行的不同历史背景,分 CAFTA 建设前、中及后三个时期的三个角度对其中的法律问题进行了系统交流。以本届会议为分水岭,前三次会议的背景和主题集中在立足过去对 CAFTA 法律合作与发展的未来进行"展望"方面;本次会议是立足 CAFTA 新建运行后的现在,承前启后地"瞻前顾后",衔接 CAFTA 建设的过去与未来。

第四,中国—东盟法律研究中心于 2010 年 11 月在重庆正式成立,成为第一个专业性、专题性、实体化的 CAFTA 法律研究机构。

可以说,通过上述四大方面的法律合作,中国与东盟之间双向多边的法律认知、普及与研究业已达到了一定的规模和水准,但此种法律合作最大的弊端有两点:第一,它主要是面向法学研究层面和民间实务层面,并不直接转化为司法合作的成果;第二,这些法律合作项目分别来看都具有各自的特色和定位,但彼此之间尽管都是探讨 CAFTA 相关协定及中国东盟 11 国的国别法律知识的,然而很遗憾的是,迄今仍然缺乏一个综合各大合作项目之成就,总结其效果,规划其发展,最终形成系统的法律研究、整理成果、并向 CAFTA 及各国提交权威法律报告的统一行动。这不能不说是一个意味深长、值得反思的问题:各法律合作项目的宗旨在于促进 CAFTA 下的法律合作,但这些合作项目自身首先便缺乏合作的自觉,在条块分割各自为战的进路之中却奢求一体化地解决 CAFTA 的问题。

解决这个问题的有效方案便是，将已经建成的中国—东盟法律研究中心建设成为一个集大成者的机构，综合中国—东盟之间所有法律合作的成就，进行系统梳理和战略审思，定期公布研究报告，并适时作为 CAFTA、东盟各成员国及中国在此方面的法律智囊团。尤其是，可通过特定制度的设计，让中国—东盟法律研究中心凭借此种智识优势成为具有提供权威的法律资源检索与证明的准官方机构，以此方式建构一个以该院为中心和枢纽的、统一化的、对东盟各国、中国及 CAFTA 的法律资源提供查明功能的外国法查明机制，而这正是本文思考的出发点和落脚点。

(二)CAFTA 化查明机制之初构

1. 三种方案

中国—东盟之间的既有法律合作已经为这样的统一查明机制奠定了最坚实的基础，经过多层次、持续多年的法律合作之经营，一个统一化的查明机制之轮廓已经呼之欲出，其点睛之笔便是寻找一个能综合各方面资源的实体性机构。这个机构不仅能够汇集涉及中国、东盟各国及 CAFTA 的所有法律资源的能力，而且还必须具有权威的理解和解释能力；它不仅能够谙熟 CAFTA 11 国之法律体制、法律精神、法系归属、法律语言，能够及时更新最近的立法变动、司法动态和法院判例，而且为了能够直接为各国审判行为提供法律适用之依据，它还最好能够得到 11 国之官方统一授权。这样的机构既可以在现有体制之外进行新设，也可以在现有体制之中对特定机构之功能进行增容。笔者以为，最适当的机构便是会议之后拟议建设的中国—东盟法律研究院，并且根据不同情况可以为其设计三种具有不同理想性和现实性程度的方案.

第一种方案是最具现实但不够理想的“统一辅助机构”方案，即原则上大体维持 CAFTA 下各国现有争议解决处理方式，只是在查明涉及各国或者 CAFTA 层面的法律文献时，不再依靠各国零散的查明力量，而是将中国—东盟法律研究院提供的查明服务纳入进去，当作为权威的专家学者查明服务。相应地，为使该查明功能得到认同且具有法律依据，既可以由各国分别在其国内立法之中就查明方式问题增加此一内容，也可以通过本次会议或者后续会议由 CAFTA 11 国签署一个联合查明授权，同意各国司法机关考虑接受该院的查明认证。

第二种方案是一种理想性和现实性均衡适中的“统一协调机构”方案，即由 CAFTA 11 国统一声明，授权中国—东盟法律研究院作为统一协调机构，允许各国司法机关在需要查明涉 CAFTA 及成员国立法时寻求该院帮助,由该院将查明请求转致被查明立法的所属国主管机关,主管机关应出具查明报告。在这过程中,也可以授权该院对需要查明的法律整理出一个报告,再将该法律报告送交被查明立法所属国的主管机关予以确认。确认报告或查明报告再反致回研究院,最后由研究院返回给请求机关。此种方案的核心是仅使法律研究院在 CAFTA 11 国之间起一个总协调和总交换的作用,激进一点便授权法律研究院对需要查明的内容打一个“草稿”,形成一个查明报告初稿,对法律材料进行初加工,这样可以简化被请求国主管机关的工作量,后者只需要确认或调整即可。除此之外,法律研究院还应当与 CAFTA 11 国建立时时更新的法律数据库跟进机制,围绕统一的查明机制之建设提出更稳定、成熟、协调和高效的改进方案。

第三种方案是最理想但现实性较低的“统一查明机构”方案,即由 CAFTA 11 国通过签署统一条约或协定的方式授权中国—东盟法律研究院以查明涉 CAFTA 及其成员国立法之正式功能,排除其他查明方式,而由该院垄断行使查明职责。这不仅需要各国进行统一授权,而且还需要各国相应调整其内国有关查明外国法的立法体制。这种理想方案最具查明效率,但因太过于强调和突出研究院的查明功效,所以很可能不易为 11 国所接受。这种矛盾向来便存在,即为了效率常常需要凝聚起力量,而为了凝聚起力量则往往伴随着分散权力的集结,集结的力量反过来很可能异化成为伤害民主与自由的独裁或暴力。妨碍各国统一接受此种方案的理由大抵如此,因为统一接受这种方案的核心和本质乃是要求各国对中国—东盟法律研究院予以充分放权和信任,但这往往难以在短期内被做到。但不论如何,这种最 CAFTA 化的模式——不一定非得由中国—东盟法律研究院来担当,也可能由其他机构来担当——终究是 CAFTA 的终极走向,因为它与 CAFTA 的一体化精神是一脉相承的,是 CAFTA 精神在外国法查明领域之中最透彻的实现。如果此种模式得不到实现,那么就不仅仅是外国法查明方式 CAFTA 化进程的挫折,而且其本质也就是 CAFTA 的遗憾,它证明的是功效被打了折扣、跛了脚的 CAFTA,它还证明的是 CAFTA 的不自信。

2.定性分析

比较三种方案,理想性是指效率性,而效率性是通过集中的模式来实现的;现实性是强调 CAFTA 下 11 国的民主,在民主基础之上进行分散式的合作。进一步的启示便是:各种不同方案之间的取舍在本质乃是民主与效率的核心取向之争,不同的“民主—效率”匹配模式是通过合作路径的“分散—集中”之不同程度实现的，而通过不同程度的“分散—集中”状态所实现的不同程度的“民主—效率”效果，则彰显了该种合作模式的不同程度的“现实—理想”性。对于 CAFTA 下外国法查明方式的合作模式之择定，既不应该满足于保守在各国主权的“坚果”[1]里不肯承让，也不可在仰望星空之际遗忘了脚下的大地，在不懈追逐最高理想性的同时还得考虑主权者可能接受之限制的极限。要知道，在合作过程中除了效率之外还有各国所坚守的、不可触碰的、它们认为属于神圣不可侵犯的东西。明白了这一临界点并且尊重这一临界点的情况下，对于 CAFTA 下 11 国而言其余下的责任便是致力于探究在这一合作趋势线上能够实现“理想—现实”、“效率—民主”、“集中—分散”完美结合的黄金分割点。

五、余论：刺猬的依偎

CAFTA 化的外国法查明机制之建构问题，不过就是那个老生常谈的命题：民主中的集中问题。这并不奇怪，毕竟 CAFTA 的建设与建成首先便是要求各国放下自己的自负与孤傲，走到一起在让渡之中形成统一体。统一体有效率，但它通常会对参与国形成压迫力量。参与国之所以愿意接受此种压迫并且享受这压迫，原因有二：一是它知道这压迫的根据在于自己的主动接受，基于这种内在的自愿，此种压迫就不再是压迫；二是它知道为了维持乃至扩大自身的现有自由，就必须得担当起这压迫。这两点理由事实上构成一切以放弃自由走向约束、限制民主走向集中的行为依据。因此，CAFTA 下外国法查明的 CAFTA 化看起来就不再显得那么天方夜谭，因为 CAFTA 化既然是赢得自由之道，那么 CAFTA 化的查明方式就不是通往奴役之途。有了这点共识，外国法查明方式要不走 CAFTA 化的道路也是不行的。

---

① Albert A. Ehrenzweig, David W. Louisell, Geoffrey C. Hazard. *Jurisdiction in a nutshell: State and Federal*. West Pub. Co., 1980.

The Caftalization of Proof of Foreign Law under CAFTA

Zhang Chunliang

Abstract

Effective operation of CAFTA can not do without the support of dispute resolution mechanisms, but the unified private law dispute resolution mechanism has not been established. Such structural defect has to be replaced by traditional international civil and commercial dispute resolution mechanism. Therefore, the choice of law and proof of foreign laws become the core of the most essential part, which have a significant meaning for the normal functioning of the CAFTA, the harmonization of regional laws, the judicial attitude of mutual trust and cooperation and the construction of the judicial platform that East Asia springs up peacefully. Because under the CAFTA, there are co-existence of diverse languages, multi-culture and multiple legal systems, and lack of basis of historical cooperation, it is no longer suitable to prove laws each other in traditional self-help ways and should raise a revolution of Caftalization of proof of foreign laws, which will be a wise way to resolve the essential problems. The existing legal cooperation under CAFTA lays a realistic foundation for reconstruction of Caftalizaiton of proof. And the prospected establishment of the Academy of China-ASEAN Law is expected to be activated to the integrated proof program.

KeyWords: CAFTA; Dispute Resolution Mechanisms; Legal Cooperation; Proof of Foreign Laws; Caftalization

Content

- Introduction: the lagging "Teeth" of CAFTA

- The Significance of the Proof of Foreign law Under the CAFTA
- The blockade for the Proof of Foreign Law Under the CAFTA
- The Critical Thinking of the Existing Proof of Foreign Law Under the CAFTA
- The Caftalization of the Proof of Foreign Law
- Conclusion：the nestle of the hedgehog

法律服务业在中国—东盟自由贸易区运行中的作用和职能

陈云东[*]　米　良[**]

内容摘要

2010年1月1日,中国—东盟自由贸易区如期建成。自贸区的建成必将对这一地区的经贸合作带来巨大的机会,但自贸区的运行必须在法治的轨道上运行才有可能具有可持续性。中国—东盟自由贸易区的运行离不开法律服务,法律服务是中国—东盟自由贸易区正常健康运行的保障。

关键词:法律服务;中国—东盟自由贸易区;职能

目　次

---

* 陈云东,云南大学法学院院长、教授、博士,主要从事国际经济法研究。

** 米良,云南大学法学院教授、东盟法研究中心主任,主要从事东盟法研究。

一、中国—东盟自由贸易区运行中法律服务的体系及特点

法律服务是现代服务体系的重要组成部分，是实现社会发展的基本条件。特别是在经济全球化的历史条件下，各国、各地区吸引跨国、跨界投资竞争的根本，集中体现为包括法律服务在内的各种服务的提供与竞争。法律服务体系是否完善不仅是决定社会经济环境质量的重要因素，而且已经成为影响外商投资的关键环节，法律服务体系是一个围绕法律作用的动态系统。科学的法律服务体系从广义上理解，包括立法、执法和司法等法制运行的方方面面。从狭义上可理解为能够适应时代需求，司法行政部门所管理的各种法律服务有机联合的整体，包括律师、公证、法律援助、司法鉴定、基层法律服务以及人民调解等，这些服务渗透到社会政治、经济、文化等多个领域，形成多层次、多功能，全面适应和满足社会发展需要的法律服务格局。这些法律服务既是一种提供事务性帮助和提供具有法律意义服务的活动，具有现代服务业市场化、商业化的一般特征，同时又具有司法专属性、法律职业性等自身特点。

（一）中国—东盟自由贸易区运行中的法律服务体系

法律服务水平，特别是律师法律服务水平是衡量一个国家法治发达程度的重要标志。法治发达国家必须有成熟、完善和发达的法律服务业。因此，中国—东盟自由贸易区的运行，无论是其内在要求，还是其外在表现，必须有与之配套的法律服务体系，这既是中国—东盟自由贸易区顺利运行的重要保障，也是中国—东盟自由贸易区运行的重要内容。司法行政机关要适应新形势、新任务的需要，着力构建以律师法律服务为龙头，以公证、基层法律服务、司法鉴定、人民调解、社区矫正为骨架的中国—东盟自由贸易区运行法律服务体系，在为中国—东盟自由贸易区运行提供法律服务的同时，促进法律服务业地科学健康发展。

在为中国—东盟自由贸易区运行提供法律服务的过程中，要确立“大服务”思想，实施“大服务”战略，即律师、公证、司法鉴定行业在服务空间上应“无处不在”，应覆盖中国—东盟自由贸易区运行的各个方面、领域；在服务期间上应做到“无时不有”，要搞好超前服务、跟踪服务和延伸服务；在服务内容上应“无事不用”，围绕中国—东盟自由贸易区运行的重点领域，在培育市场主体、维护市场经济秩序、维护社会和谐稳定，在生产、分配、交换、消费

等各个环节提供法律服务;在服务对象上"无所不容",既包括公民、法人、国家机关和各种社会组织,也包括国内外的各种市场主体。因此,律师、公证、司法鉴定等法律服务行业在中国—东盟自由贸易区运行中必须积极探索、勇于实践,在优化特长、强化职能、硬化作为、深化改革上实现新突破。具体而言,有如下几方面:

1.规范和拓展律师法律服务,为中国—东盟自由贸易区运行"导航"。法律服务涉及诸多方面,但律师是提供法律服务的主体力量。律师工作是法律服务体系中最重要、最主要的要素。中国—东盟自由贸易区的运行不是单向度的,也不是平面状地,而是一个多向度、全方位内引外联、通江达海的立体状态,由此决定了中国—东盟自由贸易区的运行对于我国而言是以外向型经济为主的战略,我国法律服务业在该战略中的定位也应当确立以服务外向型经济的非诉讼领域为主,尽快转变以传统的诉讼业务为主的思想观念,不仅要精通法律、具有丰富的政治、社会、经济、科技和其他知识,还必须尽快熟悉和掌握国际经济贸易知识、东南亚国家法律知识和东盟法律制度,只有这样,法律服务业在中国—东盟自由贸易区运行中才能做到得心应手。

2.发挥公证证明作用,为中国—东盟自由贸易区运行"铺路"。公证是公证机构根据自然人、法人或者其他组织的申请,依照法定程序对民事法律行为、有法律意义的事实和文书的真实性、合法性予以证明的活动,是国际通行的证明制度。涉外经济、民事公证文书在域外具有与国内相同的法律证明力,在国际上得到广泛的承认,是进行国际间民事、经济交往不可缺少的法律文书。因此,公证行业要紧紧围绕中国—东盟自由贸易区的运行,通过公证在民事活动中规范当事人的行为,明确当事人的权利义务,最终达到预防纠纷、减少诉讼,降低中国—东盟自由贸易区的运行成本的目的。

3.发挥司法鉴定证据作用,为中国—东盟自由贸易区的运行提供科学的鉴别和判断意见。司法鉴定是指在诉讼活动中,鉴定人运用科学技术或专门知识对诉讼涉及的专门性问题进行鉴别和判断,提供鉴定意见的活动。在中国—东盟自由贸易区运行中,诉讼是不可避免的,及时、正确的解决争议有利于及时化解纠纷,从而让自贸区运行更加顺利。在这一领域,司法鉴定业同样大有作为。

(二)中国—东盟自由贸易区运行中的法律服务的特点

中国—东盟自由贸易区运行中的法律服务既具有传统意义上法律服务

的特点，包括服务性、专业性、广泛性等，同时又具有其自身的特点。就其自身的特点而言，至少具有以下两个特点：

1. 涉外性。显然，中国—东盟自由贸易区运行中的法律服务是以涉外服务为主的，这就要求我们的法律服务要改变过去以国内法律服务为主的现状，把涉外法律服务作为一个重点区研究和实践，要花大力气去研究东南亚国家的法律制度和东盟国际组织的法律制度。东南亚国家在历史上曾经有受西方殖民者长期统治的历史，有的曾是西方大陆法国家的殖民地，有的曾是英美法国家的殖民地，这些经历导致东南亚国家的法律呈现多元化、复合性的特点；这一地区还有一个区域性的政府间国际组织——东盟，这个组织也有一系列经济领域的多边条约；10 个东南亚国家除老挝外还都是 WTO 的成员，WTO 各项制度在这一地区同样具有约束力。要深入研究以上这些相关法律制度，才能使法律服务具有针对性和准确性。

2. 针对性。中国—东盟自由贸易区的运行对我国而言，主要是面向东南亚国家的，这就给我国法律服务业指出了一个明确的方向，即面向东盟国家。我国的法律服务业制度应向东盟国家延伸，拓展我国法律服务业的市场。

二、法律服务在中国—东盟自由贸易区运行过程中的重要性

2010 年 1 月 1 日，中国—东盟自由贸易区如期建成。自贸区的建成对我国与这一地区的经贸合作带来巨大的机会，我国与东盟国家的投资、贸易合作不断发展，2009 年，中国对东盟国家非金融直接投资额达 22.95 亿美元，同比增长了 5.5%，中国企业在东盟国家承包工程和劳务合作，完成营业额 115 亿美元，同比增长 26.4%。截至 2010 年上半年，双方累计相互投资总额约 694 亿美元，其中东盟对华投资累计约 598 亿美元，中国对东盟非金融类投资累计约 96 亿美元。[①] 据海关统计，2010 年 1—9 月，中国与东盟双边贸易总值达 2113 亿美元，同比劲增 43.7%，其中中方对东盟贸易逆差达 122.5 亿美元，与之相较，2009 年同期贸易逆差仅为 9 亿美元。

10 月 21 日，广西社科院副院长古小松告诉记者，目前中国与东盟 10

① http://www.tradehn.com/news/news.aspx? id=173678，访问日期：2010 年 10 月 24 日。

国经济均较去年回暖,预计今年双边贸易额将超过 2500 亿美元。[①] 但投资贸易急剧增长的过程中也逐步暴露出一些问题,其中法律服务的缺失便是一个亟待解决和事关可持续性的问题。一些有能力、有优势的企业也很想在中国—东盟自由贸易区的蛋糕里分得一块,但由于对周边国家的法律不熟悉而裹足不前,坐失良机;一些企业虽然走出去了,但由于缺乏对当地法律的了解而在经营过程中遇到了税收、金融、劳动、保险、环境保护等法律问题甚至产生纠纷,影响了经济合作的顺利进行,法律服务的重要性日益凸显。与此同时,我国法律服务业对外特别是对我国与东盟国家开展投资贸易的企业提供法律服务的能力和水平也不能满足现实需求,甚至没有把“中国—东盟自由贸易区法律服务”提上议事日程,这个问题是否能得到及时解决,将关系到中国—东盟自由贸易区能否正常运行和为双方带来利益。

三、法律服务在中国—东盟自由贸易区运行过程中的地位和作用

这里说的法律服务是指狭义的法律服务,仅指律师、公证和司法鉴定业在民商事活动中或诉讼活动中为当事人提供法律上的帮助的活动。

(一)法律服务在中国—东盟自由贸易区运行过程中的地位

中国—东盟自由贸易区的运行需要更加良好的法治环境、稳定和谐的社会秩序,因此,律师、公证和司法鉴定等法律服务业在中国—东盟自由贸易区运行中是一个不可缺少的、发挥保障性作用的、独立的重要主体。有了这个主体,中国—东盟自由贸易区才能在法治的轨道上有序运行,形成良性循环并健康发展。[②]

(二)法律服务在中国—东盟自由贸易区运行过程中的作用

律师、公证和司法鉴定等法律服务行业由于其职业的性质和属性决定了这些行业在中国—东盟自由贸易区的运行中具有提供服务、反映诉求、规

---

① http://news.sina.com.cn/c/sd/2010-10-22/181021332846.shtml,访问日期:2010 年 10 月 24 日。

② 何剑文、汪洋、米良:《桥头堡建设法律研究与实务》,中共中央党校出版社 2010 年 10 月版。

范行为等方面的职能作用。根据法律服务业的职能和中国—东盟自由贸易区的特点，法律服务业在中国东盟自由贸易区运行中可以发挥以下作用：

1. 参谋助手作用。律师、公证、司法鉴定等法律服务工作者要紧紧围绕建设法治政府的目标，完善政府法律顾问团（组），加强政府法律顾问工作，促进政府依法行政和科学决策，为各级人大、政府出台推动中国—东盟自由贸易区运行的法律法规和规范性文件以及涉及经济决策、产业结构调整、转型升级、扩大投资领域等宏观调控措施提供法律意见和建议；加强针对经济开发区、高新技术产业园区等经济转型升级要素相对集中区域政府派驻机构的法律服务，积极为各级党委政府依法决策、依法行政提供法律依据和理论参考，规范行政执法行为，提高依法行政的水平。要深入了解社情民意，利用专业优势，通过提交议案、向政府有关部门反映等形式，架好人民群众与政府间沟通的桥梁。要围绕完善社会主义法律体系的要求，积极参与法案起草、修改，努力参与立法活动和国家政治生活，促进市场经济法律体系的成熟完善，推动我国的法治进程。组织律师、公证员通过担任企业法律顾问、代理民事诉讼和非诉讼法律事务等形式，为重大工程项目建设提供全程法律服务。对建设项目的合法性、可行性等进行分析论证，参与建设项目的公示和听证，依法出具法律意见书；参与建设项目工程勘察设计、施工、监理及工程设备的招投标工作，对招投标活动进行现场监督；根据当事人的委托，审查、起草和修改有关合同和协议，参与纠纷的调解，代理纠纷的诉讼或仲裁；根据企业的委托，审查、起草和修改有关合同和协议，参与纠纷的调解，代理纠纷的诉讼或仲裁等。

2. 发挥规范作用，为市场经济主体依法经营、依法办事提供制度约束。市场经济是法治经济，特别是在对外开放中，市场经济主体的一切行为必须在法治框架下运行。律师、公证、司法鉴定工作可以为促进经济发展方式转变、推进结构调整和自主创新，规范市场经济主体的法律行为提供制度参考和专业意见，如律师可以为就招商项目进行法律可行性论证，出具法律意见书；接受招商部门或单位的委托，对投资方的法人资格和诚信状况进行调查，提供法律咨询，审查修改法律文书，排除法律障碍；为投资商担任专项或常年法律顾问，为其进行工商登记、行政许可申请及其它具体法律事务等提供全过程服务。为投融资项目的合法性、可行性出具法律咨询意见；为投融资项目的立项、投融资形式、投融资结构及投融资方案出具法律意见书；对投融资项目中涉及的经营、税收、外汇管理等方面的法律问题提供解决方案；对国际投资中可能出现或造成的法律冲突，进而引起的法律风险提供预测、防范等法律意见;协助或参与投融资项目的商务谈判。同时,律师还可以为国内外企业提供法律风险评估、融资引资、劳资关系、市场营销、产权转让、兼并重组、破产清算等方面法律事务;帮助各类企业建立健全企业重大投资、重要经营合同、资产处置、改制改组、知识产权保护等一系列企业内部经营管理制度;为企业提供法律培训、代理办理企业设立、投资、重组、改制、上市等方面的法律事务。公证机构为企业提供商标、专利、著作权的权属证明、许可协议、转让协议及保全证据等公证服务,为企业间买卖租赁、加工承揽、技术转让、建筑工程、贷款抵押、仓储保管等经济活动提供合同协议公证,保障交易安全等。

3.发挥疏导作用,为中国—东盟自由贸易区运行提供稳定和谐的社会环境。疏导和化解社会矛盾,保持社会各种利益的平衡,是构建和谐社会、保障中国—东盟自由贸易区健康运行的基础环节。随着我国社会的逐步转型,特别是利益主体多元化格局的形成和发展,社会矛盾日趋复杂化和多样化,迫切要求建立和完善包括诉讼在内的多元化的纠纷解决机制。实践证明,律师、公证等法律服务工作的特殊性在预防和减少各类矛盾纠纷、化解社会矛盾、促进社会和谐中具有不可替代的作用,律师、公证、司法鉴定人员可以为各级党委、政府运用法律手段推进社会管理创新、疏导化解各种社会矛盾提供法律帮助。广大法律服务工作者在认真做好法庭辩护、诉讼代理、公证证明、司法鉴定等业务的同时,积极参与“大调解”工作体系建设,充分发挥法律服务工作的专业优势,采取诉前调解、庭内调解、庭外和解和其他非诉讼手段,引导当事人借助法律手段调节利益关系,依法表达利益诉求,促进建立科学有效的利益诉求表达机制和矛盾纠纷化解机制,把化解社会矛盾纳入法制化轨道;参与建立社会稳定风险评估机制,为各级党委、政府制定处置重大突发事件和群体性事件的政策措施、工作方案提供法律意见。疏导群众情绪,促成事件依法有序解决;协调解决企业改制、征地拆迁、教育医疗、环境保护、安全生产、食品药品安全等领域发生的法律问题;及时为农村新型合作医疗、农民养老保险、民间借贷、抚养协议、财产继承和分割等提供优质高效服务,最大限度地消除矛盾纠纷和隐患。

4.发挥桥梁作用,为促进中国法律服务界与东盟国家法律服务界的交流与合作搭建平台。中国—东盟自由贸易区的运行涉及包括经济、政治、文化等各个领域在内的对外开放与合作,是一个复杂的系统工程,需要律师、公证等法律服务的保驾护航。同时,律师、公证等行业的对外交流合作本身也是一个重要内容,要适应新形势、新要求,通过举办论坛、搭建法律文化、法律制度交流合作平台等方式，积极、稳妥、有步骤、有计划地推进律师、公证等法律服务市场的对外开放、对外交流与合作，制定并落实与东盟国家法律服务业交流合作的具体优惠政策，开展与境外律师、公证、司法鉴定行业的交流、合作。吸引国内及外国律师事务所进入我国法律服务市场，鼓励我国律师事务所拓展境外法律服务市场，参与国际竞争。

5.发挥救济作用，预防和化解中国—东盟自由贸易区运行中的各种纠纷。中国—东盟自由贸易区运行不但涉及国内企业生产经营管理中的各种矛盾纠纷，而且涉及转变经济增长，实施“走出去”、“引进来”等对外开放中的矛盾纠纷，不但涉及中国的法律制度，而且涉及国际贸易规则、涉及相关国家的法律制度以及纠纷解决机制，律师、公证工作在这些方面都具有得天独厚的优势和作用。特别要充分发挥公证工作预防纠纷的功能作用，积极开展产权关系公证、开展事前证据保全公证等，预防和减少经济贸易中各种纠纷。①

① 何剑文、汪洋、米良:《桥头堡建设法律研究与实务》，中共中央党校出版社 2010 年 10 月版。

On Roles and Functions of Legal Service in the Implementation of CAFTA

Chen Yundong Mi liang*

Abstract

January 1, 2010, to complete the China-ASEAN Free Trade Area. The completion of the FTA will trade and economic cooperation in this region offers great opportunities, but the operation of the FTA must orbit the rule of law, be possible to have sustainable. China - ASEAN Free Trade Area is inseparable from legal services, legal services, China-ASEAN Free Trade Area of the normal operation of the protection of health.

Keywords: Legal Service; CAFTA; Function

Content

- The System and the Characteristics of the Legal Service in the Operation of CAFTA
- The Importance of the Legal Service Under the CAFTA
- The Role and Status of the Legal Service Under the CAFTA

---

* Chen Yundong, dean and professor of Law School of Yunnan University, PH. D, mainly engaging in the research of international economic law; Mi Liang, professor of Law School of Yunnan University, director of ASEAN Legal Research Center, mainly engining in the research of ASEAN law.

中国律师涉东盟法律服务面临的机遇、问题及其对策

凌 斌*

内容摘要

中国—东盟自由贸易区经济、贸易及投资合作发展的良好态势为中国律师开展涉东盟法律服务提供前所未有的机遇，律师涉东盟法律服务机遇主要表现在投资、贸易、知识产权等领域，律师把握涉东盟法律服务机遇有赖于语言能力、专业水平等方面能力的提高及信息沟通、协助合作平台的构建。

关键词：中国—东盟自由贸易区；法律服务；律师

目 次

中国—东盟自由贸易区（以下简称自贸区）系全部由发展中国家组成的世界上最大的自由贸易区，至 2010 年 1 月 1 日自贸区建立时，自贸区内人口超 19 亿，GDP 接近 6 万亿美元，贸易总额达 4.5 亿美元。为建成自贸区，中国与

* 凌斌，广西万益律师事务所律师、合伙人，中国—东盟法律研究中心研究员。

东盟分别签署了《中华人民共和国政府与东南亚国家联盟成员国政府全面经济合作框架协议》(以下称框架协议)、《框架协议货物贸易协议》(以下称货物贸易协议)、《框架协议争端解决机制协议》(以下称争端解决机制协议)、《框架协议服务贸易协议》(以下称服务贸易协议)、《框架协议投资协议》(以下称投资协议)。前述协议的签署及自贸区的建立,促进各缔约方之间的经济、贸易及投资合作,作为为经济发展提供法律服务的中国律师,面临前所未有的机遇及挑战。

一、中国律师涉东盟法律服务面临的机遇

经济基础决定上层建筑,法律服务机遇总是伴随经济贸易的发展而产生。分析自贸区经济、贸易及投资合作发展的态势,可以了解律师涉东盟法律服务面临的机遇。律师涉东盟法律服务机遇主要表现在投资、贸易、知识产权等领域。

(一)中国律师涉东盟投资法律服务面临的机遇

1. 中国与东盟相互投资现状及特点

自2002年11月框架协议签署后,中国与东盟相互间投资不断扩大。2003年,东盟对中国投资为29.3亿美元,中国对东盟投资仅为1.89亿美元。2009年,东盟对中国投资额为46.8亿美元,中国对东盟投资为30亿元。截至2009年底,中国与东盟相互间累计实际投资额接近600亿美元。

中国与东盟相互投资存在如下特点:

(1)投资由单向性发展为双向性。框架协议签署前,中国与东盟投资关系基本上是单向进行,中国是投资目的地,东盟是投资来源地。框架协议签署后,中国与东盟投资关系逐渐呈现双向发展态势。中国企业已将东盟作为主要投资目的地之一。

(2)投资地域分布不平衡。东盟对中国投资的来源地相对集中,主要是新加坡、马来西亚、菲律宾等国,投资的目的地亦相对集中,主要是珠三角区域、长三角区域、福建省、山东省等地。中国对东盟的投资目的地主要集中在新加坡、缅甸、柬埔寨、印尼、越南等国。

(3)投资产业结构有所差异。东盟对中国投资基本上投向制造、房地产及旅游等劳动密集型和资金密集型行业,较少涉足技术密集型行业。中国对东盟的投资除投向机械制造、交通、能源等劳动密集型和资金密集型行业外,重

点向技术密集型行业发展，近年来涉足生物制药、电子信息、化工、电气等行业，与东盟投资的产业结构有所差异。

2. 涉东盟投资法律服务的机遇

(1)为东盟企业在中国投资提供法律服务的机遇

①东盟对中国投资逐年稳定增长，越来越多的东盟企业进入中国的各个领域进行投资，其需要知悉涉及市场准入、投资壁垒、土地管理、税收优惠、投资保障、外汇管理等中国的相关投资法律、政策，而向中国律师购买前述法律服务是其了解中国相关法律规定及保障其合法权益的最佳途径。

②在中国经济转型的大背景下，东盟已在中国投资的劳动密集型及资金密集型企业将不可避免的进行调整甚至发生产业转移。在企业产业调整及转移的过程当中，劳资整合、易地搬迁、关停转产、投资建设等经济事件层出不穷，需要在中国法律的框架内和谐处理，法律服务与企业寻求发展和进步过程中共生共赢。

(2)为中国企业在东盟投资提供法律服务的机遇

中国对东盟投资迅猛发展，投资目的地已遍布东盟各成员国。中国企业赴东盟投资前，需要了解中国对有关境外投资管理规定、境外投资行为规范；投资目的地国对市场准入、投资壁垒、土地管理、税收优惠、外汇管理的法律及政策；WTO 投资机制及争端解决机制、自贸区投资协议及争端解决机制等，中国律师可向中国企业提供咨询服务及其他法律服务。

(二)中国律师涉东盟贸易法律服务面临的机遇

1. 中国与东盟贸易现状及特点

2003 年以来，中国与东盟的贸易一直保持逆差态势。2009 年中国对东盟贸易额为 2130.11 亿美元，其中出口 1062.97 亿美元，进口 1067.14 亿美元。2010 年截至 8 月份，中国对东盟贸易额为 1854 亿美元，其中进口 973 亿美元，同比增长 54%，出口 881 亿美元，同比增长 40%。在服务贸易方面，东盟是中国对外承包工程的重要市场，2003 年至 2008 年中国对东盟承包工程完成营业额由 17.61 亿美元增至 46.7 亿美元，平均增长 21.5%；东盟是中国最大海外劳动市场，新加坡、印度尼西亚、马来西亚、缅甸、泰国和越南是中国对东盟劳务输出的主要国家。

中国与东盟贸易存在如下特点：

(1)基本实现“零”关税。自贸区建成后，中国对东盟的平均关税从之前的 9.8%降至 0.1%，东盟 6 个老成员国文莱、印度尼西亚、马来西亚、菲律宾、新加坡、泰国对中国的平均关税从12.8%降低至0.6%。

(2)贸易额增长较快。如前述,2010年截至8月份,中国对东盟进出口贸易额同比均增长40%以上,远远高于中国整体进出口增幅。

(3)贸易对象相对集中。中国主要的贸易国为马来西亚、新加坡、泰国。

(4)服务贸易发展良好。为满足服务贸易发展的需要,2010年第七届中国—东盟博览会增加了服务贸易专题。与东盟相比,中国在旅游、建筑、计算机与信息服务、个人文化与休闲等行业存在比较优势。

(5)贸易的商品结构优化。进出口商品结构日益改善,逐步由初级产品向工业制成品尤其是机电产品和高新技术产品方向发展。

2. 涉东盟贸易法律服务面临的机遇

(1)为中国企业出口贸易提供法律服务的机遇

中国企业开展出口贸易主要关注中国出口管理、出口退税、相关规定及出口目的地成员国的进口管理、海关管理、检验检疫、关税制度、贸易壁垒、外汇管理、贸易救济措施、贸易争端解决机制等相关规定。出口贸易量的增长将导致买卖合同、货物运输、信用证、通关、退税、诉讼、仲裁等传统法律业务的增长。此外,自贸区建成后关税壁垒基本消失,反倾销、反补贴、保障措施、技术壁垒已成为各国贸易竞争的主要手段,为出口企业提供相关预防及应诉服务将成为律师业务增长点。

(2)为中国企业进口贸易提供法律服务的机遇

中国企业开展进口贸易主要关注出口国出口管理、中国进口管理、海关管理、检验检疫、关税制度、贸易壁垒、外汇管理、贸易救济措施、贸易争端解决机制等相关规定。律师可为之提供咨询及相关法律服务。譬如:服务贸易协议签署后,各成员国之间自然人流动更加便利,与部分经济发展水平较低的东盟成员国相比,中国的工资及社会福利水平具有明显优势,将吸引东盟部分成员国大批劳动力。自然人的跨国流动对大多数中国企业而言是新生事物,如何趋利避害有赖于律师的专业服务。

(三)中国律师涉东盟知识产权法律服务面临的机遇

1. 中国与东盟知识产权现状及特点

自贸区各成员经贸活动的进行,与知识产权的流动相辅相成;相对成熟的国际贸易和国际投资活动中都蕴含着知识产权的成分。中国—东盟博览会自举办以来,一直将高新技术作为会议主题之一。自贸区各成员国中,除老挝尚未最终加入WTO外,其他成员国均已经是WTO正式成员国。自贸区各成员国都是世界知识产权组织（WIPO）的成员国，但加入的公约不尽相同。中国、柬埔寨、印度尼西亚、老挝、马来西亚、菲律宾、新加坡、越南系《保护工业产权巴黎公约》成员国；中国、新加坡、印度尼西亚、菲律宾、柬埔寨、老挝系《世界版权公约》成员国；中国、菲律宾、泰国系《伯尔尼保护文学和艺术作品公约》成员国；中国、新加坡、越南系《马德里协定议定书》成员国；中国、印度尼西亚、老挝、马来西亚、菲律宾、新加坡、泰国、越南系《专利合作公约》成员国。

中国与东盟知识产权存在如下特点：

(1)自贸区各成员都是 WIPO 成员国并分别加入部分公约，加入公约的各成员国权利及义务的行使及救济有法可依。中国是自贸区加入 WIPO 公约最多的国家之一。

(2)自贸区各成员国之间知识产权发展水平与保护水平参差不齐，中国知识产权发展水平与保护水平较高。

2. 涉东盟知识产权法律服务的机遇

“经济贸易投资，知识产权先行”，框架协议第 7 条将知识产权作为合作扩展的领域并把技术转让作为加强合作的措施。中国与东盟之间的投资和贸易迅速发展以及贸易商品结构的优化必然导致各成员国企业在本国及在他国获得知识产权保护的需求。各成员国企业日益重视知识产权战略的制定与实施，以获取并保持市场竞争优势，知识产权的创设、运用、管理、保护等业务将持续增长。

(1)为中国企业对东盟投资、贸易提供知识产权法律服务的机遇

中国企业对东盟投资、贸易关注如下涉及知识产权尤其是涉及商标和专利的规定：中国知识产权部门法、知识产权边境措施、中国与投资贸易目的地成员国共同加入的 WIPO 公约、投资贸易目的地国家知识产权边境措施、该国知识产权部门法及该国知识产权司法政策等。

(2)为东盟企业对中国投资、贸易提供知识产权法律服务的机遇

东盟企业对中国投资、贸易关注如下涉及知识产权尤其是涉及商标和专利的规定：东盟企业本国知识产权部门法、知识产权边境措施、该国与中国共同加入的 WIPO 公约、中国知识产权边境措施、中国知识产权部门法及知识产权司法政策等。

二、中国律师把握涉东盟法律服务机遇面临的问题

(一)语言能力不足,阻碍有效交流

东盟各成员国除新加坡和菲律宾官方语言为英语外,各国官方语言均不相同且属小语种。中国精通东盟各成员国语言特别是小语种的律师极少,与东盟企业沟通存在隔阂,难以进行有效交流。

(二)缺少权威译本,东盟信息不全

中国精通东盟各成员国小语种的法学家或精通法律的小语种翻译家极少,东盟各成员国相关法律、法规、政策的中文译本匮乏且未经权威机构认定。由于权威信息的缺失,中国律师对东盟各成员国相关法律、法规、政策缺乏准确、全面的了解。

(三)律所品牌有限,专业能力不强

中国律师事务所品牌知名度不高,缺乏完善的内部管理制度,承担执业风险能力较差,难以满足与东盟各成员国特别是较发达成员国律师事务所业务接轨的需要。中国律师参与中国对东盟经济贸易、投资合作机会不多,专业化程度不高,缺乏在国际法、国际条约、WTO规则、国际贸易、投资融资、反倾销、反补贴、保障措施、技术壁垒等方面学有专长的律师。

(四)竞争处于劣势,服务机遇流失

服务贸易协议虽然没有法律服务的具体承诺,但却约定适用《服务贸易总协定》。《服务贸易总协定》中,界定了服务贸易的四种方式:跨境服务、境外消费、商业存在和自然人流动。除商业存在较难实现外,其他三种法律服务贸易方式容易实现,客观上存在竞争。由于东盟各成员国华侨较多,中国改革开放较早,东盟各成员国部分律师精通中国语言,了解中国法律及政策。东盟律师在东盟各成员国对中国投资、贸易相关非诉讼法律业务承接上较中国律师而言具备竞争优势,导致本来属于中国律师的业务流失。

三、中国律师把握东盟法律服务机遇的对策

(一)加强语言学习,消除交流障碍

中国律师应加强对东盟各成员国语言的学习,尤其是对中国与东盟投资、贸易的主要国家新加坡、菲律宾、马来西亚、泰国等国语言的学习,提高语言水平。中国律师事务所还可以利用中国经济、社会发展程度较高的优势,吸引部分东盟国家既懂中文又懂法律的人才为中国律师事务所工作。

(二)构建专业团队,提高专业水平

随着自贸区各成员国经济、贸易、投资合作的深入发展,企业对法律服务的需求日益细化。中国律师事务所应找准定位、统一理念、完善管理、树立品牌、专业分工、团队协作,为企业提供优质、高效的法律服务以满足企业的实际需要。

(三)借助社会力量,获取东盟信息

律师应主动与对东盟法律有研究的政府机构、社会团体、高等院校、各国使领馆及商务代表处等联系,取得东盟各成员国相关尤其是投资、贸易、知识产权方面的权威法律、政策等资料。

(四)建立协作网络,实现资源共享

个体的力量无疑是有限的,有志于涉东盟业务的中国律师事务所之间应加强联系、交流信息、取长补短、深化协作,避免重复建设,实现资源共享。中国律师事务所还应积极与东盟各成员法律服务机构建立战略合作关系,互通有无,实现利益共享。

参考文献

1. 邓志勇、文彩云:《水润花开、共享硕果》,载《南国早报》2010 年 10 月 20 日,第 4 版。

2. 陈宇航:《中国与东盟国家间投资法律保障问题的研究》,载《中国—东盟诉讼法律理论与民事行政检察制度专题的研讨会优秀论文汇编》。

3. 易在成:《构建中国与东盟自由贸易区知识产权协调制度》,http://

blog.sina.com.cn/blog_69da7edf0100kkys.html。

4. 张晓君:《中国—东盟〈服务贸易协议〉与中国服务业的发展》,载《河北法学》2010年第3期。

5. 陈承帼:《法律服务贸易的发展前景》,载《西部律师论丛第三届西部律师发展论坛的优秀论文集》,广西教育出版社2010年版。

6. 刘树森:《中国—东盟自由贸易区丛书2》,广西师范大学出版社2009年版。

Opportunities, Problems and Strategy of Chinese Lawyers in Providing Legal Service Involving ASEAN Affairs

Ling Bin *

Abstract

The prosperous development of the economy, trade and investment co-operation in China-AESAN Free Trade Area has provided good opportunities for Chinese lawyers. The opportunities have manifested themselves mainly in the spheres in investment, trade, IP etc. To grasp those opportunities depends on the improvement of the language capacity and professional standard, as well as the construction of the information communication and the assistant co-operating platform.

Keywords: China-AESAN Free Trade Area; Legal service; Lawyer

Content

- The Opportunities facing the Chinese Lawyers related to the CAFTA Legal Services
- The Problems and the Challenges for the Chinese Lawyers
- The Relative Countermeasures the Chinese Lawyers may consider

* Ling Bin, partner & lawyer of Guangxi Wanyi Law Firm, researcher of the China-ASEAN Legal Research Center.

加强区域合作 构筑中国—东盟法律服务大通道

马 巍*

内容摘要

目前,中国已成为东盟第一大贸易伙伴,中国与东盟也互为主要投资国家。中国与东盟国家如此巨大的经贸往来,中国企业广泛参与东盟贸易和投资,必然需要法律保驾护航,这其中蕴涵了巨大的法律服务需求,为中国的国际化法律服务提供了巨大的增长空间,给中国律师拓展国际法律服务创造了历史性机遇,同时也对中国律师提出了较大挑战。拓展东盟法律服务市场,构筑中国—东盟法律服务大通道,需要中国律师和法律服务机构的积极参与,需要律师不断增强专业服务能力、创新法律服务方式、提高法律服务质量。积极探索与东盟各国优秀律师事务所合作模式,构建法律服务网络,推进中国—东盟法律服务大通道建设。

关键词: 区域合作;中国—东盟;法律服务通道

目 次

---

* 马巍,一级律师,北京大成(昆明)律师事务所主任,大成律师事务所高级合伙人,东盟专业委员会主任,全国优秀律师,云南省律师协会副会长,中华全国律师协会理事,云南省法学会常务理事,博士。

在经济全球化的推动下，中国与东盟的合作领域日益拓宽，相互投资日渐增长，无疑给双方的发展带了更多的机遇。自 2002 年中国与东盟签署建自由贸易区基本文件以来，双方逐渐减免关税、开放市场，一个由 11 个国家组成的统一大市场正在形成①，中国与东盟各国的自由贸易政策广泛惠及这一区域内传统的货物贸易领域和服务贸易体系。

回顾 2008 年全球金融危机，世界诸多国家的经济增长受到严重影响。然而，中国经济的继续增长不仅让在全球主要经济体侧目，在亚太地区，中国也继续发挥着经济增长火车头的重要作用，中国与东盟国家之间的经贸往来呈现出一派经济复苏的景象。温家宝总理在 2010 年 10 月 29 日越南河内举行的第十三次中国与东盟领导人会议上谈到："无论国际风云如何变幻，中国与东盟的政治互信不断加深，战略沟通与协作更加密切，维护了地区和平与稳定。中国已成为东盟第一大贸易伙伴。"

一、中国及东盟各国法律服务业面临巨大机遇，承担着历史性使命

(一)中国与东盟国家的经贸往来密切

中国与东盟国家的双边贸易额与日俱增。在 2002 年，双边贸易额为 500 亿美元；2004 年，突破 1000 亿美元；2005 年，增长到 1303.7 亿美元；2010 年 1 月至 8 月，双边贸易额已达 1854 亿美元。其中，中国从东盟进口 973 亿美元，同比增长 54%；对东盟出口 881 亿美元，同比增长 40%。

从投资领域来看，中国与东盟间相互投资迅猛增长。2010 年上半年，东盟对中国直接投资约 31 亿美元，中国对东盟非金融类直接投资约 12 亿美元。截至 2010 年 6 月底，双方累计相互投资 694 亿美元，其中东盟对中国投资累计 598 亿美元，中国对东盟累计投资 96 亿美元。

目前的中国已成为东盟第一大贸易伙伴。同时，中国与东盟也互为主要投资国家。中国与东盟国家如此巨大的经贸往来，必然蕴涵着巨大的法律服务需求，这是市场经济的基本规律。

---

① 《中国东盟自由贸易区开放时间表》，http://baike.baidu.com/view/351255.htm，访问日期：2010 年 8 月 1 日。

(二)亚太地区的法律服务市场,中国的国际化法律服务具有巨大的增长空间

回顾2005年世界法律服务业市值分布,美国占了49.1%,达到1927亿美元;欧洲地区占37.7%,为1480亿美元;亚太地区所占比例较小,仅为5.7%,市值为230亿美元。

另外,从2005年世界法律从业人员分布情况上看,美国和欧洲占了绝大多数比例,两者的比例分别为40%和37%,即法律从业人员数分别为81.78万和76.78万;亚太地区则占15%,法律从业人员仅有30.39万人。

可见,欧美法律服务业发展较成熟,同时反衬出了亚太地区法律服务业具有巨大的开发空间。

(三)企业走向国际市场,迫切需要法律手段保驾护航

当国内企业选择走向国际市场时,必然面临一系列风险,对于破除企业在国际贸易往来中可能面临的各种风险,消除各方分歧,促进各方合作,使中国—东盟自由贸易区保持快速、稳定和健康的发展,法律手段的保护显得尤为重要。

目前,企业在面对国际市场时,主要存在以下风险:

首先,对东道国政策法律不熟悉而导致风险:国家征用制度、外商投资制度、商贸制度、特许经营权制度、金融制度、税收制度、土地制度、技术转让制度、知识产权制度、劳动制度、环保制度、海关制度、争端解决度等政策的连续性、法律的稳定性。

其次,对国际法不熟悉而导致风险:本国与东道国的投资保护、避免双重征税等条约、促进跨国投资的政策。

最后,对本国国内备案(审批)不熟悉而导致风险:发改委、商务部、外汇管理局的审批备案,财政、税收、金融、外汇等政策。

国家之间的经济交往主要通过企业来实现,法律是为国家的社会经济发展服务的,在中国与东盟友好往来、互利共赢的过程中,为各国企业的国际经济交往提供法律保障,就成了中国及东盟国家法律从业人员的历史性使命。

(四)中国—东盟合作下各国律师迎来极佳的发展契机

目前,中国政治环境稳定,法律体系和制度健全并日益完善,市场经济繁荣,这不但为中国律师业的蓬勃发展奠定了良好的基础,同时也为外国律师及外国律师事务所的国际化发展带来了难得的契机。各国律师为中国—东盟的

经贸往来提供法律服务，既有助于加强跨国投资者对东道国投资环境、投资政策的了解，又有利于缩小因文化、语言、法律体系不同造成的跨国投资阻碍，还有利于增加跨国投资者在东道国投资的信心。

随着中国和东盟各国投资者的法律服务需求日渐增多，法律服务的内容和方式也随之变化和丰富，这无疑给各国律师带来了巨大的发展机遇。

二、中国律师业为中国企业走向东南亚、南亚保驾护航的能力亟待提高

从2010年底至2011年初，笔者多次出访东南亚各国，研究发现，现阶段中国律师面向东南亚、南亚的法律服务基本上处于缺乏系统组织和管理的单打独斗阶段，难以满足中国企业的法律服务需求，普遍表现为：

第一，法律服务团队没有实现规模化、集群化。笔者认为，就西南地区而言存在律师人力资源的怪圈，表现为小个体成长为大个体，大个体孵化小个体，小个体又成长为大个体，它继续孵化小个体；循环往复，以至无穷。法律服务团队没有实现规模化、集群化作业。

第二，信息滞后。中国多年来把对外投资重点放在以美国、日本为首的发达国家国债和能源等矿产资源采掘上，购买了大量的美国和日本的国债和金融产品，并在非洲等石油矿产资源丰富又与西方保持距离的国家进行了大量的投资。对东南亚国家的中国国家形象和汉文化的宣传明显不足，对东南亚国家投资和贸易增长相对缓慢，明显呈现政治热而经济冷的局面，导致对东南亚国家的法律体系、文化背景、经历贸易管理、国家战略等信息知之甚少，不能稳、准、快地为中国与东南亚国家的经济贸易提供充分的法律服务。

第三，熟悉东南亚、南亚国家法律、语言的人才匮乏。目前就全国而言，学习英语和其他欧盟国家语言的人才较为集中，而大学教育培养东南亚国家的语言的人才较少，且这类人才毕业后因为投资环境尚处于起步阶段，未更进一步对较为高端的法律语言进行学习和研究，故能掌握东南亚国家小语种特别是法律外语的人才缺口巨大。

第四，尚未深入、系统地了解东道国风土人情、社会文化、法律制度。

第五，虽然对国外法律制度有了一定程度的了解，但难以将其真正运用自如，难以有效地为中国企业排忧解难。立足国情方能放眼世界，而我们律师的固有观念仍未能与时俱进，未有充分的热情和机会充分了解国情，了解我国企业特别是中小型企业的现状，故不能做到想客户所想，满足客户所需，导致律

师团队服务与企业发展战略的断裂。

第六,虽然有不少律师在为企业提供法律服务,但服务效率、服务深度和广度均有待提高,量不大、质不高。

可以说,中国的法律服务机构目前针对东盟的法律服务,无法满足中国—东盟法律服务大通道的需要。尽快提高面向中国—东盟法律服务大通道的法律服务水平已经刻不容缓。

三、抓住机遇,践行使命,构筑中国与东盟法律服务大通道

针对现阶段中国法律服务机构面向东盟的法律服务现状,笔者认为提升中国律师业面向东盟法律服务的能力,构筑中国—东盟法律服务大通道应当从以下几个方面着手:

(一)要建立与构筑中国—东盟法律服务大通道相匹配的法律服务网络

1. 突出该法律服务网络的功能

该法律服务网络要突出其互联互通的功能。这主要体现在:一方面,实现国际业务本土化,充分运用东道国的服务资源(包括:人力资源、信息资源、社会资源等)来满足客户的服务需求;另一方面,可以随时调动该法律服务网络内的一切优势资源进行优化配置,为政府、为企业提供法律法规政策研究、个案处理、风险防范等优质服务。

该法律服务网络还将囊括若干国内外机构、人员,例如:本国外贸主管部门、本国法律服务机构、国外的优秀律师事务所及律师、本国驻外国使领馆、相关科研及教学机构,等等。

2. 明确建立法律服务网络的基本方法

目前,构筑中国—东盟法律服务大通道主要是通过在外国设立自己律师事务所的分支机构、与外国的律师事务所签署松散型的合作协议的传统方法。该传统方法的主要缺陷为增加了律师事务所的运营成本,难以实现国际业务本土化,难以及时、有效地配置东道国的优势资源(人力资源、信息资源、社会资源等),且很难以最快的速度满足客户的需求。

针对传统方法的不足与缺陷,很多优秀律所作出积极探索,如大成律师事务所创新提出了与东盟各国优秀的律师事务所之间"签署实质性的合作协议,结成紧密型战略合作伙伴关系,共铸优质法律服务网络"的有效方法。这一方法的优点在于:第一,不用去外国设立自己律师事务所的分支机构,节省人力

资源、物质资源;第二,协议双方可以及时调动对方享有的各种优势资源(人力资源、信息资源、社会资源等),为客户提供优质高效的法律服务,真正实现国际业务本土化,用最快的速度满足客户的需求;第三,相比传统方法,能够有效地控制律师事务所的运营成本,降低财务风险。

(二)构筑中国—东盟法律服务大通道,中国律师业提升法律服务能力基本思路

首先,实行与中国—东盟法律服务大通道法律服务需求相匹配的专业化团队作业模式。

法律服务市场要求法律服务专业化、精品化。这就要求律师事务所着力于推进法律服务团队化作业模式。

推进专业化团队作业,需要具备以下条件:(1)要有在业内有影响,在团队内得到高度认同的业务带头人;(2)业务要有相对稳定的市场份额;(3)要有一批优秀的专业律师;(4)要形成具有特色的法律服务产品;(5)团队成员要形成权益共同体。

其次,制定发展战略,制定战略规划,确定工作目标及工作措施。

律师事务所应当从战略性高度,积极研究东盟法律服务市场的现状、走势,谋划开拓东盟市场的途径、方法。要制定并实施开拓东盟市场的规划;研发及推广面向东盟市场的法律服务产品;要组织、调动各种资源去拓展东盟法律服务市场。例如,北京大成律师事务所在2010年6月成立了“大成律师事务所东盟专业委员会”(以下简称“东盟专业委员会”)。成立至今,东盟专业委员会已走访了东盟国家的泰国、老挝、印度尼西亚、马来西亚、越南、新加坡、柬埔寨等国,对东盟各国经济、文化、产业及涉外投资、法律制度及法治环境等进行了考察,并与相关国家的优秀律师事务所签订了战略合作协议或建立了区域合作伙伴关系。对加速中国—东盟法律服务大通道建设,为推进与东盟国家的全面合作奠定基础。

最后,提高自身素质和业务能力。

对于律师个人而言,应当针对自身实际,扬长避短努力提高自身素质和业务能力。具有大局意识、责任意识、忧患意识,具备团队精神。同时提升自身外语能力,对东南亚各国较为高端的法律语言进行学习和研究,掌握东南亚国家小语种。提升相关领域的专业技能,进一步达到整合资源拓展业务、解决问题的综合能力。

构筑中国—东盟法律服务大通道,将有助于东盟各国之间跨国投资者对东道国投资环境、投资政策的了解,有利于缩小因文化、语言、法律体系不同造成的跨国投资阻碍,有利于增加跨国投资者在东道国投资的信心。通过法律服务,可以防范交易风险,消除各方分歧,促进各方合作,为经贸往来保驾护航,促进中国—东盟自由贸易区的持续、快速、稳定和健康的发展。

Strengthening Regional Cooperation, Constructing A China-ASEAN Legal Service Channel

Ma Wei*

Abstract

Currently, China has become the biggest trade partner of ASEAN. ASEAN and China are the main investment targets of each other. Since economic and trade exchanges are such frequent between China and ASEAN nations, Chinese enterprises are going to widely participate in ASEAN's trade and investment activities. They must require legal escort and consultant. The whole process contains huge legal service demands which will bring a great growth space and a historical opportunity for Chinese lawyers to expand their international legal services. However, it is also proposing a great challenge to the Chinese lawyers. To expand the ASEAN legal service market and to build the great Channel of Legal Service between China and the ASEAN nations, the active participation of all Chinese lawyers and legal service agencies are required. Moreover, the lawyers have to constantly strengthen their professional service ability. Meanwhile, the lawyers shall innovate their legal service mode and improve their legal service quality. We believe that we can explore a cooperation pattern which will help us work with the most outstanding law firms in ASEAN nations actively and efficiently to establish the legal service network and to build the great legal service channel between China and ASEAN nations.

Keywords: Regional Cooperation; China-ASEAN; Legal Service Channel

---

* Ma Wei, first-grade lawyer, director of Beijing Dacheng Law Firm(Kunming), senior partner of Dacheng Law Firm, chief of the ASEAN professional commission, vice-president of the Lawyer's Association in Yunnan Province. Member of council of ACLA., standing director of the Law Society of Yunnan Province, PH. D.

Content

- The Great Opportunity and Historical Work for the Legal Service Sector of the China andASEAN Nations
- The Legal Professional Ability to help the Chinese Enterprises Developing the Southeast Asian and South Asia Market of the Chinese Lawyers Needs Urgently Improving
- The Construction of the Great Channel of Legal Service under the CAFTA

学术综述

ACADEMIC SUMMARY

第四届"中国—东盟法律合作与发展高层论坛"学术综述

中国—东盟法律研究中心秘书处

2010年11月10日至14日，由中国法学会和重庆市人民政府主办，中国法学学术交流中心、重庆市法学会和西南政法大学共同承办的第四届"中国—东盟法律合作与发展高层论坛"在重庆市召开，200余位来自中国和东盟国家的司法界官员、律师、仲裁员和学者，其中包括10位部级以上官员在内的91名东盟外宾参加了本届论坛。本届论坛的开幕式由中国法学会常务副会长刘飏主持。中国法学会会长韩杼滨、重庆市委副书记张轩、柬埔寨司法部大臣昂翁瓦塔纳、泰国最高法院大法官布恩洛德·唐普拉塞尔先后作了热情洋溢的致辞。论坛期间还成立了由中国法学会创设，以西南政法大学为依托的"中国—东盟法律研究中心"，并聘请100余名(家)来自中国和东盟国家的咨询单位、咨询委员和客座研究员。

2010年正值中国东盟自由贸易区建成第一年，为开展中国—东盟各国法学法律界之间的对话、交流与合作，厘清自由贸易区法制建设中基础性理论问题，更好解决法律合作的实践问题，本届论坛设定的主题为"走向互利共赢：中国—东盟自贸区建成后的法律合作"，为便于参会人员广泛地展开研讨，研讨会确立了涵盖主题框架下法律合作的环境、立法和司法等三个单元，即"中国—东盟自由贸易区相关法律问题研究"、"中国—东盟自由贸易区建成后各国国内法的调整"和"中国—东盟自由贸易区建成后法律实务合作的新趋势、新特点"。各国代表分别就三个方面的内容开展了专题演讲和讨论，共同为促进中国—东盟自由贸易区的发展献计献策。

现将本届论坛学术研讨的内容按专题单元综述如下，以飨读者。

一、中国—东盟自由贸易区相关法律问题

这一单元分别由西南政法大学校长付子堂教授与印尼雅加达中心地区法院副院长伊法·苏德维女士以及西北政法大学副校长王瀚教授与马来西亚梁潘及黄律师馆合伙人黄子靖共同主持。

本单元涵盖了中国东盟自由贸易区所需的法制环境的各个方面。问题主要集中在中国—东盟自由贸易区运行中的公平竞争问题、东盟对国内经济结构的影响、运行中的反倾销和竞争问题以及自由贸易区协定的东盟投资协定、争端解决机制等问题,其中,对争端解决机制运用及设计成为各方重点研讨的内容。

如何处理投资自由化与国家主权的关系是国际投资法领域的重大问题,由于其敏感性,国际社会包括 WTO 尚无统一的投资规则。中国—东盟自由贸易区的投资协议统一了区内的投资法制,为中国与东盟各国间的投资提供了制度性保障。但是也出现了许多问题需要关注。中国商务部条约法律司司长李玲发言主要涉及在中国—东盟自由贸易区投资协定的执行中加强交流与合作的问题。她评价投资协定与中国及东盟各国发展水平相适应,既充分保护外国投资者的权益,也注意尊重各国政府对外资管理的权限。但是,当前投资协定领域出现了一些新的变化,如投资协定的内容和条款日趋复杂,超出了传统的投资保护协定范围;投资者与东道国之间的程序条款的设计日趋复杂;东道国的调控和管制制度更多地得到关注。与此同时,投资领域的潜在风险不断增加,投资者和东道国之间争端的案件迅速增多,有必要进一步改革投资者与东道国的国际仲裁机制,加强其公开性、透明性,以及对国际仲裁员的纪律约束。她认为,就中国—东盟自由贸易区《投资协定》而言,应该正确看待其作用。对于投资者与东道国之间的争端,执行中应该慎用协议规定的争端解决仲裁机制,充分利用磋商交流谈判等方式来解决分歧。广西大学法学院魏艳茹教授认为,《投资协议》在中国—东盟自由贸易区范围内创建了统一的国际投资保护法制,在保护外国投资者私益的同时试图兼顾东道国国家主权,此为其成就。但该协议也存在重大不足,如所约束的国家行为范围过于狭窄、缺乏审慎措施条款、根本安全例外条款未受到必要的制度性约束等。《投资协议》的修改和后续谈判应扩大受约束的国家行为之范围,增设审慎措施条款,对根本安全例外条款予以必要的程序性的制度约束。

中国—东盟自由贸易区各成员国政治体制和经济发展水平各有差异，更彰显自由贸易区的法律合作和对话的重要性。有多位东盟国家代表从地缘政治及经济的视角来探讨中国—东盟自由贸易区的法律问题。菲律宾司法部总检察长办公室代表诺那图斯·凯撒·里奥图科·奥贾斯认为，2010年中国—东盟自由贸易区进入务实阶段，各参与国已经调整了他们的经济结构，让所有的商业团体与企业能够更具有竞争力，经济规模变得越来越大。中国—东盟自由贸易区通过消除关税和非关税壁垒，推动了中国与东盟之间的贸易自由化和投资自由化，促进了中国与东盟之间的经济、政治、安全、法律等方面的合作。相信通过进一步发挥彼此之间的地理、历史、文化优势，中国—东盟自由贸易区将会给本地区带来和平与繁荣，成为亚洲乃至世界区域合作的典范。印度尼西亚高级法官索托尼·穆罕达利讨论了中国—自由贸易区运行过程中的反倾销问题和良性竞争问题。中国经济的增长将会影响到印度尼西亚的增长，中国也会从印度尼西亚的快速增长中受益，印度尼西亚是中国产品的潜在市场。自贸区的建成明显带来了一些重要的法律问题，特别是在公平竞争贸易法领域。虽然印度尼西亚政府已经建立了相关的技术委员会来监督框架协议的实施，并建立了反不正当竞争法等法律制度，市场公平竞争问题仍然是印度尼西亚政府的关注点。因此，中国和印度尼西亚需要制定有关垄断和不正当竞争的法律框架来促进双边合作，需要有法律框架支持中国和印尼在自贸区建立有竞争力的市场，实现贸易双赢。中国和印尼在自贸区的另外一些重要的法律问题还包括保护消费者以及知识产权等。

完善的争端解决程序既是中国—东盟自由贸易区各个协议的执行的重要保障，也是实现中国—东盟自由贸易区的目标及其安全运转的重要支柱。各国代表围绕着中国—东盟自由贸易区争端解决机制协议存在的问题及其完善的建议展开了研讨。如针对中国—东盟自由贸易区《争端解决机制协议》适用的争端主体仅限于解决国家的问题，中国法学会常务理事、上海大学法学院院长沈四宝教授认为，需要建立有私人主体参与的中国—东盟商事纠纷解决机制，通过该机制可以打破由西方世界在商事仲裁领域内的垄断局面，减少解决商事纠纷的成本、提高中国与东盟各国之间的商贸效率。为此，他还进一步从各国的仲裁法制、仲裁经验和仲裁队伍等方面论证了这一机制的可行性。文莱仲裁协会会长王科林围绕着争端的仲裁规则，详细分析了规则的宽泛和程序的缺失，比如争端解决仲裁机构的缺失、仲裁庭组成以及第三方的确定等方面存在的问题。此外，由于成员方的双重身份，对一项争端可以适用WTO争端解决机制和中国—东盟自由贸易区争端解决机制的冲突如何解决的问题。对此,他提出了一些具体化仲裁机制的建议,如他认为,应成立一个由独立的非政府法律和仲裁专家组成的轮值委员会,由这个组织的负责人指定仲裁庭主席;对确定第三方与争端是否有"实质利益"应进行客观而不是主观的解释,如果现有行为的结果会对第三方产生影响,可以认为涉及第三方的实质利益;鼓励各成员国在同时涉及WTO和自贸区义务的争端时,首先使用自贸区争端解决机制,而不是求助于更为激烈的WTO争端解决机制。

区域贸易协定下争端解决模式主要有外交、仲裁和司法三种模式,因其具有本土化、灵活性和选择性、非政治性、低成本和高效率等主要优势,能够提供一种更适合本土情况、一种更加多样化的争端解决平台和备选方案,这有助于加强区域贸易协定内部的凝聚力,有利于推动区域内的稳定发展。中国商务部条约法律司处长陈雨松在分析了区域贸易协定下争端解决模式及其优势后,认为中国—东盟争端解决机制采取的是磋商到仲裁的模式,这个模式是介于传统的模式和司法之间的模式,没有上诉的机构,仲裁庭具有临时性。目前为止还没有一个争端递交到中国—东盟自由贸易区的争端解决模式之下,这与对争端机制的不了解、不熟悉以及认为争端解决效果有一定的不确定性等有关。随着自贸区经济规模地不断扩大,势必产生争端。因此,需要进一步完善中国和东盟争端解决机制,使之在促进中国与东盟经济发展一体化的进程中发挥更大的作用。中国法学会理事、广西师范大学法学院杨丽艳教授对自由贸易区划分了超国家组织型如欧盟、南北经济合作型如北美自由贸易区、南南经济合作型、南北经济松散合作型等4大类型,她认为,中国—东盟自由贸易区存在着定位和不足的问题,如争端解决方面缺少有关社会事项和知识产权的内容,自由贸易区具体归于何种模式还需要进一步观察分析。对此,也提出了进一步改善和改进的建议。

复旦大学法学院何力教授从中国—东盟自由贸易区发展的视角,对中国区域经济一体化及其法律构建作了较为深入的发言。他认为,中国自改革开放以来开始了区域经济一体化进程,进入21世纪以来成功地和东盟建立了中国－东盟自由贸易区,为双方发展贸易和投资等经济交往创造了最佳外部条件。CAFTA的成功推动了日韩与东盟的自由贸易区的成立,并向包括东南亚和东北亚在内的东亚自由贸易区发展,最后有可能建成接近欧盟模式的东亚共同体。其法律制度的设计以现今的CAFTA法律制度为出发点,然后是建立NAFTA模式的东亚自由贸易区法律机制,最后升格到欧洲共同市场模式的法律机制。如果实现这一步，不仅对于东盟国家甚至对于全世界的经济体系、经济结构、法律制度都有很大的作用。

对于中国—东盟自由贸易区在货物贸易、服务贸易及投资等领域的法律问题，提交论坛的相关论文较多，从不同视角来进行较为广泛的探讨，如货物原产地，服务自由化、投资准入等法律问题，不一而足。

二、中国—东盟自由贸易区建成后各国国内法的调整

这一单元分别由西南政法大学副校长刘俊教授与印尼最高法院院长助理普里·邦布迪·德古以及西南政法大学教务处处长刘想树教授与泰国中央知识产权与国际贸易法院庭长纳塔蓬·朱拉克萨主持。

中国—东盟自由贸易区的建成前提是拥有一套规则，要求各成员方保证这套规则在国内的有效实施，这是一项国际条约义务。通常而言，这套规则的实施是通过各成员国的国内法而适用的，这就要求各成员国进行国内立法调整。本单元涵盖了中国—东盟自由贸易区国内立法的调整所涉及立法、执法和司法等方方面面的内容。

东盟国家代表们还就本国就融入国际经济一体化和区域一体化体制所进行的国内立法调整的经验作了主题发言。柬埔寨司法部国务秘书占·索思威介绍了柬埔寨调整国内法使其与国际法接轨的经验。她认为，中国—东盟自由贸易的建成与运行要求各国必须改变和调整国内法，以适用于双边贸易协议，促进双边合作，推进一体化进程及相应的活动。在这方面柬埔寨已经做了充分的准备，加入东盟和加入世贸组织后已经完全地融入了一体化。柬埔寨自1998以来进行了一系列的深入的司法改革，对税法、经济法、金融法、土地法、企业法、消费者权益保护法、民事家庭法等方面的国内立法进行了与国际条约一致化的调整。此外，在东盟一体化进程中，柬埔寨和越南进行合作，谈判关于民商事司法援助问题的双边条约。占·索思威最后希望各国来宾能够充分地参与实现这一成就的对话，促进经济实现一体化。老挝司法部部长扎伦·叶宝和以“老挝法律制度的发展”一题进行了发言。老挝正在逐步健全法律体系，积极实施《2020年之前建成法治国家总体规划》，进一步发展法律，使其能够应对社会的需求，符合经济和社会发展的趋势，并使它能够达到国际标准，保证老挝能够真正地融入地区和全球（包括中国—东盟自由贸易区）的发展之中，为老挝加入世贸组织创造良好的司法条件和基础。为此目的，老挝已经制定并且修改了很多法律，老挝支

持建立中国—东盟自由贸易区,致力于调整国内法律以推动自由贸易协议的贯彻,希望各方都能够有效、严格和逐步地贯彻中国—东盟自由贸易协议。缅甸总检察长办公室副主任温·敏特围绕“缅甸商法的发展”作了发言。他指出,缅甸非常重视与中国东盟之间的经济贸易合作,为适应国内经济发展和自由贸易区运行,缅甸构建了一些新的法律政策机制,以保护私有部门和商界利益。同时,随着贸易自由化原则的确立,缅甸的进出口政策也作出相应调整,以鼓励产品出口并对进口机械和工业产品予以平等对待。中国—东盟自由贸易区要发展完整的体系才能支持经济的进步。中国—东盟自由贸易区在有完善的法律制度基础上才会进入新的阶段,缅甸将进一步修改和完善外商投资法以及国有经济企业法、知识产权法、商务法等一系列法律制度,使之能够完全地融入中国—东盟自由贸易区的法律框架。越南—中国—东盟法律信息咨询中心副主任阮春英介绍了越南遵守中国—东盟自由贸易协议、东盟自贸协议以及 WTO 等协议所进行的国内法调整情况。越南在执行中国—东盟自由贸易协议的过程中也面临着巨大挑战,在货物贸易出口和进口方面面临一些负面影响,如针对东盟新四国关税减让的“五年宽限期”在 2015 年到来之前将会结束,相关国家政府必须能够制订出相关法律有效地管理本国经济,同时也需要自贸区各国通力合作,共同克服挑战,以法律工具实现共赢结果。

民商事司法协作是各国国内司法制度的重要内容。西北政法大学副校长王瀚教授在分析中国—东盟自由贸易区建成民商事争议的国际私法属性后,认为此类争端的处理无法通过自由贸易区的争端解决机制,因此,要优先加强各国双边民商事条约的缔结,缔结区域性的民商事司法协助的多边公约维护东盟自由贸易的框架,推动自由贸易区经济的发展和繁荣。中国和东盟各国由于历史文化传统和制度的差异,使得争端解决机制框架下的司法协助问题需要有计划和有步骤地进行。他认为,目前中国与东盟通过政府间签署条约并不现实,可以尝试由各国的法院系统出面来就涉及仲裁的司法协助问题进行协商,成功后向争端解决机制框架下的其他方面扩展。争端解决机制框架下的司法协助必须遵循平等互利原则和效率原则,并注意将其和一般的外国仲裁裁决加以区分。泰国中央知识产权与国际贸易法院秘书帕里查特·蒙斯古尔和庭长塔纳叻·瑙瓦拉和先后介绍了泰国中央知识产权与国际贸易法院处理知识产权及国际贸易案件的诉讼调解制度,认为法院在中国与东盟签订自由贸易协定后将发挥作用。他们特别指出,世界仅有几个国家建立有如泰国中央知识产权与国际贸易法院这样的法院,建设这样的专门法院对经济的发展是非常重要的。

代表们的发言还涉及中国—东盟自由贸易区建成后公司法和证券融资市场的法制问题。西南政法大学民商法学院院长赵万一教授以“中国—东盟自由贸易区下中国公司法的发展”为题作了发言,他指出,中国与东盟之间的贸易投资有较大发展空间,但仍然有一些法律方面的障碍需要克服。2005年修改后的中国公司法为吸引外资提供了有效的法律保障,中国公司法所确定的一些基本的理念和原则,为东盟国家的公司立法提供了一定的借鉴对象。对于中国—东盟自贸区建成后给公司法带来影响和法律对策可以概括为以下5个方面:一是创新企业的组织形式;二是改善公司的生存环境;三是完善对外商投资者的法律保护,明确社会公共利益的适用对象、适用范围和程序及救济方式;四是通过合理的设计降低外商投资的风险;五是充分发挥司法的引导功能强化给外商投资的法律救济。马来西亚梁潘及黄律师馆合伙人梁柏林律师认为,转型期经济容易产生利益冲突,只有用公共秩序、法律法规原则约束利益冲动,在这些法律制度的实现当中营造一个相互共同繁荣的原则,这样才能使经济繁荣。东盟证券交易所如马来西亚和新加坡证券交易市场允许中国和东盟的公司上市,实现融资有利业务扩张。通过这样一种在新兴国家的投资,使得共同利益和共同优势的实现取得了充分的成功,也使得自由贸易区获得了成功。如何加强上市公司的内部和外部监管,以及不同国家间监管机构的协调,是当前面临的重要挑战。会议所提交的论文探讨范围还涉及规则的效力层级问题,如WTO规则、东盟组织规则、中国—东盟自由贸易区规则以及区内11个成员国的国内法冲突和协调的问题。

三、中国—东盟自由贸易区建成后法律实务合作的新趋势、新特点

这一单元分别由西南政法大学国际法学院副院长张晓君教授与马来西亚律师公会副主席林志伟以及重庆市律师协会副会长、索通律师事务所执行合伙人韩德云与文莱仲裁协会会长王科林主持。

中国—东盟自由贸易区建成后法律实务合作进一步拓展了领域和主体,呈现出更实务、更紧密的新特点。代表们围绕着这些新趋势和新特点,进行了主题研讨,其中,中国—东盟自由贸易区建成后如何发挥政府、企业、律师和法学团体的作用是本专题重点关注的问题。

关于中国—东盟自由贸易区法律合作与发展问题。文莱总检察长哈雅提认为,在加强中国—东盟自贸区各国法律合作方面,不仅仅是政府从中扮演重要的角色,其他的利益相关者包括私人部门(各国的律师、法学会等)也能在促进东盟国家或中国的法律合作方面贡献力量。法律一体化在中国—东盟自贸协议框架下将切实促进各国关系以及贸易的良好发展,这将是各国法律合作的未来发展趋势。为了促进东盟与中国的贸易,有必要保证现有的法律框架不仅有利于贸易,还有利于确保在实践中法律得到了正确的实施。这就需要法律在实践中更具便捷性、实用性,需要一个独立公正的司法机关,需要对法治的尊重。为此,各国法学会要团结一起,共同促进各国间的相互理解、友谊和合作。可以考虑成立一个地区性的法律家协会或者是地区性的法律职业者、相关人士以及利益相关者的协会,并加强法律信息、专业知识和经验的交流。《争端解决机制协议》中规定的一些争端解决的综合性手段可以当作东盟和中国的律师在实践上或学术上进一步探索该问题的入手点。各国间不仅在法律领域加强合作,还应该在东盟—中国这个大集体的保护伞下发展其它方面的合作。重庆大学法学院院长陈忠林教授认为,法律合作是中国和东盟自贸区正常发展的坚强支柱之一。中国和东盟组织的发展趋势决定中国—东盟自贸区下法律事务合作的趋势:一是从国际到区际;二是从双边到多边;三是以官方为主,到官方与民间。越南最高人民检察院高级检察官邓氏梅香以"越南最高人民检察院为中国—东盟自由贸易区所做出努力"为题进行了发言。她的发言分三个方面:一是越南检察院在国家机关中的地位和功能;二是越南人民检察院对中国—东盟自由贸易区具有重要法律保障作用;三是越南人民检察院在执法过程中广泛进行国际合作,维护自由贸易区正常的法制环境。

民商事纠纷解决司法合作的问题直接涉及中国—东盟自贸区民商事纠纷解决机制的完善。来自西南政法大学国际法学院两位年轻的学者就此问题进行深入的研讨。徐鹏副教授归纳了中国—东盟自贸区民商事争议的解决呈现出的多样化、分散化和复杂化等特点。他认为,不同国家对机制建立后所获相对利益的关注,以及东盟方面对建立国际法律规范体系的犹豫和迟疑,成为构建民商事争议解决机制的重要影响因素。为此应做好以下几方面的工作:一是推动法律文化交流和合作,促进观念转变,在合作共赢中强化共同利益;二是采取先易后难的对策,促进自贸区成员国通过双边公约逐步建立民事司法协助体系,并推动最终建立多边统一的民事司法协助公约;三是根据需要丰富、完善和推广自贸区民商事交往中产生的各种替代性纠纷解决方式。张春良副教授以外国法查明来阐明了司法合作的问题。他认为，CAFTA的有效运行离不开纠纷排解机制之支撑，其统一私法纠纷排解机制并未建立。此种结构性缺失致使传统国际民商事争议解决机制成为替补路径，而法律选择及其必然涉及的外国法查明因此成为其中不可或缺的核心环节。它对于CAFTA功能的正常发挥、区域法律的协调、互信合作的司法态度以及东亚和平崛起的司法平台之建构具有举足轻重的意义。由于CAFTA下多元语言、多元文化、多元法系的并存和历史合作基础的匮乏，以传统国别自力救济方式查明彼此法律的做法业已不合时宜，必须因应经济的CAFTA化而伴生一场外国法查明的CAFTA化之辅佐运动方为标本兼治之进路。

代表们还围绕自由贸易区框架下仲裁机制的合作问题展开了研讨。中国国际经济贸易仲裁委员会西南分会秘书长陈敏以"国际仲裁在解决中国—东盟自由贸易区经贸纠纷中的作用与优势"为题进行主题发言。他总结了仲裁方式解决CAFTA经贸纠纷中所具有优势，如有利于建立各国对自贸区的信心，消除投资和贸易中的障碍，建立良好的信誉，鼓励诚实信用，避免国家和商人之间的商业关系受损，积累解决纠纷的经验，推动自贸区人员的文化交流，有助于相互的信任和友谊等。仲裁是促进发展的手段之一，是公平正义的国际惯例，是全球性的规则，在中国—东盟贸易区的使用将发挥重要的作用。为提高中国—东盟自由贸易区的实施法律的有效性，马来西亚律师公会副主席林志伟提出以下建议：一是建立涵盖自贸区十一个国家的仲裁中心；二是推动实现民商事判决在自贸区内的承认和执行；三是朝着欧盟的方向努力，即促进超越国家之上的更加有效的国际组织的建立。他认为，随着自贸区正式启动，各成员国应该灵活应对，不断调整适应变化的情况。从长远来看，自贸区的成功取决于我们是否有能力制定相关的法律措施管理贸易活动。

律师、公证和司法鉴定等法律服务业在中国—东盟自由贸易区运行中处于一个不可缺少的、发挥保障性作用的、独立的重要地位。云南大学法学院院长陈云东教授对此作了认真的分析，他认为，现行中国—东盟自贸区框架协议在具体的承诺方面实际上是没有法律服务贸易业准入规定的，但这些协议之中包含着对法律服务业的宏观作用，根据法律服务业的职能和中国—东盟自由贸易区的特点，法律服务业在中国—东盟自由贸易区运行中发挥的作用可以归纳为规范作用、桥梁作用、决策参谋作用、疏导作用和救济作用五个方面的内容。云南律师协会副会长、北京大成律师事务所（云南)主任马巍博士提出了构建"中国—东盟法律服务大通道"的问题。他认为,中国—东盟自由贸易区的启动,使各国法律服务业在面临着巨大的机遇同时也承担着历史性的使命,中国和东盟的法律服务从业人员应该抓住机遇,构筑中国—东盟法律服务的大通道。即建立与中国—东盟共谋发展过程中的法律需求相匹配的法律服务网络。该法律服务网络将囊括若干国内外机构、人员,例如:本国外贸主管部门、本国法律服务机构、国外的优秀律师事务所及律师、本国驻外国使领馆、相关科研及教学机构,等等。广西律师协会知识产权委员会副主任、广西万益律师事务所主任凌斌从中国律师的视角,讨论涉东盟法律服务的问题。他认为,中国—东盟自由贸易区经贸合作发展的良好态势为中国律师开展涉东盟法律服务提供前所未有的机遇。中国律师在提供涉东盟法律服务面临着语言隔阂、法律资料匮乏、律师的品牌和专业能力有限、竞争劣势等诸多问题。中国律师要把握涉东盟法律服务的机遇,有赖于语言能力、专业水平能力的提高以及信息沟通、律师联盟等协助平台的打造等。

加强知识产权保护的合作中发展创新型经济非常重要的法制基础。泰国泰中法学会会长刘华源围绕这一主题进行了发言。他指出,创新性经济、创新性教育和创新性基础设施在社会发展中的重要作用。政府如何保护知识产权非常重要。中国一东盟必须建立统一的知识产权和信息保护法律制度。泰国政府力争从投资、软件、硬件、技术等方面,提升知识产权和信息保护水平。实施了创新经济项目,并建立媒体渠道以促进创新性经济的发展。同时,政府推动建立创新型企业和高速信息技术网络,实施信息通讯技术计划。中国和东盟国家应共同合作,建立新的知识产权保护机制促进信息技术产业发展。

本单元论题提交的论文较多,探讨的视野也较为开阔,比如法律实务界的工作网络构建等,代表们提出了许多具建设性的对策和建议。

四、小结

本届论坛立意高远,主题紧跟时代发展,具有时代特征。近30名来自中国和东盟成员国共专家、学者、法律实务部门代表做了精彩发言,有12名中国和东盟国家代表参与主持和点评。研讨交流中提出的一些创新性观点和对策建议,具有很强的针对性和可操作性,为各国政府和相关部门提供了很好的参考和借鉴。代表们认为,中国—东盟自由贸易区的建成来之不易,各国要有效执行和贯彻自由贸易区协议。各国要通力合作，充分认识到加强法律合作比任何时候都更为迫切，更为重要。加强中国与东盟国家间的法学法律领域的交流与合作，有利于增进中国与东盟成员国的相互理解和信任，有利于保障中国与东盟国家间的经贸合作，以法律工具实现共赢目标。正如中国法学会常务副会长刘飏在论坛闭幕式致辞中指出，这是一届"扩大共识、深化合作的盛会"。代表们就加强法学法律合作，促进区域经济一体化，推动共同发展达成了广泛的共识。

A Summary of The 4th China-ASEAN Top Forum on Legal Cooperation and Development

The Secretariat of China-ASEAN Legal Research Center

On November 10—13, 2010, the 4th China-ASEAN Top Forum on Legal Cooperation and Development was held in Chongqing Municipality. Up to 200 legal professionals, government officials, lawyers, arbitrators and scholars from both China and ten ASEAN member states attended the grand Forum. The Forum focused on the theme "Toward a Mutual Benefit and Win-win-Legal Cooperation after the Establishment of China-ASEAN Free Trade Area (CAFTA)".

As the ceremony adjourned, representatives of China and ASEAN countries unveiled for the China-ASEAN Legal Research Center together and awarded letters of appointment to the representatives of advisory organizations and advisory members of China-ASEAN Legal Research Center.

Session 1: Research on Legal Issues Related to China-ASEAN FTA (Section 1)

Chairperson: Mr. Fu Zitang, President of Southwest University of Political Science and Law

Ms. Ifa Sudewi, Vice-Chief of District Court of Central Jakarta of Cambodia

1. Li Ling, Secretary of Department of Treaty and Law of Ministry of Commerce of P. R. C

Strengthen Communication and Cooperation, Implement China-ASEAN Investment Agreement

2. Representative of Office of Prosecutor General of Department of Justice of Philippines

The Geo-political and Economic Imperatives of the China-ASEAN Free Trade Area (CAFTA)

3. Shen Sibao, Dean of Law School of Shanghai University

Design and Suggestion on Commercial Dispute Settlement Mechanism in

CAFTA

4. Mr. Soltoni Mohdally, Senior Justice of Supreme Court of Indonesia

The Legal Issue Related to China-ASEAN FTA-From Indonesian Judge Perspective

Session 1: Research on Legal Issues Related to China-ASEAN FTA (Section 2)

Chairperson: Mr. Wang Han, Vice-President of Northwest University of Political Science and Law

Mr. Wong Chee Chin, Partner of Messrs, Jeff Leong, Poon&Woon

5. Mr. Colin Ong, President of Arbitration Association of Brunei Darussalam

Dispute Settlement Mechanism for CAFTA: Any Room for Future Refinement?

6. Chen Yusong, Head of WTO Division Two, Department of Treaty and Legal Affairs of the Ministry of Commerce

Dispute Settlement Mechanism in RTA and the Practice of China-ASEAN Agreement

7. Mr. Chung Ting Fai, Principal of Chung Ting Fai & Co., Singapore

Views and Outlook on the Dispute Settlement Mechanism of China-ASEAN Free Trade Area

8. Wei Yanru, Professor of Law School of Guangxi University

China-ASEAN Investment Agreement: Achievements, Shortcomings, and Improvements

Session 2: Amendment of Domestic Laws after the Establishment of China-ASEAN FTA (Section 1)

Chairperson: Mr. Liu Jun, Vice-President of Southwest University of Political Science and Law, Professor

Mr. Pri Pambudi Teguh, Assistant to Chief Justice of Supreme of Court of Indonesia

1. Wang Han, Vice-President of Northwest University of Political Science and Law

Civil and Commercial Judicial Assistance in China-ASEAN Economic and Trade Cooperation

2. Mr. Ang Vong Vathan, Minister of Justice of Cambodia

Cambodia Experience Reforming Domestic Law to Comply with International Law

3. Mr. Chaleune Yiapaoher, Minister of Justice of Lao PDR

The Development of Lao System

4. Chen Yundong, President, Professor of Law School of Yunnan University

Study on the Counter-policies for Legal Service Industry after the Establishment of China-ASEAN FTA

5. Zhao Wanyi, President, Professor of School of Civil and Commercial Law of Southwest University of Political Science and Law

The Development of Company Law in CAFTA

6. Mr. Jeff Leong, Senior Partner of Messrs, Jeff Leong, Poon & Woon

Listing Chinese Companies on the Malaysian Stock Exchange

Session 2: Adjustment of Domestic Laws after the Establishment of China-ASEAN FTA (Section 2)

Chairperson: Mr. Liu Xiangshu, Director General of Teaching Affairs Department of Southwest University of Political Science and Law, Mr. Natthapol Chullakesa, Presiding Judge of the Central Intellectual Property and International Trade Court

7. He Li, Professor of Law School of Fudan University

From CAFTA to East Asian Community: China's Regional Economic Integration and the Legal Construction

8. Mr. Thanarak Naowara … Central Intellectual Property and International Tra… Munsgool, Judge and the Secretary of the Cent… nd International Trade Court

The Intellectual Property an… ation in the Central Intellectual Property and Inte… rt

9. Mr. Win Myint, Deputy Director General of the Attorney General's Office of Myanmar

Development of Business Laws in Myanmar

10. Yang Liyan, Professor of Law School of Guangxi Normal University, Director of China Law Society

Study on Module-Selection in CAFTA

11. Mr. Nguyen Xuan Anh, Deputy Director of Center for Vietnam-China-ASEAN Legal Information and Consultancy

The Adjustment of National Laws of Vietnam in Conjunction with the Implement of ASEAN

Tea Break

Session 3: New Trends and New Features of Legal Practical Cooperation after the Establishment of China-ASEAN FTA (Section 1)

Chairperson: Ms. Zhan Xiaojun, Secretary General of China-ASEAN Legal Research Center

Mr. Lim Chee Wee, Vice-President of Malaysian Bar Council

1. Ms. Datin Paduka Hajah Hayati binti POKSDSP Haji Mohd Salleh, Attorney General of Brunei Darussalam

2. Mr. Sanguan Lewmanonont, President of Thai-Chinese Law Society

Thailand's Vision of IT and the Creative Economy for China-ASEAN Countries

3. Chen Zhonglin, President of Law School of Chongqing University

Relevant Issues in Legal Cooperation after the Establishment of China-ASEAN FTA

4. Dang Mai Huong, Senior Legal Expert of Supreme People's Procuracy of Vietnam

Efforts for ASEAN-China Free Trade Area (ACFTA)

5. Xu Peng, Associate Professor of School of International Law of Southwest University of Political Science and Law

Problems and Strategies in Settling Civil, Commercial Disputes in CAFTA

Session 3: New Trends and Features of Legal Practical Cooperation after the Establishment of China-ASEAN FTA (Section 2)

Chairperson: Mr. Han Deyun, Vice-President of Chongqing Lawyers' Association, Deputy to the National People's Congress

Mr. Colin Ong, President of Arbitration Association of Brunei Darussalam

6. Chen Min, Secretary General of Southwest Branch of CIETAC (China International Economic and Trade Arbitration Commission)

The Significance and Advantages of International Arbitration in Settling Disputes in CAFTA

7. Mr. Lim Chee Wee, Vice-President of Malaysian Bar Council

8. Ma Wei, Vice-President of Yunnan Lawyers' Association, Director of Beijing Dacheng Law Firm

Strengthening Regional Cooperation, Constructing A China-ASEAN Legal Service Chanel

9. Zhang Chunliang, Associate Professor of School of International Law of Southwest University of Political Science and Law

The Caftalization of Proof of Foreign Law under CAFTA

10. Ling Bin, Partner, Executive Director of Guangxi Wanyi Law Firm, Deputy Director General of Intellectual Property Commission of Guangxi Lawyers' Association

Opportunities, Problems and Strategy of Chinese Lawyers in Providing Legal Service Involving ASEAN Affairs

Mme. Liu Yang ,Executive Vice-President of China law society, Mr. Liu Xuepu of Vice Mayor of ChongQing , Mr. Tran Dai Hung, Director of Center for Vietnam-China-ASEAN Legal Information and Consultancy and Mr. Claro A. Arellano, Prosecutor General of Department of Justice of Philippines delivered speeches in the Closing Ceremony respectively. Mr. Liu Xuepu pointed out that the success of the forum has a positive significance in promoting the legal system construction and implementing the scientific notion of rule by law in practice. There will certainly be more and more cooperation between Chongqing and ASEAN member states in political, economic and cultural aspects after the complete establishment of the China-ASEAN FTA. Drawing lessons from the other countries' great achievements including the legal system construction is extraordinarily crucial to the future development of Chongqing. He "sincerely welcomes continuous advices from the ASEAN countries' guests in legal system construction and new developments breakthrough". Mme. Liu Yang appreciated all the organizations and individuals' great supports to the Forum in the first place. She said this was a"“great gathering that extends the consensus and promotes the cooperation”. The delegates reached extensive agreements in various aspects including enhancing the cooperation in academy and practice, promoting the integration of regional economies and pushing joint development. She pointed out that searching for “a regional cooperation method with Asian features” is “our pressing common demands” and also our “missions and responsibilities”. The setup of China-ASEAN Legal Research Center, the Alumni of China-ASEAN Legal Training Base and the website of the Alumni will inject dynamics and energy into the development of the forum. As representatives of ASEAN countries, Director Tran Dai Hung and Prosecutor General Claro A. Arellano expressed their resolution of strengthening the regional cooperation and their hope for realizing the joint development based on the actual situation and the challenges they are faced with, and emphasized that the closing ceremony was “not an end but a beginning of a more thorough cooperation”.

附　录

APPENDIX

中国—东盟法律研究中心简介

为加强对中国—东盟自由贸易区法制及东盟国家法律的研究，促进区域内各国法律学术交流和资源共享，将法学、法律领域的务实合作提高到新的水平，2010年10月，中国法学会在第四届“中国—东盟法律合作与发展高层论坛”期间，正式创设了“中国—东盟法律研究中心”。

研究中心依托西南政法大学，整合中国和东盟国家的学术和实务的专家，开展对中国与东盟法律的系统性、基础性和前瞻性的研究，为中国与东盟各国相关法律研究者提供学术交流平台，为各国政府、商业团体和其他机构提供咨询建议，为本地区的繁荣发展提供法律和智力支持。

研究中心设理事会，理事长为中国法学会常务副会长刘飏。研究中心设咨询委员会，由咨询单位和咨询委员组成，咨询单位来自东盟各国实务界、学术界和中国的律师协会、行业社团及涉东盟经贸企业。研究中心设客座研究员，由来自中国和东盟国家的学术界和实务界专家组成。

研究中心秘书处位于中华人民共和国重庆市。

Introduction of China-ASEAN Legal Research Center

To enhance researches on laws and regulations of China-ASEAN FTA and ASEAN countries, promote academic exchange and resource sharing in the legal field and raise the practical legal cooperation between China and ASEAN countries to a high level, China-ASEAN Legal Research Center will is set up during the 4th China-ASEAN Top Forum on Legal Cooperation and Development.

The Center locates in Southwest University of Political Science and Law and will conduct systematic, basic and prospective researches on the legal issues related to China-ASEAN countries, build an academic exchange platform for legal researchers of China-ASEAN countries, supply consultation and suggestions for governments, business groups and other agencies and provide legal and intellectual support for the prosperous development of this region.

Mme. Liu Yang, Executive Vice-President of China Law Society, is named for the Chairman of the First Council Meeting of China-ASEAN Legal Research Center. The Advisory Committee Meeting is subordinate to the China-ASEAN Legal Research Center, consisting of advisory organizations and advisory members from practical and academic field of ASEAN countries, China's Bar Association, industry associations and business enterprises. Furthermore, visiting research fellows are invited, all of which are specialists from academic and practical field of China and ASEAN countries.

The Secretariat of China-ASEAN Legal Research Center locates in Chongqing Municipality of People's Republic of China.

中国—东盟法律合作与发展高层论坛简介

"中国—东盟法律合作与发展高层论坛"成立于2005年，是全面涵盖中国和东盟政府界、司法界、法学界、法律界及商界的高层次、开放式、具有一定影响力的法律交流对话平台。前三届论坛分别于2005年至2007年在中国南宁、越南下龙湾、中国重庆举行。为促进中国—东盟自由贸易区快速健康发展，进一步增进中国—东盟法学法律界的友好互信关系，中国法学会和重庆市政府于2010年11月10日至14日在重庆市举办第四届"中国—东盟法律合作和发展高层论坛"。

"中国—东盟法律合作与发展高层论坛"以合作、发展、共赢、和谐为理念，在互相学习和尊重的基础上，开展中国—东盟各国法学法律界之间的对话、交流与合作，为推动本地区各国法制建设和法学研究，促进和保障本地区政治、经济和文化等各领域的健康发展做出积极的贡献。

Introduction of China—ASEAN Top Forum on Legal Cooperation and Development

Established in 2005, China—ASEAN Top Forum on Legal Cooperation and Development is a high—level, open and influential platform for legal professionals, government officials and entrepreneurs of China and ASEAN countries to conduct legal exchange and dialogue. The first three Forums were held in Nanning of China, Halong Bay of Vietnam and Chongqing of China. To promote the fast and sound development of China—ASEAN FTA and further enhance the friendship and trust among China and ASEAN legal professionals, China Law Society and Chongqing Municipal Government will hold the 4th China—ASEAN Top Forum on Legal Cooperation and Development in Municipality of Chongqing of China from November 10—14, 2010.

Following the idea of Cooperation, Development, Win—win and Harmony, China—ASEAN Top Forum on Legal Cooperation and Development encourages dialogue, exchange and cooperation for China—ASEAN countries, and contribute to the positive development in politics, economy, culture and other areas between China and ASEAN countries.

《中国—东盟法律评论》稿约

作为第四届“中国—东盟法律合作与发展高层论坛”的重要成果，“中国—东盟法律研究中心”集聚了中国与东盟国家法学法律界的相关研究资源，开展对中国与东盟法律的系统性、基础性和前瞻性的研究，为“中国—东盟自由贸易区”的可持续发展保驾护航。

经研究，由“中国—东盟法律研究中心”组织出版《中国—东盟法律评论》法学学术刊物，通过以书代刊的形式按年分期连续公开出版。《中国—东盟法律评论》将会秉承会通中外和而不同的传统精神，发扬宽容为本的组稿理念，提倡多元交流、学术争鸣，鼓励创新性学术成果。

刊物的研究内容主要涵盖：东盟国家的法律制度及与中国法律制度的比较研究，中国与东盟国家相关的立法及其实践研究、东盟组织法律制度研究、中国—东盟自贸区法制建设研究，等等；开展对国别法、组织法、比较法等领域的具体专题研讨，并将结合相关的学术焦点问题组织稿件、专刊出版。其主要特色在于：既注重法学理论的分析和研究，也兼顾对法律实践问题的探索与讨论。

《中国—东盟法律评论》诚挚地邀请邀请国内外各界专家、学者赐稿，为中国—东盟法律法学交流合作奉献力量。为提高刊物质量，就相关事宜说明如下：

1. 请将投稿文章以 Word 文档（英文或中文文字）电子版发至以下《中国—东盟法律评论》编辑电子邮箱（供选择）：

【中国】《中国—东盟法律评论》编辑部：edofcalr@supsl. cn

【文莱】Colin Ong，onglegal@brunet. bn

【印度尼西亚】IFA Sudewi，ifa. sudewi@yahoo. co. id

【柬埔寨】khemlin ku，khemlinku@yahoo. com

【缅甸】Kyi Kyi Than Aung

【马来西亚】Lim Chee Wee

【菲律宾】Maria Cristina P. Rilloraza 女士,attycristina@yahoo.com

【泰国】Thanarak Naowarat,thanarak.n@coj.go.th

请注明“《中国—东盟法律评论》投稿”字样。为便于中英文双语出版,鼓励论文以中英文两种语言形式投稿。

2.《论坛》文章注释采用脚注,每页重新编号,以阿拉伯数字加圆圈标识。英文注释依其注释习惯。来稿需有文章摘要及关键词(中英文);请注明作者姓名、单位、职称(或职务)、学位、研究方向、联系电话、通讯地址、邮政编码和电子邮箱等,以方便联系。

3. 稿件一经采用,寄送样刊两本以示谢意。原则上不支付稿酬。

4. 本刊反对抄袭,来稿文责自负,请勿一稿多投,在三个月内未收到用稿通知,可自行处理稿件。来稿均应为未在公开出版物发表之成果。

5.《评论》编辑部有权对来稿做适当文字修改。拥有对在《评论》上发表的作品出版权,任何转载、收录等须事先获《评论》编辑部书面许可。任何来稿视为作者、译著者已同意本《评论》约稿条件。

《中国—东盟法律评论》编辑部

Call for Papers

As an important outcome of the fourth China-ASEAN Forum on Legal Cooperation and Development, the China-ASEAN Legal Research Center highly enjoys corresponding research and study resources both home and abroad, esp the law sectors from the ASEAN countries and Chinese government. Accordingly, the China-ASEAN Legal Research Center would like to develop and explore the China-ASEAN Legal Research to a systematic way, making a good balance between the theoretical academic topics and the foresighted importance frontiers. With such a solid research foundation, the China-ASEAN Free Trade Area will be possibly in good operation and maintain a sustainable development.

Pursuant to relevant consideration, the China-ASEAN Law Review is in publication under the administration and management of the China-ASEAN Legal Research Center. The China-ASEAN Law Review is publicly in circulation yearly continuously with the means of book instead of periodical. The China-ASEAN Law Review will stick on the traditional spirit of "he er bu tong" and cordially welcome the diverse ideas and concepts home and abroad. The Law Review calls for papers in the conception of tolerance and advocates the collision and merger of different viewpoints as well as encourage the creative and original academic research works.

The contents of the China-ASEAN Law Review have a wide coverage, mainly including the legal system of the ASEAN nations and the comparative research between Chinese law and the former. Besides, the contents also contain the relative legislation and practice study in the China-ASEAN area; legal system of ASEAN organizations; legal construction research under the framework of China-ASEAN FTA etc. The China-ASEAN Law Review also develops many specific discussions concerning the national law, organizational law as well as the comparative law and so on. Meanwhile, the China-ASEAN Law Review much concerns the academic focus and concentrations , considering to organize excellent papers and publish in special volume of great importance. the China-ASEAN Law Review enjoys very clear characteristic—giving emphasis on the analysis and research of the theoretical legal principles and jurisprudence, as well as showing wide compatibility to the discussions of the topics of strategic importance in practice.

The China-ASEAN Law Review sincerely calls the professionals and scholars of various sectors home and abroad for good papers, making great contributions for the legal exchange of China-ASEAN legal research. To guarantee the academic quality of the China-ASEAN Law Review, the editor notes the corresponding information as follows:

I. Please email the electronic version of your paper(in English or Chinese)in file of word to the China-ASEAN Law Review editor's mailbox respectively(Both available):

[China] Editorial Board of China-ASEAN Law Review, edofcalr@supsl. cn

[Brunei Darussalam] Mr. Colin Ong, onglegal@brunet. bn

[Indonesia] Ms. IFA Sudewi, ifa. sudewi@yahoo. co. id

[Cambodia] Mr. Khemlin Ku, khemlinku@yahoo. com

[Myanmar] Kyi Kyi Than Aung

[Malaysian] Mr. Lim Chee Wee, ago. h. o@mptmail. net. mm

[Philippines] Ms. Maria Cristina P. Rilloraza, attycristina@yahoo. com or clarellano@lycos. com

[Thailand] Mr. Thanarak Naowarat, thanarak. n@coj. go. th

Please note clearly the words"the China-ASEAN Law Review paper ". For the convenience of bilingual publication, the editor encourage the authors providing papers both in Chinese and English.

II. The China-ASEAN Law Review requires all the papers to use footnotes each page by new Arab No. repeat with circle around. English notes uses according to the customer. Each paper is expected to be complete with abstract and key words both in Chinese and English. For communication convenience, information such as author's full name, unit, professional level (or work status), degree, major and research direction, telephone, letter address, code No, and email address shall be clear noted.

III. Once recruited, the editor would post two samples to the author for gratitude. No capital profit in principle.

IV. The China-ASEAN Law Review is against of any form of academic piracy. Author's self-responsibility is the only means for the any piracy-related issues. The editor reminds that one paper shall not be provided for more than once at the same time . Not receiving recruit letter within three months, the author could deal with the paper freely. Furthermore, each paper should be the unpublished work of the author in public.

V. The editor of the China-ASEAN Law Review has the right to properly revise the paper. Besides, the editor has the right to publish the works that have published in the China-ASEAN Law Review. Any form of trans-publishing , paper recording should get the consent permission of the China-ASEAN editor in written form in prior. Each paper emailed to the editor's mailbox shall be regarded as a consent of agreement from the author to the calling requisition for paper of this Law Review.

Editorial Board of China-ASEAN Law Review

图书在版编目(CIP)数据

中国—东盟法律评论. 第1期/张晓君主编. —厦门：厦门大学出版社，2011.9
ISBN 978-7-5615-3961-3

Ⅰ.①中… Ⅱ.①张… Ⅲ.①法律-东南亚国家联盟-文集 Ⅳ.①D933-53

中国版本图书馆CIP数据核字(2011)第106901号

厦门大学出版社出版发行
(地址：厦门市软件园二期望海路39号 邮编：361008)
http://www.xmupress.com
xmup@public.xm.fj.cn
厦门集大印刷厂印刷
2011年9月第1版 2011年9月第1次印刷
开本：787×960 1/16 印张：15.5 插页：2
字数：270千字 印数：1～1 500册
定价：35.00元